This book is one of a collection donated by
Morris International Associates
in memory of the company's founder
writer and publisher
Claud Morris

Public Land Distribution in Saudi Arabia

Longman
London and New York

Public Land Distribution in Saudi Arabia

Hassan Hamza Hajrah

in association with the Municipality of Jeddah
and
The University of Durham: Centre for Middle Eastern and Islamic Studies

Longman Group Ltd
London

First published 1982

ISBN 0 582 78301 1

British Library Cataloguing in Publication Data

Hajrah, Hassan H
Public land distribution in Saudi Arabia.
1. Land tenure – Saudi Arabia
I. Title
333.1 HD853.Z7 80–40608

ISBN 0–582–78301–1

Printed in Great Britain by
Butler & Tanner Ltd, Frome and London

Acknowledgements

It is a great honour to have had the opportunity of conducting this research under the supervision of Professor H. Bowen-Jones whose valuable advice and continuous guidance were instrumental in making this research possible.

I am indebted to King Abdul Aziz University and its Rector Dr M. A. Yamani for the sincere support and facilities which I received to complete this book.

If I have been able to furnish the public land management department with some useful thoughts on land distribution and development this is due to the generosity of H.E. H. Al-Meshari, Minister of Agriculture and Water, H.E. the Deputy Minister and to the co-operation that I received from my colleagues during my work as a director general for that department.

I wish to express my gratitude to all whom I applied to for information or help and for the generous assistance that I received from the Geography Department, University of Durham and Saudi Ministry of Agriculture and Water.

Contents

List of Tables

List of Figures

List of Appendices

Glossary

Arabic words:

All such terms, such as "Mawat", meaning dead land not used or owned by anyone, are explained when they are used for the first time in the book. It is, however, useful to note the meanings of some place names since they provide shorthand descriptions of some localities; in addition the words "Hejrah" and "Donum" are translated because of the high frequency of use and their specific meanings in this content.

Shari'a:	Islamic Law
Nafud:	A large continuous body of sand which is formed by sand dunes deposited by the action of the wind.
Wadi:	Valley.
Al-Hassa:	Land with sealed ground water.
Najd:	Plateau.
Hijaz:	Barrier.
Asir:	Hard.
Hejrah:	A Bedouin village or a Bedouin settlement.
Donum:	A measure of land used in Saudi Arabia. It is equal to 1000 m^2 ($\frac{1}{10}$ hectare).

Definitions:

In this book certain terms are used to mean specific processes or situations:

Ownership of land:	The right to use land together with the right to transfer that right to others.
Lease:	An agreement written or verbal, which establishes a relation of tenancy.
Arable land:	The land suitable for cropping under irrigation.
Land classification:	The inventory of land and its division into qualitative classes.
Land tenure:	The rights to ownership and control of land.

Abbreviations:

CDC:	Community Development Centres.
CDP	Community Development Programme
FAO:	Food and Agriculture Organization.
GDP:	Gross Domestic Product
GNP:	Gross National Product
g/m, gpm:	gallons per minute
H:	Hejrah year.
Ha:	Hectare.
IBRD:	International Bank for Reconstruction and Development.
ILO:	International Labour Organization.
m:	metres.
MAW:	Ministry of Agriculture and Water.
NASA:	National Agricultural Settlement Authority, Libya
NPK:	Nitrogen, Phosphorus, Potassium as fertilizers.
PLD:	Public Land Distribution.
PLDO:	Public Land Distribution Ordinance of 1388H (1968).
PLMD:	Public Land Management Department.
SAFCO:	Saudi Arabia Fertilizer Company.
SR:	Saudi Riyals
TPLU:	Temporary Principles for Land Utilization.

In this book, the *Hejrah* Calendar is normally used. This refers to the movement of Prophet Mohammed from Makkah to Madinah in AD 622. It follows the Moon Cycle and is about 12-days shorter than the Gregorian Year. Thirty of its years constitute a cycle and are almost equal to twenty-nine Gregorian years. The commencement of year 1364H almost coincided with the beginning of year AD 1945 and the next year 1395H ends almost at the same date as AD 1975.

Gregorian Year = Higriah—(3 × Higriah Year)/100 + 621.6 (Omit fractions).

References are listed under "Bibliography" at the end of this study and attention is drawn to the Bibliographical Note. Arabic references are translated into English.

Preface

This book examines the historical and recent aspects of Public Land ownership in Islam, explains the various kinds of public ownership and re-examines several problems of Public Land policy. Historically, both ownership of, and the wealth accruing from, public land belongs to the community as part of Saudi Arabia's tribal and nomadic cultural inheritance. Traditionally, for the most part, the land was partly or irregularly cultivated, depending upon rainfall, away from areas where groundwater was available to simple technology irrigation. Dry land could not be cultivated or utilized for grazing as of individual right. The absence of cultivated large estates has facilitated a form of stability based on a fairly even distribution of rights in land. Since the creation of the Saudi State the Government, in its efforts to develop the agricultural sector, has adopted a policy of distributing "Public Land", once virtually all land for use by individuals and groups of utilizers.

Fundamentally, ownership of Public Land is based on utilization. The Public Land Distribution programme is based on the same foundations as the general development of all systems and programmes in Saudi Arabia. It is based on *Shari'a*, that is, law based on the Muslim religion, and modified according to human needs. The slow process of developing land distribution, started fifty years ago by King Abdul Aziz, avoided early friction and paved the way for recent more rapid promotion. According to the present formalized programme, all public lands which have water and soil potential can be distributed to different types of population. Particular attention is devoted to the complex matter of alienation of Public Land in the State's agricultural policy.

This programme is essentially a means to increase the expansion of agriculture economically; Bedouin settlement is co-ordinated with it. The small farms found in traditional areas of irrigated agriculture can be helped less by this programme because there is an emphasis on modern agricultural techniques. Saudi Arabian authorities are perpetually examining and reviewing legislation and carrying out investigations for furthering the policy.

The Public Land Distribution Ordinance is based on the precepts of Islam: land is considered the property of all Muslims and the leader of the Muslim community has the right to distribute the holding of land with a view to maximizing its use. For these reasons the State now distributes land but requires actual utilization. All distributed land should be developed within a period of approximately three years. Since many factors affect success of this policy, not only arising from the nature of land resources but also of a social and economic nature, complex arrangements with many different government bodies have become necessary.

Observations have indicated that land distribution will benefit not only the settled population in rural and urban areas, but also those Bedouin who are willing to lead a settled farmer's life, provided physical, economic and social factors permit them to do so.

Three case studies, out of eighteen which executed all kinds of land distribution are chosen for comprehensive study. These represent Bedouin, urban and rural settled areas in Saudi Arabia.

Analogous approaches to land distribution in some other countries are considered.

This study concentrates on applied principles rather than on a pursuit of purely theoretical ideas, yet theoretical principles are referred to for the purpose of comparison.

There is considerable potentially fertile land in Saudi Arabia, usable with limited groundwater resources. In the interest of more effective rationalization of land and water use, planning and Public Land development, an analysis of Saudi Arabia's economic and financial position is made. The evaluation of land distribution, necessary even though production evidence for assessment is lacking, is made by examining some key variables.

It will be interesting in time to observe the effects of Public Land Distribution and of the economic changes which have been introduced into areas since the programme started and development has taken place. It is too early to evaluate the actual work of the programme, or how it is ideally supposed to work. The benefits for most areas are still to come and they do not generally offer possibilities for constructive evaluation. We can, however, conclude that it is of little use to try to make a development programme for Public Land development based on one existing resource in one sector without foreseeing and providing for those side effects and consequences which will affect all other sectors. The establishment of sedentary agricultural settlements is an important and valid objective; the increased use of agricultural potential resources is equally valid. Each of these and other specific approaches however has in-built limitations.

This book gives a glimpse of the continuity between the past and the present and indicates possibilities for the future according to the flexible process of development in Saudi Arabia. The major question arises of deliberately making investment in the utilization of *Mawat* or in dead land, not used or owned by anyone, which should be written off as capital. It is my theme that Public Land development should be a matter of general development rather than solely a financial measure or specific resource development. It must be basic for Public Land Distribution that the aim is to develop the national agricultural resources to their greatest potential for the benefit of the national community, severally and collectively.

In this book, Arabic names of places, references etc., are used, most of them transliterated in various ways into English. I have transcribed Arabic words according to most frequent and recent usage. In some cases a Saudi Arabian transliteration system has become "officially" adopted and is used here. Standard English versions of certain Arabic words and names have also been used. Government employment since 1954 in agriculture, followed by studies for B.Sc., and M.Sc., degrees in soil, and my position in charge of Public Land from the first establishment of a Public Land Agency to becoming Director General of PLMD has provided me with a background knowledge both relevant to my study and useful for interpretation and analyses. This has also given me familiarity with the original texts of decrees, regulations and ordinances of the Country.

This study is based on field research carried out in Saudi Arabia during the period between October 1972 and May 1973. During these months I not only spent a considerable amount of time searching for available information at governmental agencies but I was also able to visit all the areas where Public Land distributions are made. Most of these areas I have visited more than once and I am well acquainted with the actual working of the Public Land Distribution programme.

Data relevant to this work is practically non-existent in published literature. The largest part of the material used consists of unpublished data obtained from the Ministry of Agriculture and Water.

Chapter One

Traditional Position Regarding Rights to Use and Own Lands

Any examination of a deliberate policy of land allocation or distribution must recognize that fundamental legal questions are involved. In any society, once the question of the right to use, control or allocate land is assumed by either individual, community or institution, some structure of law has to be designed in order to bring order into the situation.

When we consider Public Land Distribution in Saudi Arabia, we must start by examining the broad background of relevant Islamic law before we look at the particular national situation.

Nothing has ever affected Arabian society since its earliest history so strongly as the Muslim faith. When the Prophet Mohammed (Peace be upon Him) came with the message of Islam in the year AD 622 and presented this faith to the mainly Bedouin Arabian society there began a new era of civilization. Islam brought a unifying force following ages of discord to a great variety of peoples over a vast area, and part of this force was expressed in religion-based law: *Shari'a*.

All Saudi citizens without exception are Muslims, and Islam and the social life of individuals are fundamentally integrated. The *mores* of the religious institution in Saudi Arabia are very powerful. The individuals in the community are believers in and are controlled by these *mores*; the sanction of the religious leaders is not easily evaded.[1] It is therefore essential to recognize the involvement of the religious institutions in all community affairs. Religious leaders are the heads of kinship groups, naturally strong in Arabia, and therefore they are automatically members of Community Councils. Their opinions in council are considered of great importance, especially in all matters concerning change.

The codification of Muslim law has two main bases:

1. The *Shari'a* or Muslim religious law.
2. The decrees and ordinances issued by the government ruler.

The fundamentals of Islamic law, *Shari'a*, are four in number:

1. *The Holy Qur'ān* which is the first foundation and basis for all legislation.
2. *The Sunna and the Hadiths,* the second of these fundamentals, represent the sum total of the habits or general pattern of life of the Prophet Mohammed – Peace be upon him – (his words, acts, and tacit approvals as embodied in doctrine: in Saudi Arabia, the *Sunna*).
3. *Ijma al-ummah*, the consensus of opinion of the nation or Muslim community, producing given solutions to specific problems at any given time. This is justified by a *hadith* which recalls the words of the Prophet: "My people will never agree on an error".
4. *Qiyas̄*, deduction by legal analogy. This allows the following of precedents in deciding new cases

Rulers' decrees and ordinances are made fundamentally to satisfy and control public interest. They are:

Ijtihad (Investigation), which refers to the research necessary in order to apply the relevant rule to each and every case.

Istihsan (Preference), new judgements and principles according to public interest and welfare. This is based on the fact that every principle in *Shari'a* which is founded on custom can be changed or modified when such custom is changed. It therefore provides a flexible system of civil law for non-religious matters, drawn from experience and decision-making.

The vitality of Muslim law and its capacity to meet the exigencies of changing patterns of life have been dramatically demonstrated in the award of the Arbitration Tribunal held at Geneva on 23 August 1958. The Tribunal described the legal system of Saudi Arabia in the following terms:

"According to the doctrine and the information submitted by both parties to the Tribunal, Saudi Arabia belongs to one of the great legal systems of the world, namely Muslim law in which several rites of schools are distinguished. The principal Sunni School are the Hanafi, the Maliki, the *Shafi'a* and Hanbali. They do not differ in fundamentals but disagree in several points of detail."[26]

First a brief description of the manners, customs (*Urf*) and ways of life of the Arabs before Islam, relevant since law is more or less affected by these customs. *Urf* is a custom associated with a group of individuals where *Adah* is a habit of individualism. The majority of Arabs led a nomadic life. The nucleus of social life was the tribe, which was composed of blood or classified relatives. They lived in tents, easy to move whenever the tribe travelled in search of water and grazing. If they did not find enough of both, they lived near towns earning their living either by work or by plunder. Each tribe had, and still has, its chief who had absolute authority over its members. The head of each household similarly had absolute authority over the family.

Man recognized religion before he recognized the law, but Islam reconciled them. Islamic law combines as far as possible the advantages of both individual and social theories and avoids the disadvantages.[26] It combines morality with law in that it enacts for every act of Man two principles: one governing the act from its appearance and the other governing it from its motivation. In most advanced societies in non-Muslim countries religious laws were separated from civil laws in order to diminish the influence of the Church, which would not permit the changing of laws according to the needs of the society. In Muslim societies this was not necessary as Islamic laws were flexible and permitted changes as needed by the advances of the society.

In the economic field, the *Qur'ān's* conception is based upon the fact that ownership is a social function and that Man is the representative of *Allah* in the world. Therefore, he must dispose of his property in such a manner as to guarantee the satisfaction of the original owner who is *Allah*. He must refrain from abusing his right in such a manner as to cause harm to others. He must share in public expenses, be neither extravagant nor parsimonious. He must neither monopolize nor employ his wealth in acquiring political influence in the administration of the State and directing it to his profit in detriment of the interests of others. He must look to money as a means of production, not as a God to be worshipped.

Islam looks at matters from the objective point of view; and considers that everything inside or upon the Earth was created for the benefit of Mankind, each individual having his share. Therefore, ownership in Islam is divided into two parts:

Allah's ownership which benefits all society; the Holy *Qur'ān* indicates this "He who created for you all that is in the Earth". (*Surat Al Baqarah*) This means that all the Earth had been created by *Allah*, created for all people without preferences. The following paragraph asserts this also: "He created Earth for people." (*Surat Al Rahman*)

Utilization ownership: this originates from our legal right to what is created for us, the "owner" having the right to use it freely and enjoy it as beneficiary.

The Holy *Qur'ān* describes it as follows: "Spend from what *Allah* made available for you" (*Surat Al Hadid*).

Islamic principles in ownership rights and utilization

The Prophet Mohammed (Peace be upon Him) restored the old principle on which land ownership on earth was established. When human beings began utilizing the world the principle which was followed was that as land was used, reclaimed or made utilizable by a person, then he would have priority in its use. Thus a distinction was made between land in a state of nature or abandoned, "dead" land *mawat* or *mushaa*, and land made fruitful by its cultivation or other appropriate use. This principle is the basis of all human rights of ownership in *Shari'a* (legislation). The Prophet asserted on more than one occasion that the earth is *Allah's* earth, people are *Allah's* servants, and he who makes land fruitful has the right to use it, as it was stated in the following *Hadiths*:[8]

"That land which had inhabitants in the past but whose inhabitants died will come to be appropriated by the Imans; land not owned or utilized by anybody is of the proprietorship of *Allah* and His Prophet, and I give it to you Muslims."

"Who revives non-owned land has priority to use or own it."

"Who revives a dead land, it becomes his own; if another person attacks him by planting in his land he should remove the plants."

"Who surrounds a land by a wall, that land becomes his own."

"Who reaches first to what is not reached by another Muslim, the subject reached becomes his own."

The Prophet added to this instinctive principle another two bases. The first was: if a person utilizes a land owned by others, he does not obtain its ownership just by utilizing it. Instead, he says: "Whoever plants in the land of others without obtaining their permission, the costs he incurs should be repaid but he does not own the harvest."

The second deals with the individual's right to ownership: "He who utilizes *mawat* land that land becomes his own", and, "He who arranges to use *mawat* land becomes its owner. All land not belonging to anyone belongs to *Allah* and his Apostles, and to you afterwards."

Shari'a further defines the condition of full possession as the actual use and development of land for the purpose intended.[40] For example, if the land was intended for building a house, the actual building of the house fulfils the condition of possession. Or if the land was intended for cultivation, basic preparation which should include providing water for irrigation is sufficient.

Iqt'a – Donation

Another method of acquiring a title to ownerless land is through its bestowal upon an individual by the Imam. This is referred to as *Iqt'a* (donation) and many examples are cited.

The Prophet himself donated ownerless lands to many people. The following are some relevant *Hadiths*:

The Prophet donated lands to his followers and predecessors. Some of them sold his or their share of the donation. The Prophet donated lands in Hadramout and Khaiber. The Prophet donated land in Madinah to the two Caliphs (Abu Bakr and Omar).

From the days of the Caliphs have come the following *Hadiths*:

Abu Bakr (the first Caliph) donated land to one follower and gave him a deed, and brought witnesses among whom was Omar ibn Al-Khattab (the second Caliph). When the follower came to Omar to stamp the deed he said: "Stamp? is this all for you who have no people?"

Omar wrote to one *Wali* (Governor) asking him to donate land on Dijla riverside to one person if the land was not *jizyah* land or had water passing through it. (*Jizyah* land is property taken from non-Muslims by legal means.) Omar donated land to some people in Damascus for the purpose of keeping their horses on it, but they farmed it instead, so the Caliph took back the land and fined them.

Othman (the third Caliph) donated lands to five of the Prophet's followers.

From this body of caselaw and precedents finally emerges a system in which the following elements in land donation can be identified.

Firstly, whoever leaves a donated land without utilization for three years loses his donation. The basis for this was that the Prophet donated land to some people but they did not utilize it; then others came and utilized the land. When the two parties disputed the matter before Omar ibn Al-Khattab, he said: 'If it was donated from me or from Abu Bakr, I would take it back, but it is from the Prophet himself." Then he said: "Whoever has land and leaves it without utilization and then other people come and utilize it, then the latter will have priority in its ownership." He then made the appropriate period three years and thus created a firm precedent which is still recognized.

Secondly, if the donatee does not utilize the land properly, his donation will be reconsidered. The basis for this was that the Prophet donated to one of his followers the whole Aqiq area in Madinah but when Omar became Caliph he said to the follower: "The Prophet gave you the land not to deprive people of it but to work on it, so take the area you are capable of utilizing and return the rest of the land to us."

Thirdly, the government can donate only ownerless land; it has no right to withdraw land from some and give it to others. As for that "dead" or "white" land which is used for a common interest even though ownership is not established, this may not be donated. The *Hadith* says: "The Prophet gave one of his followers a 'white' land to utilize; afterwards it appeared that there was flowing water (a spring) in this land; the Prophet then withdrew it because his principle was that all people are partners in fodder, fire and water."

Fourthly, the government donates land only to people who have contributed good service to the common interest, or who are related to such service or to people where the donation fits the common interest. Equally, donations to persons not deserving it could not be considered legal gifts.

Fifthly, evidence of utilization must be firm and in one important respect it is based on environmental and social needs. Omar said: "Water is the basis of revival, such as digging a spring or well; if a person did this, then built or farmed the land, his work creates the complete revival. If he did nothing on the land except extract water, he will, however, have the right of ownership only for the area of the spring or well."

We can thus summarize the principles of donating land as follows:

1. Donation is in moderation and in the light of natural justice.
2. Donation is to those who contribute services to religion and the nation.
3. Donation is to those who perform useful works.
4. Donation is only from lands over which the donor has the right of gift.

Iqt'a (donation), in the light of this last pint and also since there exists the right of every person to develop dead land without the need to obtain the consent of the ruler, seems unnecessary. *Shari'a*, however, confirms *Iqt'a* fundamentally because it is useful in two respects: it enables the ruler to exercise some authority over the ownership of land, and it enables those who acquire the title to dead land in this way to gain full possession for appropriate utilization as soon as the title has been bestowed upon them. So, in Islamic law, dead land may be declared to be State property reserved for public use. *Iqt'a* does in fact provide a practical means of recognizing the dynamic and ever-changing nature of land use while retaining the spirit of the concept of equality of right, yet avoiding anarchic individualism.

Muslims have responsibilities as individuals and as members of communities. Islam believes that benefits should be directed both to the individual and to the community because, firstly, the individual is the origin of action in the community, so he should act without prejudice being directed against him; secondly, the community is the purpose to which the individual's action is directed. The individual is free in his behaviour and in benefiting from its results; thirdly, the community is responsible for the individual and for encouraging him and recognizing his status both as an individual and as a member of the community.

There are, however, three limitations on the use of an individual's rights in general and ownership rights in particular. Firstly, the right should be used to fulfil a stated purpose. Secondly, the right should be used for good purposes and not to bring direct harm to others. Thirdly, the use of the right is considered illegal if it brings unusual or even indirect harm to others. This principle has been applied on dead public land tenure.

In general, therefore, we can say that the Islamic creed reconfirmed the fact that utilization of land is the only reason accepted by primary communities for ownership. Islam revived this principle which modern Man has almost cancelled. Consequently an individual cannot become the owner of land by force, but conversely the investment and utilization of land by an individual or community results in the ownership of such land.

Islam and land tenure

Developing out of this Islamic concept of rights in land and also pre-Islamic systems is customary law or tenure.[54]

A characteristic feature of any such tenure system is the absence of the concept of land as a marketable commodity; nor is there any distinction between community ownership of land and the right of an individual or group to occupy and use a piece of land at any given point within the framework of the community. Traditional community control over individual land use, in the context of a subsistence type of agriculture, is one of the more important underlying objectives of this tenure system. In the past this pattern of distribution of rights facilitated conservation of land and phased extension of cultivation in accordance with the increased pressure of population. Under the impact of the modern economic systems the original pattern has, however, undergone such modifications that new problems have arisen which need specific and urgent action.

Both custom and religious law have in the past played, and still play, a major role in matters relating to land tenure, and this is hardly surprising since in any community land tenure is merely one aspect, though in agricultural communities it is one of the most important aspects in the socio-economic life of the people. Islam depends on custom as a basic concept for guiding the trends and behaviour and for judging problems. One *Hadith* says, "you people know best for your social life". However, the disadvantages of customary tenure are:

It does not provide legal security of tenure.
It can discourage improvement of natural resources.
It can hinder agricultural development.
It has resulted in unequal distribution of land in many countries.
It presents a paradox in some areas of land shortage coupled with poor utilization of available land.
It does not encourage investment, as individuals have no incentive and sometimes are even penetrated by tribal chiefs from making improvements.
It perpetuates tribal rivalries.

On the other hand, there are some observable advantages in customary tenure:

It has often prevented the development of the phenomenon of absentee landlordism and landless peasantry.
It has discouraged land speculation.
It has facilitated social control over private land use.

Whatever the tenurial system, wherever it has been based on a sense that the community as a whole is rightfully the ultimate owner of land, then, as with rights to land, we find the need for qualifying or limiting the control of specific land by specific people.

The concept of qualified ownership

As States, countries and governmental systems have developed, Islam, through the various Islamic institutions, still deals mainly with personal requirements such as food, housing or land holding—a range of requirements found in the earlier more simply equipped societies. The specialization in making use of any of these things is called either property, ownership, or the right of proprietorship.

No doubt, this right varied from time to time. In early and ancient situations this right was spread among all the members of the tribe. This common ownership was later narrowed to the extent that every family had its own specific property which related especially to the father and his children (males and females) without any specialization or distribution. The most recent stage of development was the appearance of the individual personality and his independence of personal possession.

Implicit throughout is a concept of social good. In *Shari'a* when certain rights are described as belonging to *Allah*, this means they belong to the community or public right, and the people are only agents of *Allah*. An individual is one who belongs to the community. So one can refer to this right as a private right and once this right is vested, then it consequently can be referred to as ownership right. Since the community is particularly considered to be a group of people in blood relationship to each other then the security of ownership is linked with blood relationships, with all that they imply in strength, continuity, and so on.

The concept of private property itself varies according to individual and group attitudes from one country to another. Those countries which adopted freedom in ownership did not place limitations on the range of things possessed while others adopted limitations preventing the possession of lands or large estates. However, the presence or absence of limitations, as we shall see, did not in themselves prevent or cause the appearance of large landed estates.

Land is one of the natural resources without which Mankind cannot achieve any kind of production.[26] Islam contributes positively to the distribution of natural resources by controlling the freedom of individuals to possess these resources, but at the same time recognizing that individuals have the right to select certain kinds of production.

In this concept, Islam is in contradiction with capitalism, which believes in the freedom of control of natural resources and production, and also with communism, which controls both centrally.

Islamic theory believes in beneficial utilization: benefit for the community and utilization for individuals. Competition is a promotion of utilization. Utilization is usually as extensive as the individual's power to utilize and there is no benefit to the community when any individual holds large areas without utilization.

Shari'a believes that all forms of ownership, community, public, and private should be in equilibrium. It does not give an individual the right of ownership for temporary utilization but only for continuous utilization, and insists on its return to communal ownership if utilization ceases.

So, there are three forms of land ownership which are appropriate under Islamic law:

1. Community ownership.
2. Public domain.
3. Private appropriation.

In Islam, the community ownership and public domain (State domain) appear superficially the same from the social point of view but differ in legislation and control.[12] The owner of the former is the whole community and the ruler has no apparent status to let or give it away. In the second, the owner is still the community, but the ruler has legislative status to control its use or dispose of it under Islamic law.

Community ownership originally extended over land conquered by Muslims which was already cultivated, and also over forests. Public domain extended over conquered fallow land, unutilized land and land carrying forest. Unutilized land is then public domain (State domain) and when it is utilized it becomes either community or private land.

In general Muslim legislation, it is the right of an individual to utilize the land whether this is authorized by the ruler or not, but the individual has the right of appropriation only as long as he maintains his utilization. However, in addition to the *Iqt'a* system other means have been found to regulate the situation (see p. 7)

Environmental and social influences of land control

Systems of land control necessarily reflect in some way or another the characteristics of specific societies and their interaction with their environments. The traditional systems of many of the Arab lands were evolved above all to suit societies in which both nomadic and sedentary peoples were represented.

In general, the Arabs could be divided into two main groups:

1. Nomads, *El-Badia*, who own livestock and live in black hair tents. These in turn could also be divided into two groups. First, the true nomads who move great distances in regular transhumant patterns and live in black hair tents away from towns. These are the camel breeders and true Bedouin. Second, there are the semi-nomads who live mostly in tents close to villages, towns or wells during summer and who move partially or wholly to the desert steppe grazing lands with flocks of sheep and goats. These are called in Arabic, *El-Dar*, which means "arabs of the house". Some of them are semi-sedentary and grow wheat, etc., as rainfed cash crops and have palm groves or natural jungle date palms.
2. Urban, *El-Hadar*, the sedentary people who dwell in permanent stone or mud houses in towns and villages, as cultivators, merchants, etc.

The pastoral nomadic land has certainly always been more extensive than cultivated land in the Arab countries, and the Arabian Peninsula in particular has been used since time immemorial as grazing land. Both in the past and today, more than eighty per cent of the area has been and remains pastoral land. Nomads are the sole means of utilization of the vast regions of range land. Traditionally, desert nomads move their flocks to almost any place where they can find forage and water. Traditionally, (and the Prophet Mohammed - Peace be upon Him - confirms this) such people are partners in three things: water, pasture and firewood. This is why pastoral land is always regarded in some sense as an area where communal rights must be dominant.

It is also an old Arab concept that communities should maintain huge areas of land surrounding this central territory to be their own tribal grazing reserves, for their sole benefit and utilization, such land being considered as communal and tribal property and maintained as such by force. This custom has been known since pre-Islamic times, originally called *Hema*. When Islam came, this practice was modified by the Prophet, who is reported in a *hadith* to have said: there is no *hema* except for *Allah* and his Apostles. During the lifetime of the Prophet, *hema* land was used as pasture for the horses and camels used in wars.[40] Later, during the days of Caliph Omar, it was made available also for the animals of individual poor Muslims as well as for the common interest of the community.

From the point of view of the nomad, then, it would appear that any territory regarded as necessary for the survival of his group is, by definition, utilized, is held as some form of property by the group and to some extent can be spatially identified. All this makes functional sense in a tribal society and is to some degree incorporated into *Shari'a* law, but it obviously leaves a legacy of problems to any system of public land distribution.

Even before the Prophet Mohammed - Peace be upon Him - (during the period of ignorance) some Arabs preferred to live in areas where they were wild palm jungles. If these palm jungles were situated in low lands or at the bottom of wadis, where occasionally there would be surface water or where ground-water was near the surface then natural oases would exist. The oasis dwellers call themselves the "people of the palm". The high water-table oases are best represented in the eastern province of Saudi Arabia in areas such as Al-Hassa and Qatif, but smaller oases of this type are also found in Najd, lowland Hijaz and wherever geohydrological conditions are favourable (see Fig. 6–3).

In the western highlands, however, the presence of springs, some running surface water and higher precipitation produced relatively favourable conditions of agriculture in which many tribes adopted a semi-settled life and supplemented pastoralism with cultivation. Such conditions are found in Hijaz and become increasingly favourable southward to the Asir, mountainous areas along the Red Sea coast. This was, and still is, the most thickly inhabited area of the Arabian Peninsula.

All the Arabian Peninsula was in political and cultural isolation for many centuries in the past. Into this traditional and Islamic situation in the Arabian Peninsula there came from outside the intervention of the bureaucratic needs of the Ottoman Empire.

In the early years which followed the establishment of the Islamic Empire, Muslim law applied in full the principles laid down by the Prophet, together with the administrative principles improvised during the Muslim Conquest. Local customs and geographical factors also had a profound influence.

The decrees, ordinances and legislation issued during the Ottoman Empire (AD 1300–1922) by the Sultans, were applied to the Muslim countries under their control for centralist and imperialist reasons. The rich fringes of the Arabian Peninsula, Hijaz and Asir on the Red Sea and Al-Hassa (which had a garrison in Hafuf) were under the Ottoman Empire for more than a century from the mid-eighteenth century onwards, but they were still governed by local leaders (Fig. 1–1). In the interior and the inner deserts, the Turks had no power or control; they knew the difficulties of climatic conditions and so the tribal areas, especially in the centre and the north, were unaffected, the tribes maintaining their traditions and social unity. The agricultural areas in the east were, in fact, little affected in comparison with the inhabited areas in the south-west and in particular the Holy area in the west, the latter being regarded as of great importance to the Ottoman Empire.

It was particularly during the period of Ottoman influence that the terminology describing land tenurial systems became most firmly established in the Arab countries.[18] The Ottoman land code was introduced to our region in 1858 (1274H). Other Arab countries such as Libya, Egypt, Syria and Iraq were also ruled by the Ottomans (see Chapter Ten) and the terminology set out below became generally used.

1. *Miri* Property (*Amiri* property) denotes land held in some degree of communal ownership and which the State has the right to supervise. The forms of these collective ownerships are as follows:

(a) *Mawat* or *Mushaa*. These are the "dead" lands, desert, vacant or empty. They are considered to belong to the public domain of the Muslim community.

(b) *Kharaj* or Conquered Land. These are cultivated and productive lands conquered by Muslim force of arms, but the lands still being left in the hands of the inhabitants, no matter whether they were converted to Islam or not. However, such land is strictly the property of the Muslim community which enjoys the usufruct and administrative responsibility.

(c) *Waqf*. This is usufruct land, once given as endowment to the Holy

THE OTTOMAN DOMINION IN SAUDI ARABIA IN 13th H (19th) CENTURY

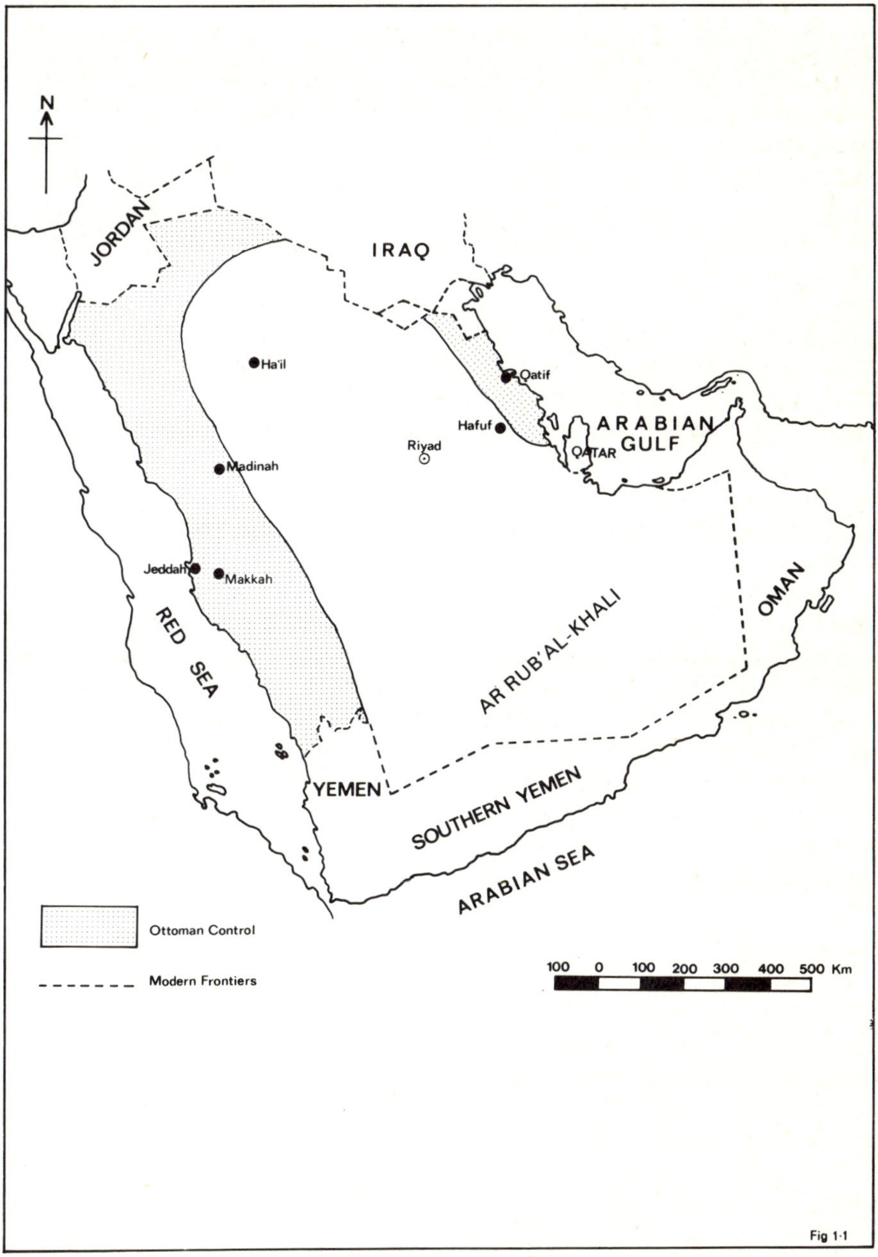

Fig 1·1

places and for other purposes, now administered by the State; its revenues are allotted to pious foundations, mosques, cemeteries, fountains, (*sabeels*), schools.

2. *Mulk*. Denotes private property including land over which full right of disposal and alienation are exercised.

The Ottoman Imperial Code was originally derived from *Shari'a* but it was reformed twice in major ways to hold Muslim and non-Muslim institutions together, and was developed on the lines of secular European models to make it more adapted to actual Imperial needs. *Shari'a* retained restricted jurisdiction in the panel and procedural sections only. Identification and registration of land titles had been recognized and recorded in this code. It was finally translated into Arabic and put into force throughout the Ottoman Empire. The present-day modern states which were once affected by Ottoman control have therefore inherited a double legacy as regards land-holding laws, the first being the ancient traditional and Islamic-based system, the second, the bureaucratic codification of the Ottomans. As we shall see, the needs of the modern nation state have required further modification of these systems.

To summarize the position as it has come to affect Public Land allocation systems:

The term "dead" land, generally refers to unutilized land to which there is no identifiable claim based on use. The general Islamic principles as described by *Qur'ān*, the *Sunna* of the Prophet (*Hadith*), the conduct of the Prophet's companions and their pious followers, all encourage dead land utilization through individual enterprise and through donations to potential users. As long as such land is utilized it is considered as being in the private ownership of the new user.

The important consideration in this respect is that *Shari'a* embraces important principles regarding dead land utilization by individuals and facilitates the Imam being in a position to be involved in land use.

Chapter Two

Position of the Modern State Exerting Control over Rights to Use and Own Lands

Following World War I and the liquidation of the Ottoman Empire the movement towards the creation of a major sovereign State in the Arabian peninsula culminated in the proclamation of King Abdul Aziz (Ibn Saud) as King of Saudi Arabia in 1932. The new State was formally an Islamic State in which full unity between diverse regions in the peninsula had still to be attained.

Within the kingdom some forces and elements relevant to fundamental aspects of land holding had to be accepted and incorporated into the workings of the new State with its own specific statehood needs.

It is clear that in the Arabian Peninsula Islam always reflects the hardships of tribal life in arid and semi-arid environments, and stresses equality and brotherhood. The Arabs accepted and followed the *Shari'a* precept that everything on the earth belongs to Allah and his people are his representatives who share the utilization of what had been found. The Imam in the past, the Sultan later, and the King now is the qualified representative of the community, who has the authority of controlling community proprietorship.

Individuality and separation are the main characteristics of any one tribal group. The area occupied by a tribe is regarded as being in its absolute possession – as long as the tribal group can maintain by force this possession. It recognizes pre-existing situations. Oases and palm groves are symptomatic of permanent utilization; and the people belonging to them have the right of ownership, in the sense of *mulk*. Hijaz, especially Holy areas, is important for pilgrimage and is affected by Muslims meeting annually in these Holy areas and surroundings.

Ottoman Empire concepts applied for a short period in small spatially important areas. Registration of some specially defined lands took place and responsibility was given to the existing internal organization. Particularly in the east (Al-Hassa Oasis), water distribution and registration took place for a short period according to the concepts of Ottoman law in an area where, along with other parts of the Gulf Coast, traditions had been partially affected by Persian influence.

Other important elements have also to be recognized in the evolution of the Kingdom of Saudi Arabia. First, King Abdul Aziz was the formal religious leader (*Imam*) in the country. Saudi Arabia had regions with different backgrounds; for example, Hijaz was relatively modern while Najd was religiously restrictive. The people of Hijaz and the people of Najd were anxious to see real Muslim rule in the country.

As a man well capable of recognizing the differences and contradictions implicit in the situation, King Abdul Aziz, with his limited experience in administration and his great enthusiasm to build a vast Kingdom, had to go through a long process of reconciling the regional interests.

Saudi Arabia, as a twentieth-century State needed a modern constitution, but it was not very easy to produce one because the country had no experience in this field. The King had to deal first with Hijaz. At the same time he had to take into consideration the opinion of *Ulema* (the body of religious learned men) in Najd, representative of Wahabism, and the converted Bedouins of Najd, devoted Muslims calling themselves *Ikhwan*. Both had great power.

Since most aspects of law and administrative rules are not strictly defined by the *Shari'a*, King Abdul Aziz was able to incorporate, to a certain degree, elements from the Ottoman system which existed in Hijaz, and Saudi Arabia continued using procedures of that law according to *Shari'a*.

New supplementary rules and regulations amplifying this control were issued. In particular, the government accepted appropriations of government land if claimants had official receipts registered in the Islamic Court. Ordinary certification or older appropriations of government land had to be investigated by Islamic Courts. (Consultative Council Resolution No. 430 dated 23/8/1349H (1930), approved by Royal Order No. 3013 dated 28/8/1349H.) The previous Ottoman procedures were adapted for housing registration. (Consultative Council Resolution No. 104 dated 22/4/1349H (1930), approved by Royal Order No. 1209/1055 dated 27/4/1349H.) The concept of property ownership used by the previous government in Hijaz as *Amiri* property, remained as Amiri property. (Property Ownership Ordinance in Hijaz, Chapter Five, Article 9, issued by Royal Decree No. 26/2/12 dated 29/6/1353H (1934)). Also, where *Waqf* property followed Hijaz procedures, they were then accepted.

The new country had to nurture its own modern institutions, a difficult process in a basically conservative and traditional community.

In Saudi Arabia, then, the monarchy combines authority from three sources. The monarch is simultaneously the propagator of the faith (*Imam*), responsible for upholding the law (*Shari'a*), and the leader (*Sheikh*) of the tribes and commanding tribal allegiance; also, by extension, the King (*Malik*) should lead and act as would a western ruler. These sources provide great religious and secular powers to a ruler who is capable of appreciating them. In the monarchical state of Saudi Arabia the concept of State land is very important. Under the King the power of the new State institutions appeared to conflict with the power of the *Ikhwan* groups, the interpreters of Islam.

Extreme *Ikhwan* thought called for a return to the simple fundamental sources of Islamic religion and the *Ikhwan* criticized King Abdul Aziz for the following:

Not returning the new Kingdom to the ways of life typical of the first Hejrah century.
Making contact with the enemies of Islam.
Meeting with non-Muslim delegates at conferences, etc.
Using recent technology (like telegraphs and telephones).
Sending his sons to foreign countries.
His lenient attitude towards applying the teaching of the Wahhabi movement.
His imposition of secular taxes and accepting taxes on forbidden things such as tobacco.

Slowly, the King, by his far-sightedness, experience and virtues, overcame opposition from the rebels from *Ikhwan* and obtained acceptance of the country's new rules and regulations. Usage of the recent technical ways and means necessary for civilization and for religious reform is a vital factor in the development of old social codes and the creation of a more pleasant and co-ordinated society. The power of the new State institutions to initiate change or to plan development were designed to be compatible with traditional ways of life and not lead to the neglect of the Islamic concept and the beneficial use of previous regulations.

Inherent in the situation was, however, a conflict between some aspects of the old and the new and, once oil revenues started flowing, socio-economic change inevitabiy became a fact. Therefore, even more power had to be lodged in the hands of the State and in some institutions through which the new State must accept responsibility for controlling change. In this situation the King gathered around him groups of consultants and liberation movements in the Arab countries, tribal leaders and religious people, the *Ulema*, the interpreters of Islam.

In the case of land, new institutions, such as the Public Land Management Department (PLMD), were established but, even before the present-day structure could appear, some particular problems had to be faced.

The end results were of course judicial decisions. The translation of new or modified concepts into judicial language in Saudi Arabia has required that the judicial bureau, through the cumulation of decisions, build up case law referring to land ownership. For example, utilization of public lands leads to ownership. Utilization differs according to the purpose thereof. If it is for urban purposes, the surrounding of the perimeter of the land with all its contents, brick, stones, or palm leaves, according to the customs pertaining therein, is deemed compulsory. But, if farming is the purpose of utilization, then levelling the land and piling the soil round it, is deemed compulsory. In a case where it is meant for a barn or a well, then surrounding the land according to the customs as a protective procedure is considered compulsory. On the other hand, if the utilizer cannot reach the object of utilization, for example, water if he drills a well, then the land is not considered his property, but he or his inheritor has the right of priority. But if land is neglected for three years without relevant justification for such negligence, then the utilizer shall be asked either to utilize the land or to leave it to others who are capable of such work.

Behind such decisions, however, lie problems of interpretation and identification of claimed rights, and the balancing of interests, regional, individual, personal and, above all, national. Some illustrations of these problems arising from the needs of the new State can now be given.

First, land for new resource development: Land not clearly in qualified individual ownership is the main potential for new resource development. The lands of the tribes, which were in the past prohibited to others, are now receiving tribal societies alien to them. This phenomenon can be observed on coastal areas and in many parts of Najd.

The immovable property wealth, the land, of tribes had become the property of the State. But the situation in Hijaz and other parts of the State is different and each region had to be dealt with on its own merits.

In fact the *Ikhwan* captured Hijaz in 1924 by a religious war, and according to this concept, they have to divide the property among themselves. One part of this property is the land itself. But King Abdul Aziz, the head of the State and the inheritor of the *Ikhwan* rights did not want to be viewed as a conqueror of land. Nevertheless, he is supposed to control the land and to use the power in a way similar to that which happened in Western Europe in the seventeenth century to build up the State national plan.

According to this type of control, we quote from Hobbes' *Leviathan*, besides the title: "All private Estates of land proceed originally from the arbitrary Distribution of the Sovereign. ... Wherein the Sovereign assigneth to every man a portion, according as he, and not according as any Subject, or any number of them, shall judge agreeable to Equity, and the Common Good." Though people coming into possession of land by war do not exterminate the ancient inhabitants, but leave to most or all of them their estates.

At this point we can examine the position of the State and the evolution of Governmental machinery, in the context of land distribution, under three main headings.

The State in relation to specific claims to and demands for land

Where claims already exist, the State's responsibility has to be faced through insisting on its right to control.

First there can be the acceptance or rejection of pre-existing land claims. King Abdul Aziz accepted many of the administrative customs in the new State temporarily to avoid friction, but he changed the administration gradually to put all powers in his hands as Head of State. This was acceptable as a custom of all rulers as *Amirs*, where they managed the whole affairs of a community, large or small, as absolute rulers.

When tribal claims were affected, because according to the belief of some tribal groups that *any* devolution of authority gave them total power in their territory, the King gave some of these tribal leaders, the *Sheikhs*, limited rights of disposition for the purpose of settlement or distribution among their people. This concept was thought of as an attraction for tribes to substitute calm and peace for aggression; this is still effective in *Hejar* in Mada-in Saleh and Mughiyra in Al-Ula. (See Fig. 3–4.)

In Hijaz Ottoman-granted titles to land were of particular importance. As previously stated, the King did not want to create hatred by depriving tribes of the social status and influence acquired from the previous government and at first accepted the situation as long as they respected his orders, kept away from main roads and prevented crimes. He did not reject former titles as long as they were not clearly against religion. These titles related to ownership of areas including mountains, valleys and water channels; many cases were taken to and warranted by the Islamic Court and its judgement was accepted. Dry farming areas were managed according to custom and *Shari'a* so that the rights fell to the first seasonal occupant.

The land property of previous governments was located in Hijaz, Al-Hassa, Qatif and other areas. Regarded as community property, this land became utilized under a contract lease system applied to agricultural areas, and also to unutilized land. Responsibility for it is held by the Ministry of Finance and National Economy for the national community.

Secondly, there was an insistence on the illegality of any land claim made without State permission; this was based on a strict interpretation of *Shari'a*. The official faith of Saudi Arabia is *Hanbali*, but the present authorities have made an end to the numerous faiths. They have unified them and kept to the basic principles of Islamic faith which conforms with the *Qur'ān* and the Prophet's sayings. An ordinance of *Shari'a* Courts was issued in 1372H (1952) to unify and organize systems of courts in the whole State and to counsel others. In the same year an ordinance governing the organization of the functions of *Shari'a* law departments was issued. Articles 85 and 86 are the most important to the control of land appropriation.

Article 85 of the Organization of the Functions of *Shari'a* Law Departments provided that if a Court were requested to issue an appropriation deed for a real property, it should write to the Municipality, the *Waqf* Department, the Ministry of Finance (and recently to the Ministry of Agriculture and Water Branch in the area where the Court is located), and enquire from them as to whether they have any objection regarding the same. If they have no objection, the appropriation deed may be issued after being published in the official gazette for a period of one month.

Article 86 also provided that in case the Court is requested to issue an appropriation deed for undeveloped land, it should refer the matter to the financial authorities for guidance, in addition to the procedures contained in Article 85.

This institutional and bureaucratic procedure, however, was not universally accepted. The *Hanbali* school of Qur'ānic interpretation maintained that any action – in this context any grant of land – of the Prophet Mohammed – Peace be upon Him – was made by him as Prophet in the name of *Allah* and therefore was perpetual. For differing reasons, however, two other schools, *Maliki* and *Hanafi*, believed that in the matter of land the Prophet acted solely as Head of State and that therefore the normal need to show use would operate. In 1377H (1957) the Chief Justice (*Grand Mufti*) made a final ruling and confirmed that the dead land can be owned with utilization. "He who utilized the land claimed it as his own, whether or not he had permission from the *Imam*. He who surrounded a land by stones, it became his own free of charge. When an interested person got it he had to utilize it or leave it. Any dispute or interpretation by municipality or another will refer to *Shari'a*. Anybody trying something else is not going in the right direction." This was the decision of the Chief Justice of Saudi Arabia and still remains authoritative, but other jurists still prefer a requirement of permission for the benefit of land control.

The appropriation of utilized and unutilized land by individuals and groups who claimed that their titles had a legal basis gave rise to other problems. In some cases it seemed that jurists had confirmed proprietorship or division of utilized land by written documents or deeds. Similarly the disposition of unutilized land sometimes appeared to be confirmed by deed or written document. It became necessary first to insist that lands without ownership documents or with only incomplete ownership registration documents (since those were only confirmation of witnesses' evidence) could be claimed by the State. Private appropriation of these lands and ownership claims were rejected. A Royal Decree of 1387H (1967) ruled that anybody who henceforward alleges land appropriation would have his allegation disregarded. Another Decree of 1388H (1968) also ruled that undeveloped lands are owned by the Government, that the appropriation of such land by anybody is not recognized, that any deed supporting such appropriation is cancelled and that the claimant shall be made to understand that this is a trespass for which he may be penalized.

Many regulations, orders and instructions were issued to control appropriations, due to problems that arose in this context, the most important ones relating to this vexed question of land deeds. It is now necessary to ascertain, for example, a donor's ownership to land before the realization of any donation, and that the jurist shall, when writing the deeds, ascertain the proper names of individuals in the light of the details shown on personal identity cards. No deeds of appropriation for agricultural lands and waters may now be issued except by the State. Furthermore, the *Shari'a* law upheld by the Chief Justice provides that land which has no sign of life or development cannot be appropriated by merely lodging a case or giving an oath even though the claimant has appropriation deeds for the same, but shall remain in its original uncultivated status.

The concept of public interest has had to be updated and codified. Public interest reflects the rights of a group or groups, utilization and exploitation in which groups of individuals jointly participate. Public and community ownership recurs as a constant theme and affects many types of land and land use. Thus there are the following:

High grade pasture land capable of meeting the demands of tribes, smaller groups or individuals for considerable periods and with relatively high carrying capacity. Such land has long been identified and preserved for the use of particular groups.

Dry farming areas with a natural water supply. The constant here is the regularization of the traditional behaviour in each area. When conflict arises it will be settled by the local Court.

Collective facilities, including the important public animal drinking water supplies, e.g. *Birak Zobeda* (basins). Constructed over one thousand years ago these basins are scattered all the way from Iraq to Madinah. They are filled by rainfall and their supply lasts several months. Wadis and water channels leading to farms and palm groves are also considered public facilities. Bedouins are prohibited from establishing even temporary encampments in Wadi channels (e.g. Wadi Qassibah) to prevent the further development of what has happened previously, the slow growth of unplanned sedentary settlements. Any wish to be allocated even temporary rights in such areas must be referred to the King himself and any dispute of this sort should not be referred to the Court.

Forestry areas which in the past were managed and conserved by appropriate tribes for their individual benefit. Usually these have normal property documents but the State has exerted the right of management and conservation and tribal utilization is restricted in order to conserve resources.

Land with mineral rights includes that which has superficial minerals such as salt, oil, etc., which do not require development; the land is therefore considered public property. Concealed minerals near the surface or deep underground are and have been normally considered property held in the public interest according to *Shari'a*. In this case, as in that below, the group with a relevant "public interest" is extended to mean the national community whose interest is represented by the State.

Railways' Right of Way is a novelty resulting from technical innovation. The Royal Decree No. 21 dated 3/4/82H (1962) considered that the right of way for a railway is a zone with a width of 200 metres measured from the centre of the railway track on each side. This "right of way" land is Government public property, Government here representing the national community, and it is called "The Zone of the Railway Lands".

The Right of Way zones for main and subordinate roads have been regulated as follows:

> The width of the right of way inside cities and villages is determined in accordance with the planning decisions of the municipality concerned. If there is neither a municipality nor a planning auth-

ority, the width of the right of way is limited to 30 metres. The width of the right of way outside cities and villages is limited to 60 metres in ownerless lands and to 40 metres in privately owned lands.

Urban areas. Outside the established built-up areas lie the surrounding districts which have become the most attractive zones for illegal appropriation. These hinterland zones are attached to the municipality institution, if one exists, or under the control of *Amirs* in the case of villages. In about 1380H (1960) such zones were held to extend over 10 Km outward from the boundaries of the inhabited areas of a town, and 5 Km for a village. This concept has since been changed (see pp. 70–71). No appropriation within these hinterland zones is accepted unless the *Shari'a* law departments are satisfied, especially with reference to Articles 85 and 86 (see p. 20).

One group of lands held in the public interest is called "the restricted ancient areas". These include areas of important cultural interest (mostly pre-Islamic) and are especially located in Madinah, Mada-in Saleh, Al-Ula, the Taif-Mecca old road, Khaiber, Ha'il, Tabuk, Najran, Al-Hassa and Qatif. In some of these areas wells lie buried, springs (often easily to be discovered and utilized), and ancient dams still holding water for irrigation. All claims, appropriations and written documents supporting individual private claims are rejected. Any deeds which may be required to be issued for these or for neighbouring areas are held until the Courts consult the Ministry of Education and the *Shari'a* law departments, and the deeds are valid only if the requirements of Articles 85 and 86 are fulfilled (see p. 20).

Protected Land (*Hema*) is a special category of some importance. Saudi Arabia was faced in its early days as a State with a confused situation concerning the *Hema* system. It became necessary to examine each regional situation and to decide upon specific policies. Although the *Hema* system as such was abolished and all relevant land became equally accessible to all, (see p. 11), there remained a type of private *Hema*, or "common land" which was always small in area and reserved for working animals or for special usage; such common land was linked to specific and identifiable communities. It is now considered that the previous interpretation of the scripture and *hadiths* applied in reality to nomadic societies and *Ijtihad* research (see p. 2) supports the rights of the whole tribe or of individual members of the tribe to use the *Hema*, where inhabitants have a more or less settled way of life. Only Hijaz and Asir have *Hema* lands of this type.

A Royal Decree confirmed the decisions of the committee which was set up for the evaluation of the *Hema* system of the Taif suburbs and made some rulings as for example:

"Six protected dry farming lands (as private *Hema*) since ancient

times should be kept as they are and accordingly protection of the same is approved.
Thirteen protected public lands are to be opened for grazing. Some others are to be opened for neighbourhood grazing, others for public grazing and the rest are allowed for the people of the area though some parts of these are allowed for grazing only. Nomads are prohibited from settling in the areas allocated to them in the parts opened for grazing. Cutting of trees is prohibited in the lands opened for grazing. Nomads and shepherds are prohibited from approaching farms and channels to avoid causing dispute."

Protected Public Lands were confirmed by a Royal Order issued (vide the letter dated 5/4/1373H (1953)), and circulated to all Amirates. The following paragraphs are quoted from it: "As you are aware, we do our best and pay the necessary funds for the welfare of the people, as stated in the sayings of our Prophet, that *Allah* the Merciful helps us as long as we help our poorer fellow men. However, it is ordered that no land should be monopolized. This means that when we are individually too strong our nation is weak. It also means that when we are weak and when our nation (nomads and settled) is strong then, paradoxically, we are strong. Accordingly Public Land should be protected absolutely. Other lands will remain as they are and if any dispute arises in this connection, it will be subject to the judicial rules." Private protected land (private *Hema*) is still allowed, as above, even though the number of working animals requiring grazing rights is decreasing due to the utilization of agricultural machines. Recently a committee representing the Ministry of Interior and the Ministry of Justice was set up and it submitted three decisions. A Royal Decree confirmed its decisions as follows: "Firstly: concerning *Hema* Al-Hajar mountain, Wadi Al-Qayyem, and *Hema* Al-Hayafin, we would like to inform you that there is no objection to the execution of what was decided concerning the three private protected lands. Secondly: if the dispute deals with rights of land as an area, it should be referred to the legal courts. Thirdly: if the dispute deals with grazing, a committee should be set up to examine the place disputed, and if it finds work animals existing there, the protected land should remain as it is, otherwise the land becomes open to all provided that no harm occurs to the villages and farms."

Restricted areas for drilling. The Ministry of Agriculture and Water is responsible for the management of water for irrigation, drinking and other public uses. This Ministry recommends that certain areas with underground water resources be declared "Restricted areas" to the State's Ruler. When a recommendation is approved, the area may be used only by the Ministry for drilling for drinking water. There are several locations where private drilling is prohibited by the State ruler. These are the Madinah area, Makkah (Wadi Fatima), Abha (Wadi Abha), Khamis Moshait and Riyad.

Riyad is illustrated here as an example of a prohibited area for private drilling. This conserves the Minjur and Wasia Aquifers and also preserves resources for existing and future settlements. This restricted area includes the lands located between 110 and 150 Km. on the Riyad-Khurays Road and a zone including Wadi Nisah and Riyad within a radius of 40 Km. This will include several wadis as shown in Fig. 2–1.

From all that has been said, it is clear that Saudi Arabia as an Islamic Kingdom and as a leader of Muslim countries, has wished to show and to prove that religion is not against development. By enforcing *Shari'a*, the State has asserted its authority for the safeguarding of the interests of individuals, specific and varied communities as well as the national community. There have emerged, therefore, by evolutionary stages the rights and interests of the State as an institution, which in economic and administrative terms we describe as the "public

RESTRICTED AREA IN RIYAD
FOR DRILLING

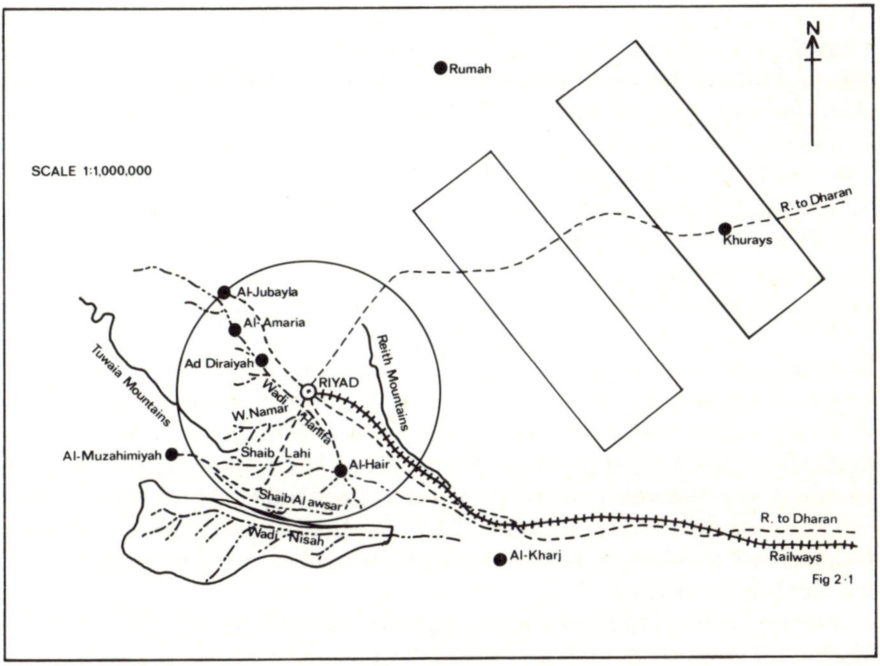

Fig 2·1

sector". So far this has been achieved by preserving a continuity with the past and without provoking, as has happened frequently elsewhere, a conflict between secular and religious attitudes.

The authority of the State and the evolution of administration

To understand the system of government in Saudi Arabia, one must see it as the result of the interaction of specific basic factors of social, economic and geographic circumstances of the Arabian community, including its beliefs and traditions. If we understand this concept, the present régime in Saudi Arabia is constantly changing and evolving according to the development of Saudi society, while still fundamentally remaining an Islamic régime.

Within this society, we must first recognize the religious element: the meaning of the government system lies in a sort of free election, *Bayà* which translated means investiture. The system of government in Islam is neither autocratic nor hereditary. In the first place, the head of state regards himself as representing the will of *Allah* on earth. Invested with this status he can do no wrong and there is no limit to his will; his powers cannot be restricted. In Western history one has the emergence of a King who reigns but does not rule. In Saudi Arabia, however, one finds in King Abdul Aziz a ruler, the founder of an Islamic State (the concept of which is essentially one of an identifiable community of believers rather than a Western political unit), and one who was invested with the Imamate before he was proclaimed King. This wide-ranging authority, to which King Abdul Aziz added his own strength of personality and state-creation, is complete provided that his rule is at all times directed towards the public good and that it is accepted that he is accountable to Allah and the people. The ruler's duties are then defined in terms of *Shari'a* law. (See p. 16).

During the early period of the development of Saudi Arabia the necessity of retaining a compatibility between the nature of Kingship and the nature of the Imamate was very great. The Ruler, in the Islamic concept, as *Imam* is supreme, however, should his rule effectively be shown to be offensive to the Islamic conscience, by, for example, a pronouncement by the *Grand Mufti*, then he can be divested of his authority. This position has been a source of strength to rulers with the ability to retain what is essentially a traditional authority rooted deep in the Islamic culture and, although not easily transformed into western bureaucratic government, it does provide a base for flexible evolution.

The position of the judiciary is equally affected by the force of religion. The main principles of judiciary are the independence of judges and equality before the law. The *Grand Mufti* (Chief Justice), the *Ulema* (learned and well-informed men of Islamic law) and other interpreters of Islam have direct contact with the Ruler whose decision would, after consultation, be final. It has been declared more than once that the country will follow *Shari'a* law as a constitutional régime. A Royal Decree in 1347H (1927) was issued to organize Islamic Courts in Hijaz; this was followed by several regulations and ended with the Ordinance of *Shari'a* Courts 1372H (1952) (see p. 20). Up to 1386H (1966) this meant that a "Presidency of Judges" (a committee of senior Islamic jurists) developed; after 1386H this became bureaucratically formalized as the Ministry of Justice. However, the separate institution of *Dar-el-Efta* (the office of religious legal opinion) exists outside the Ministry for dealing with matters in which religious doctrine is significantly concerned, for example, the morality of loan-interest.

Given, however, the creation of the State of Saudi Arabia in the twentieth century, the concept of power was forced to evolve in political as well as in socio-religious terms. In the early days, King Abdul Aziz gathered the power into his own hands. Administration at that time was very simple. He appointed his son Faisal as a Viceroy in Hijaz, and other personal representatives in regions as in Najd and Al-Hassa to deal with all matters, except military and foreign affairs which remained under the direct authority of the King. These matters included religious, administrative, financial and educational elements. Such devolution was in conformity with Islam, under which the ruler has the right to appoint four types of personal representatives.[5]

1. General duty for general work, for example, Ministers.
2. General duty for special work, for example, *Amirs* and Governors.
3. Special duty for general work, for example, judges.
4. Special duty for special work, for example, judges for a region.

The ruler in Islam can devolve power both to individuals, for example, the *Amirs* and Governors, and also to administrative organizations. He appoints Ministers and judges and allocates duties. In addition to individuals and organizations given specific authorities by the Ruler there is also derived from the *Qur'ān* the concept of a consultative council, the duties of which are to advise and to be consulted. Decisions remain in the hands of the Ruler.

In Hijaz, consultative councils emerged temporarily and a general council located in Makkah in 1346H (1927) was reorganized and strengthened in 1347H (1928) and headed by a viceroy. The latter is now the only surviving one of its type.

The General Consultative Council had general authority mainly for:

Expropriation for the general interest.
Preparing ordinances and regulations for the Ruler's decision.
Budget preparation for Government divisions.
Preparing permits for economic and urban projects.

All these authorities given to the Consultative Council only became effective after the approval of the King. The General Council acted as a legislative authority for 25 years after which this authority was transferred to the Cabinet Ministers. Before the establishment of major Ministries, a viceroy was responsible in Hijaz for Education, Finance, Security, Health and Communications Directorates, Agricultural Affairs, Minerals, Trade, Industry and Private Institutions. Also, before the establishment of Cabinet Ministries with executive power, a deputy council was established in Hijaz also in 1351H (1932) (located in Makkah) and had executive authority for:[50]

Planning and Policymaking for the whole country.
The supervision of the Ministry of Foreign Affairs (recently established).
The supervision of the Ministry of Interior (which replaced viceroyalty).
This Ministry besides its actual legal and executive authority, started as a point of reference for the Directorate of Public Health, Directorate of Education, Directorate of Wire and Wireless Communications, Directorate of Police, Quarantine, Islamic Courts and Municipalities.
Supervision of the Consultative Council (whose legal authority started to decrease).
Supervision of the Office of Finance and the other remaining directorates (district, governors and presidency of the judiciary).

Actually these authorities were similar to the authorities of Cabinet Council nowadays and sometimes covered more than that for Hijaz region.

The development of governmental apparatus also required changes in the management of finance and the economy. In 1351H (1931) as the community advanced somewhat and its needs began to become diversified, King Abdul Aziz transformed the traditional Treasury into an Office of Finance which in turn became a Ministry of Finance and then a Ministry of Finance and National Economy in 1372H (1952).[13] It had authority over a large number of State directorates already existing as well as new ones which were established. For example, Transportation Directorate 1355H (1935) Mineral Resources and General Constructions Bureau in 1355H (1935) which developed into the Directorates of Petroleum and Mineral Resources, and also the general Directorate for Constructions in 1372H (1952), *Hajj* and

Waqf Directorate (which included broadcasting) 1365H (1945); Agriculture Directorate 1367H (1947), Office of Labour 1367H (1947) and Directorate of Tribal (or Customary) Law 1372H (1952). However the viceroy, who is the head of the Deputy Council, retained supervision of the Ministry of Finance on behalf of the Ruler.

Financial improvement helped the Government to extend its administration and services. Between 1370–1373H (1950–1953), separate divisions grew into bureaucratic Ministries which now are: the Ministry of Health 1370H (1950), Ministry of Communications 1372H (1952), and simultaneously in 1373H (1953), the Ministry of Agriculture and Water, the Ministry of Education, the Ministry of Labour and Social Affairs were created. The Cabinet of Ministers replaced the Deputy Council in the same year.

Following the transformation of the Ministry of Finance into the Ministry of Finance and National Economy, there also came about the strengthening of the Ministry of Interior in 1373H (1953). This Ministry is concerned with political administration (security, boundaries, municipalities, governorates, etc). It is the Ministry of Interior's responsibility for land control, from the point of view of political administration, for example, tribal rights, municipal areas and administration concerned with nomadic population, which is of relevance to us here.

Land as a resource is obviously a vital area of responsibility of the Ministry of Agriculture and Water. However, most of the Kingdom's Ministries are concerned with land control. For example, the Ministry of Communications and later the Ministry of Petroleum and Mineral Resources separated in 1380H (1960), are also involved.

As we will see later (Chapter Four) an administrative machinery with its roots in Islam and traditional Arabia has developed in ways which are of complex importance to the whole question of control and distribution of land.

The consequences for the State in connection with land control arising from special man-land situations

Saudi Arabia, as part of the arid and semi-arid Middle Eastern heartland, was in its early days still predominantly a nomadic pastoral country. In spite of regional variations, the dominant cultural characteristics were those associated with tribal systems and on the political level a sense of nationhood had to be created and the central authority of a State had to be accepted. It could be ruled only by a strong monarchy both because of tribal groups which were always strong and separatist and because the only feeling of common citizenship among the people was their respect for religion and observance of the *Shari'a* law. If the new constitutional monarchy had been weakened the Arabian community would have returned to its previous state of discord.

On the economic and resource level the dominance of nomadic and pastoral evaluations of, and attitudes to, land and water and to the exploitation of these had produced systems of land occupation which were simply not compatible with the needs of a central Government engaged in the economic development of a State.

The social consequences of this situation were dealt with in part by the Ministry of Interior, an administration concerned with nomadic population, tribal relationships and urban areas and settlements. The economic consequences, so far as they affected rural land, became in large part the responsibility of the Ministry of Agriculture and Water. In particular, it dealt with land control from the technical point of view, for example, some aspects of nomadic sedentarization, the preparation and improvement of grazing land and the supply of water to nomads, tribes and urban areas.

However, many other sectors in the developing administrative structure were also functionally involved in this general situation, for example, the Ministry of Labour and Social Affairs which was established in 1380H (1960).

To summarize, we can distinguish the following phases and elements in the development of the Kingdom of Saudi Arabia.

During the first thirty years, 1319–1351H, (1899–1931) the only achievement was the unification of the country and the establishment of the Kingdom; all was subordinated to this goal. The second thirty years 1351–1381H, (1931–1961) saw the gradual change of the system of governmental and administrative authority from an old-style personal authority to a modern structured and bureaucratic system. After 1381H (1961), attention was given to the development of economic and social projects which went hand in hand with administrative improvement. All through the various changes, one must accept the given fact that the Ruler is the personal embodiment of the community; he is the trustee of land which ultimately is owned by Allah.

All this followed from the other given facts: the political need of the new concept of the State (through the Ruler) to exercise authority: the economic need of the State to organize use of resources: the financial power to organize resources and plan for future use: the desired transition from tribalism to non-tribal conditions (social element).

From what has been said, one can understand how various departments of government, headed by the Ruler who retains ultimate power, emerge as active in this area of land control. State land started to come under administrative governmental control and becomes technically synonymous with Government land. Since the benefit of its use is, and is intended to be, directly for the public, it may also be called Public Land.

The major result of these changes and developments was a fundamental alteration in the status of Public, State or Government Land. Even now a complete hierarchy of the regional organization of administration in the provinces of the Kingdom has not yet developed and many traditional elements still appear to survive. Thus local administration has been delegated to *Amirs* or Regional Governors, to whom many types of jurisdiction have been warranted. These Governors derived their authority in the past from the King or Prime Minister, but at present they derive their authority from the Minister of Interior. The limits of jurisdiction of each local authority are not clear. The number of Governors in the country exceeds eighteen and they are assisted by a few thousand Sheikhs (village or tribal and called *Amirs*) who practise their power mostly over nomads.

The continued existence of such means of exercising authority through *Sheikhs* and governors does not mean, however, that their traditional powers remain unchanged. In particular, and relevant to this study, their traditional and customary powers of land allocation and distribution have been removed and these powers are now concentrated in the hands of central Government. As noted on p. 18 and following, where allocations were made before power was centrally concentrated, grants and claims have to be confirmed by the courts and accepted by the government before they become valid.

The Royal Decree of 1379H (1959) was most important in that it prevented the Amirates from granting lands to people except by an order from HM the King, and that only the lands granted by the *Amirs* previous to this date are sanctioned. This Royal Decree was addressed to the Minister of Interior and to the most important *Amirs*. Official circulation of this decree to all *Amirs* then took place.

The culmination of all these developments has been the present situation in which the State, through governmental and administrative machinery, controls the management and distribution of Public Lands.

To summarize: King Abdul Aziz overcame the problems, conflicts and tribal claims of land created during the long history of the country of Saudi Arabia. He brought into being the fact and concept of *State Land* and laid down the fundamental structure of its status within general Islamic principles. Now State land excludes the community owned lands such as specifically identified pastures, dry farming land, collective facilities, forestry, oil and mineral rights, railway rights, urban land, ancient and restricted areas. It also excludes privately owned lands such as *mulk*, *waqf* and all utilized lands. State Land for utilization can now only be granted by the Ruler.

Chapter Three

The First Phase of Distribution Policies

The general national background

In this study, we are concerned only with non-urban land. A background picture is needed if we want to project our thoughts about land-use patterns.

Saudi Arabia occupies about four-fifths of the Arabian Peninsula, which covers a surface area of approximately two and a half million square kilometres. The peninsula is bounded by the Red Sea on the west, the Gulf of Aden and Arabian Sea on the south, and the Gulf of Oman and the Arabian Gulf on the east. North of the kingdom lie Jordan, Iraq and Kuwait. Several small countries are located along the coast: Bahrain, Qatar, the Trucial States (now the U.A.E.), Oman, People's Democratic Republic of Yemen and the Arab Republic of Yemen.

Saudi Arabia is divided into four provinces, and these in turn into districts. Geographically, the West, except for a narrow coastal plain, is composed of a range of mountains that reach a height of over 3,000 metres in elevation near the Yemeni frontier, but gradually decrease in height towards the north. This province includes Hijaz and Asir. Makkah and Madinah, the two most sacred towns in the Muslim world are located in Hijaz. The great central plateau, Najd, which is largely of igneous and metamorphic formation, lies at an elevation of between 1,000 and 1,500 metres and is almost co-terminous with the Central Province. Riyad, the capital, is located in this central province. From this high plateau, the country generally slopes gradually towards the Arabian Gulf. This part, the Eastern Province, contains the Al-Hassa and Qatif Oases and most of the oilfields. Large areas of gravel and rocky plains, as well as lava beds, occur throughout the northern part of the country - the Northern Province. Limestone is the principal parent material of the poorly developed soils east of the great central plateau.

The following (Fig. 3–1) shows the administrative divisions of the country.

ADMINISTRATIVE DIVISION OF SAUDI ARABIA

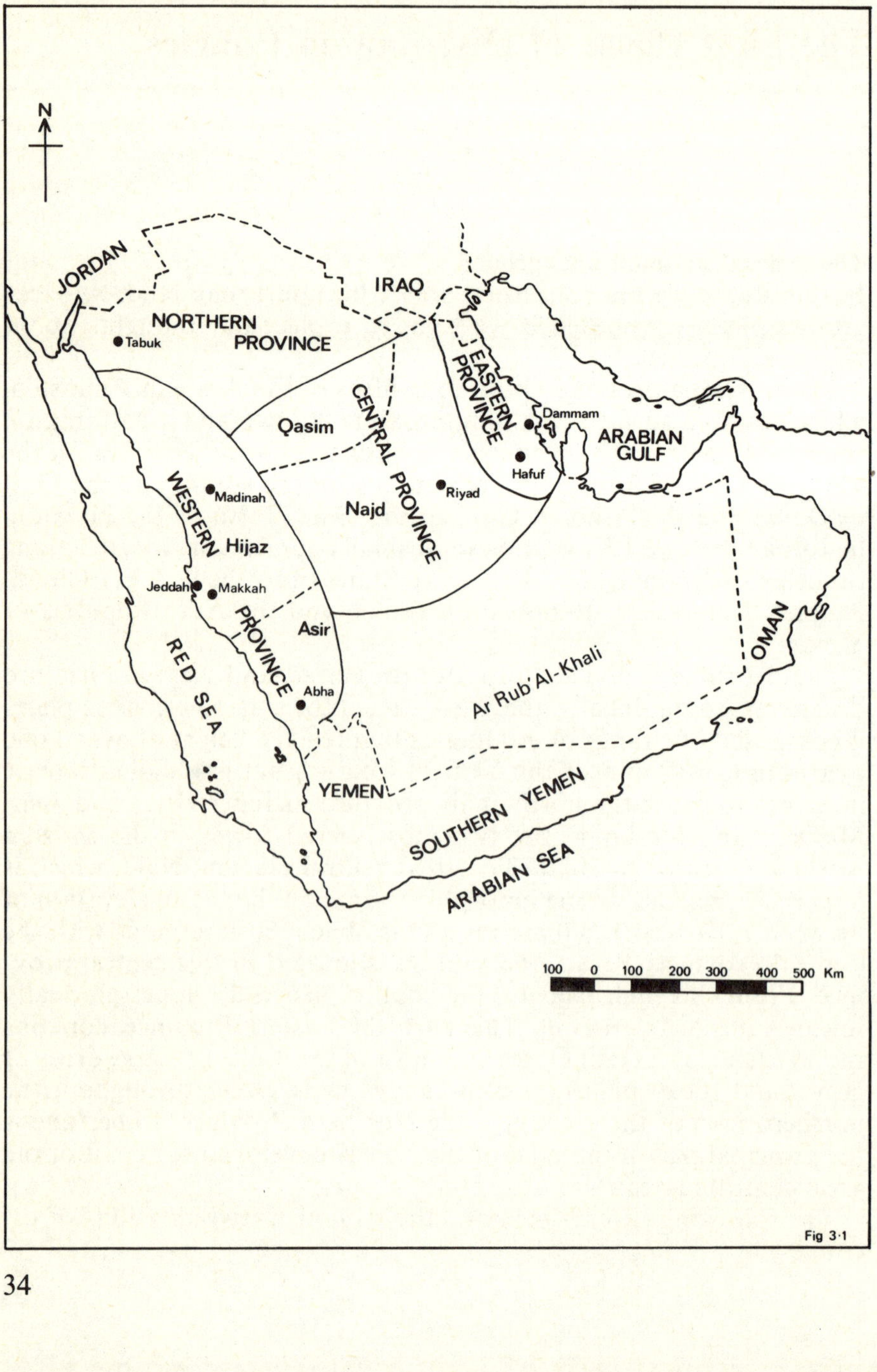

Fig 3·1

The position of Central Government as land controller

The population of the Arabian Peninsula in the past consisted mainly of Bedouins, except in the relatively few and scattered towns and agricultural oases. The number of Bedouins is diminishing year after year; whereas previously Bedouins represented 70 per cent of the Kingdom's population twenty years ago, they have diminished now to about 23 per cent and are still decreasing in number.

The distribution of the nomadic population over the four major regions of the Kingdom, namely Najd, Hijaz, Asir and Al-Hassa, varies. The northern part of Saudi Arabia contains the greatest Bedouin percentage, then comes Najd, Madinah and western coastal areas; last comes the southern coastal area (Fig. 3–2).

Table No (3–1). The percentage of Bedouins to the area populations.[28]

Area	*Percentage of Bedouins to the Area's population, 1344H (1925)*
Al-Khasrah	86.5
Afif, Qurayyat, and the North	70.0 (approx.)
Ha'il	66.8
Al-Joaf	59.3
Najran	31.9
Ranyah	25.9
Madinah	24.0
Qasim	23.4
Bishah	22.2
Riyad	17.9
Asir	16.4
Western Coastal Area	16.4
Makkah	5.3
Jizan	2.1

Estimates of the Bedouin population in Saudi Arabia must be regarded as very tentative, since no full and reliable population census exists. The total population in 1964 was estimated at 3.3 million, of which 694,000 were classified as nomads.[28] (This is regarded as a low estimate.) The total population in 1969 has been estimated at approximately 4–5 million, but no estimate is available for that year for nomadic population. The last estimation carried out showed that the population in six out of eight survey areas (see p. 105) was almost three and a third million, of which Bedouins (nomads and semi-nomads) composed 23 per cent, the rural settled population represented 43 per cent and the urban proportion 34 per cent. (See Table No. 7–2.)

Since nomads and their flocks cannot be sustained for long in any one site, they are obliged to move from place to place in search of valuable but scanty pasturage. Consequently the way of life of nomads entails a "Communal economy", since major activities are arranged on a communal rather than an individual basis, namely, the land is held in common, herds of camels and flocks of sheep are looked after on a collective basis. The communal use of the land, traditionally necessary for survival, is the most important factor that creates a feeling of equality among the nomads.

The collective spirit still survives among the Bedouin. Tribal systems are still strong and each tribe keeps to a known geographic area within which their rights to pasture and water are understood and accepted by others. Sedentarization of nomadic groups has not fundamentally affected economic aspects based on the exploitation of grazing resources, but it has resulted in deep changes in the social system. Settlers are identified with the place in which they settle and the individualistic concept of private ownership which is the basis of land control in cultivated areas begins to spread. The historical roots of the Arabian Peninsula society go back some two thousand years. Some regions near towns in the Western Province as well as much of Al-Hassa have long been affected by urban and settled life, but societies in the central regions of the peninsula remained conservative and characterized by their traditional characters until very recently, and some areas are still slow to change.

Rural economies and societies based on irrigation and occupying oases, "islands" separated by great areas of desert or semi-desert, also retained for millennia those traditional characteristics associated with early survival responses to environmental conditions.

The whole of rural life, nomadic or settled, conditioned by the harsh climatic conditions was based on subsistence motivations. There has always been exchange of surplus products of farm or of range, and links between the nomadic and settled populations did exist. However, the dominating force everywhere outside the few towns was survival and the agricultural response was subsistence orientated.

The first trial of land distribution for agriculture and settlement

In the early part of the twelfth century the great religious movement of Wahabism was born, which at one time spread from one end of the peninsula to another. During the last century there was a vigorous religious revival, the *Ikhwan* movement, which had a great effect on the whole region and one of whose features was the establishment of settlements which could serve as effective rallying points for the *Wahabi* military forces (see p. 17). More than one settlement nucleus could be established for each tribe. In these collective communities

PERCENTAGE OF NOMADS IN THE POPULATION OF SAUDI ARABIA

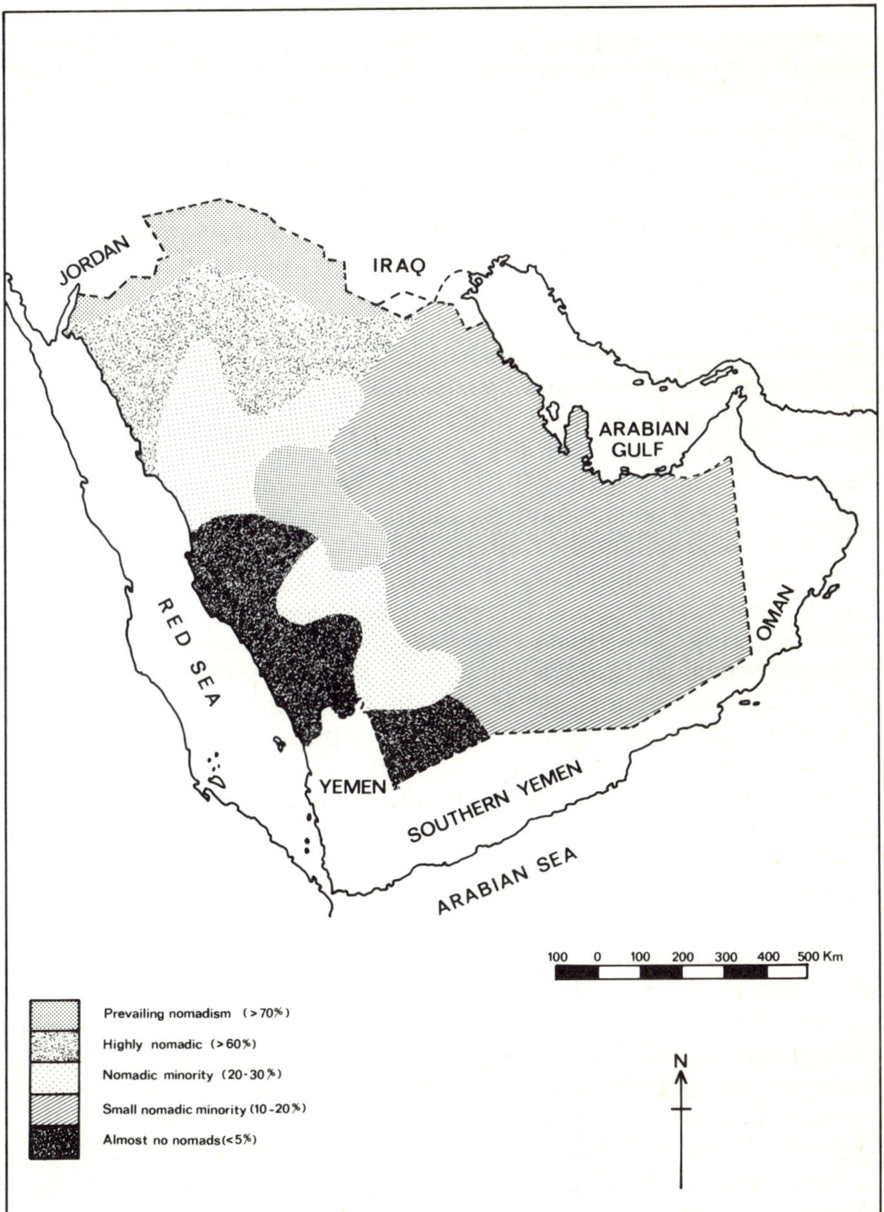

Fig 3·2

(*Hejar*), in which religious beliefs prevailed, Bedouins were to be transformed from a freely ranging life, frequently of conflict, to peace and brotherhood. They left the nomadic life, which they had followed for thousands of years, and began a settled life new and strange to them. Such settlement centres might be named *Hejar* after the movement (*Hejrah*) of the Prophet Mohammed (Peace be upon Him) from Makkah to Madinah in order to spread the Islamic faith.

During the expansion and consolidation of the power of King Abdul Aziz, the *Hejar* principle was then implemented according to the instructions of the King, who aimed at reaching a political settlement and marshalling the Bedouins to serve the unity of the country. This policy lasted from 1912 to 1932, the date of announcing the establishment of the Saudi Kingdom. The first *Hejrah* was Artawiyah in northern Najd. Historians differ in their estimates of the number of *Hejar* established, varying from 122 to 550, scattered through the centres and the north-eastern parts of the Arabian Peninsula (see chief tribes and names of *Hejar*, Table No. 1, Appendix II).

This *Hejar* policy was a first attempt to grapple with the problem of asserting central authority over the tribes. Bedouin life in the settlements is based on agriculture. Each settlement centre has its own name. In these residential centres, which were built very quickly, tens of thousands of the people of Bani Khalid, Ajman, Bani Hageer, Harb, Motir, Utaiba and Shammar tribes used to live forty or fifty years ago (Fig. 3–3). Even where these centres were abandoned, the ruined houses, the mosques, the wells which became dry, could all be taken as an obvious proof of human will and the desire of Man to put an end to nomadic life through settlement and stability.

The fruit of this policy was the settlement of more than thirteen tribes; 30,000 persons were settled in Utaiba centres, 40,000 in Motir centres, 40,000 in Harb centres and 50,000 in Shammar, Al-Awazim and Al-Murrah centres.

Since these *Hejar* centres were remote from towns and villages, they depended, from the economic point of view, on distant provision centres; water was brought to them from distances which might reach hundreds of kilometres.

At the beginning of the *Ikhwan* movement, particularly when a new *Hejrah* was established, they were dependent in large part on subsidies from the Government for daily subsistence. They had been obliged to sell their camels, sheep and goats (for which they no longer had grazing territory in sufficiency), the mainstay of their previous economic existence. Thus, even the seeds for the first season's crops were provided by the State; however, the subsidies continued long after the *Hejar* became operative. These subsidies were necessary not only

THE PRINCIPAL TRIBES OF SAUDI ARABIA

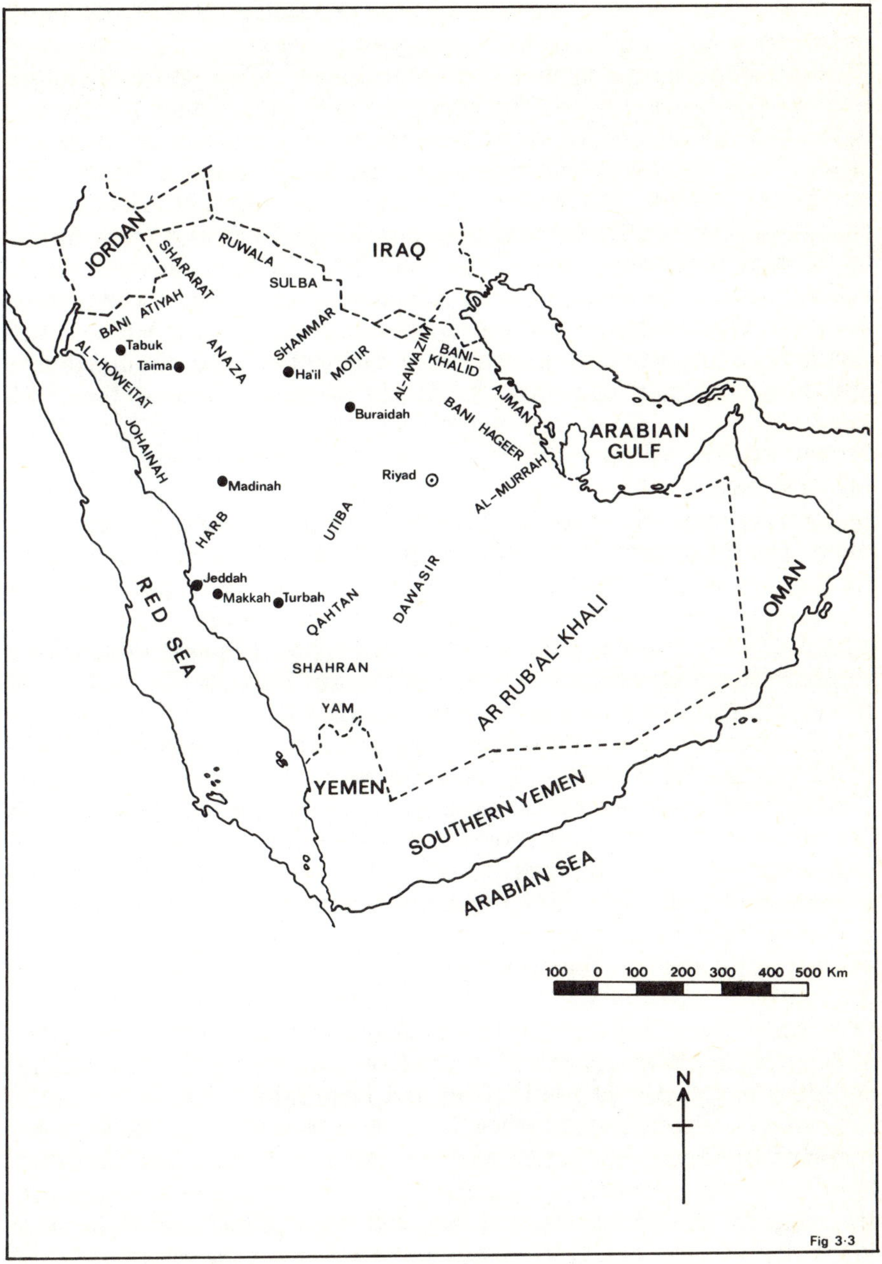

because the *Ikhwan* movement had no other means of support, but because the very nature of its existence as a para-military organization now supporting the new and growing State which required that they be ready to mobilize for war at any time precluded their involvement in full-time activities such as farming and trade.

Some *Hejar* have survived but others have collapsed, their failure due to specific causes. At the time of their establishment technical data was not available to the authorities and scientific experience was absent. The result was sometimes a choice of places unfit for farming and in which water resources were saline or not sufficient. The remoteness of these *Hejar* from main communication lines and from populated areas made them frequently very vulnerable to adverse social and economic pressures. Often it was a simple matter of the unsuitability of the settlement centres. Although the Bedouins were enthusiastic to farm, productivity was poor due to the hard circumstances and the new farmers' ignorance of farming methods. Most of the tribes after settling got rid of their herds, but when working in agriculture became an impossibility, Bedouins were often forced to return to grazing once again.

In this context, King Abdul Aziz had a cogent strategy for development. The settlement of the *Ikhwan* served to produce gains in agricultural production, although the primary purpose was political. His philosophy appears to have been one of encouraging development of a type which was not contrary to the principles of Islam, while trying to preserve traditional Arab values. This was appropriate in view of the prevailing social and economic conditions.

Filali has discussed the socio-economic and administrative difficulties facing the stability of these *Hejar*.[28]

In spite of all its hazards, the policy was positive since it was the first attempt to settle and urbanize the Bedouins, and the only real defect was that it was affected at a time when the nature of the problem had not been fully exposed. King Abdul Aziz, the initiator of this trial, knowing that a modern political State could not be realized while social disorder prevailed in the country, resolved to undermine nomadism gradually by settling the Bedouins around water points. With this plan, he took the first step towards ending tribal raids, fights and feuds. When this had been achieved, alternative and more advanced policies could be developed; a foundation had been laid.

Today, major disputes between Bedouin tribes have gone for ever, but in new policies the obstacles encountered in this first trial should be avoided. Such obstacles are economic, social, technical and cultural; the religious factor also should be taken into consideration because it provided the basic factor on which the *Hejar* scheme was based.

The political union of the country and the prevailing of peace and order within it made possible the transformation of tribal territory into land held by particular communities. During this period, the rights of tribes were reserved and the borders of tribal lands continued to be respected, the tribes from their side accepting not only this new concept of land held by particular communities but also of the larger concept of a national community (that is, the State) holding State Land.

Here then we have an example of the development in Saudi Arabia of a central concept of land, which while for all practical purposes accepting divine absolute ownership, nevertheless places land at the disposal of the State.

The first *Hejar* scheme was a general expression of the need to establish a policy towards the Bedouin nomads and pastoral groups. The problem was not and could not clearly be formulated at that time. The only problem generally identified was that of the need for limiting the fragmented land control traditionally asserted by nomads. At that time there was a shortage of finance and a shortage of administrative and technical machinery, and there could only be a general appreciation of a general problem.

Second trial, the Bedouin settlement project in Northern Saudi Arabia

This illustrates what may be regarded as a second stage in the evolution of a settlement policy for the Bedouins. It was triggered off by a specific problem, that of assisting nomadic pastoralists during a severe drought. In this case, the specific practical possibilities were limited by the nature of the physical and human factors involved. The connection between the implementation of what started as a relief project and the more general aspects of land settlement policies was to be extremely important for future developments.

This time the Government had a greater capability for seizing financial and human opportunities. In spite of the *Hejar* scheme, the vulnerability of many nomadic pastoralists to climatic hazards was still great. The drought that attacked some northern areas of the Kingdom in the year 1380H (1960) left the Bedouin there in a bad condition due to the desiccation of the range pastures and the decrease in livestock numbers on which the Bedouins depend for their living. The Government's attention was immediately drawn to the necessity of helping these people.

Accordingly, the Ministry of Agriculture and Water began the execution of a Bedouin Settlement Project in the year 1381H (1961) then regarding it as a temporary project, not open-ended in terms of government commitment. The Project aimed at settling the Bedouins as cultivators and helping them agriculturally and financially in order to raise their social and agricultural standards. In the course of this work, the Ministry of Agriculture and Water encountered many difficulties, the most important of which are given below.

Project studies were not available before the work began, due to the urgent circumstances which caused the Government to take immediate steps to help the Bedouins in the north. This is a reminder of the difficulty of basing development work on emergency schemes. The temporary nature of the project and the indefinite dating of its execution period led to an unstructured approach being adopted. As a result, technical errors, for example, selection of saline soil, inadequate layout design, etc. appeared and these were difficult to correct without considerable and continuous modification. Lastly the nature of the Bedouin who depends for his living on grazing and is unacquainted with cultivation, makes the transformation of his life from the nomadic to the settled very difficult. Great effort, skill and time are required, none of which could be rapidly applied in an emergency scheme. The sum of 2,040,000 SR was allotted in the budget of the fiscal year 1380/81H (1960/61) for this project. The continuing costs of the project were then budgeted in the following years until they reached, as a total, by the fiscal year 89/90H, 12,726,888 SR. The vast zone concerned is traversed by the Howeitat, Bani Atiya, Anaza, Sharrarat and Ruwala tribes. The project included three main areas:

1. *Tabuk and Western Coast Area* which includes 13 *Hejrah* (Fig. 3–4) and in 1390H (1970) had a farmed area of 2,568 donums utilized by 220 citizens.
2. *Al-Ula Area* which includes 4 *Hejrah* (Fig. 3–4) with a farmed area of 3,270 donums utilized by 198 citizens.
3. *Wadi Sarhan Area* which includes 12 *Hejrah* (Fig. 3–5) with a farmed area of 4,412 donums utilized by 226 citizens.

The data shown in Table No. (3–2) shows that the farmed area produced by the project is 10,253,266 donums utilized by 644 citizens, and the number of government pumps installed was 259 and private pumps 293. The average holding size does not exceed 16 donums, which is still small.

The essence of the scheme was to establish a new set of *Hejar* in the drought-stricken areas. Each of these was to consist of a block of small irrigated and cultivated farmsteads. The key provision here was that of water supply. There was insufficient time to carry out soil surveys and all that could be done was to decide on land generally regarded as usable, within each tribe's territory, and in which groundwater could be found.

Much of the project's finances were spent on water supply. Pumps

LOCATION OF HEJAR,
TABUK AND AL-ULA

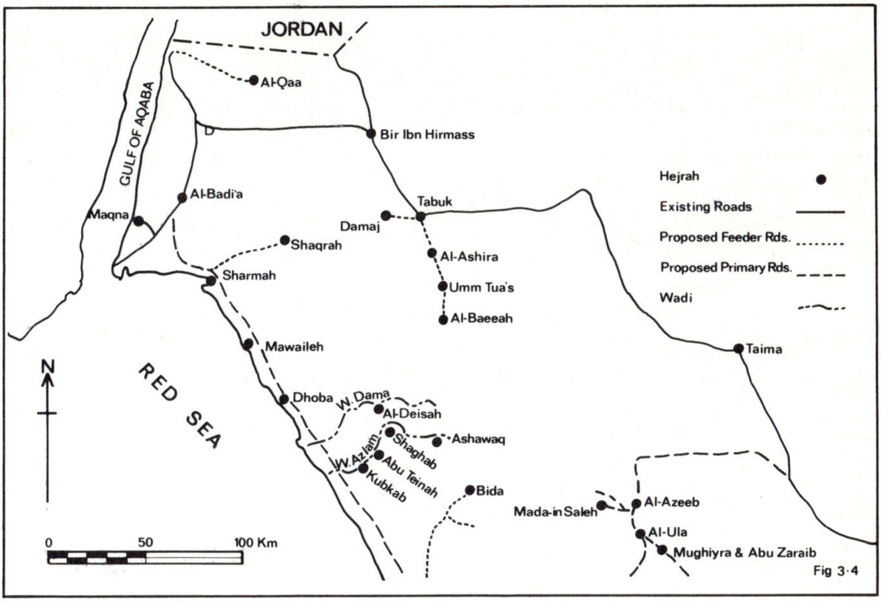

Fig 3·4

were provided free for the manually dug wells whose depths are between 2 to 7 metres. Each pump irrigated one farm or more and was under the responsibility of a settler who received 150 SR monthly for undertaking the pump's operation. This sum was later reduced to 100 SR, and then during the last year of the project's period it became only 50 SR. When the number of persons willing to have a private pump increased this was encouraged, since the project's finances were limited, a monthly payment of 100 SR was paid to each settler who installed at his own expense a private pump. The settlers were also provided with free seeds, fertilizers, fuel and ploughing in addition to the marketing of their products and technical assistance.

The project began in Wadi Sarhan, then Tabuk and Al-Ula were added. Although the project areas were supervised by the Extension Department in the central Ministry of Agriculture and Water, in fact each of these three areas was administered by the agricultural field organizations located in the area. These new *Hejar* were located on the wadis (see Fig. 3–4) to be sure of available water, as traditional agricultural areas always have been located. Most project areas have a limited

LOCATION OF HEJAR, WADI SARHAN

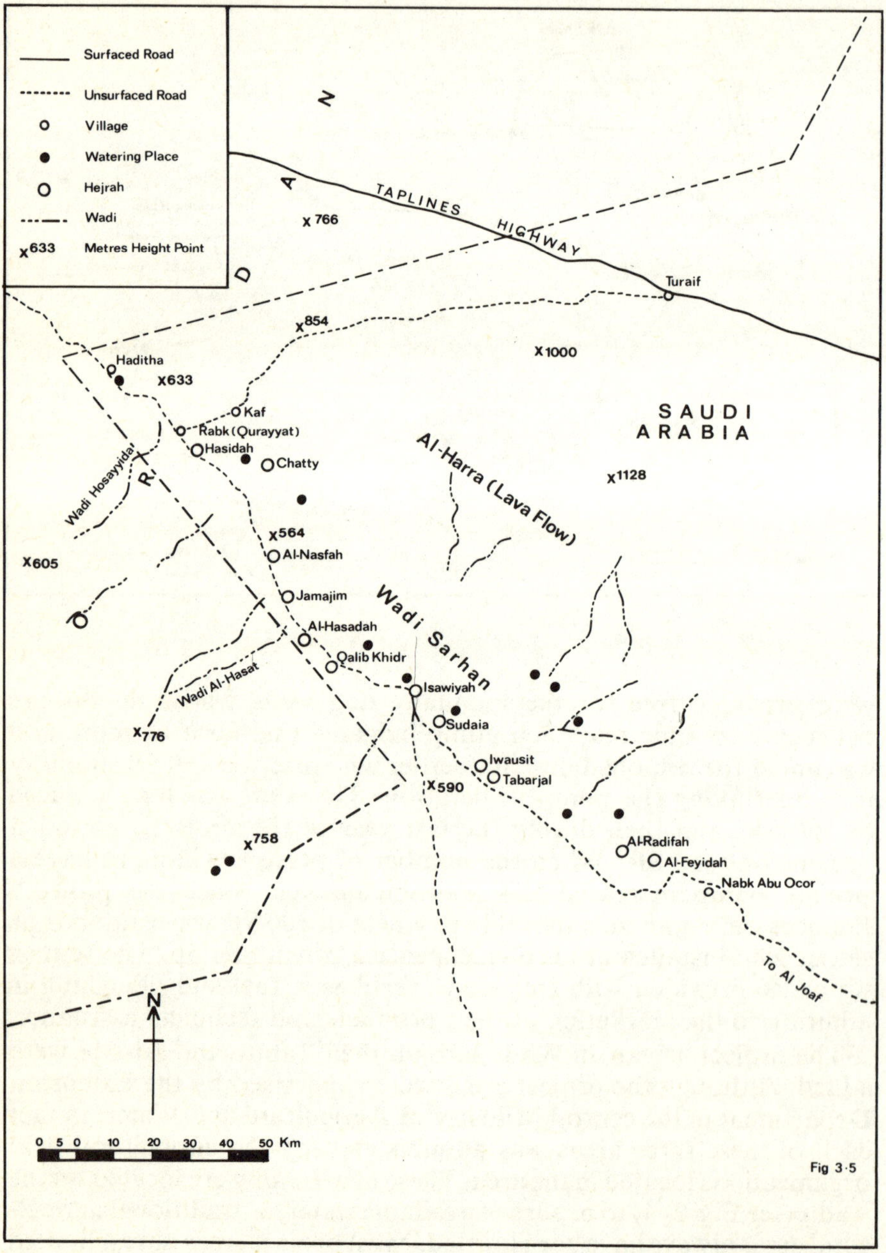

Table No. (3-2) The total farmed areas in *Hejar* Tabuk, Al-Ula and Wadi Sarhan areas.

Location	*Name of Hejrah*	*Farmed area (donums)*	*No. of Utilizers*	*No. of Pumps Government*	*Private*
1. *Tabuk*	Al-Badi'a	559.741	63	18	23
	Shaghab	434.911	29	6	11
	Ashawaq	331.678	48	15	13
	Al-Jadea	71.918	5	—	4
	Al-Deisah	667.626	33	8	7
	Al-Hamdh	77.825	4	4	—
	Abu Teinah	47.098	3	—	3
	Mawaileh	74.264	3	2	1
	Sharmah	73.534	9	—	—
	Al-A'shira	42.761	2	—	2
	Damaj	53.446	10	2	2
	Umm Tua's	59.047	3	—	1
	Kubkab	74.724	8	—	6
	Total	2568.573	220	55	73
2. *Al-Ula*	Mada-in Saleh	1659.991	78	—	78
	Al-Azeeb	1151.396	82	2	80
	Mughaiyra & Abu Zaraib	460.218	38	4	34
	Total	3271.605	198	6	192
3. *Wadi Sarhan*	Tabarjal	1347.413	66	51	15
	Sudai'a	530.023	18	15	3
	Al-Nasfah	379.555	29	28	1
	Iwausit	10.550	3	3	—
	Jamajim	88.625	9	9	—
	Qalib Khidr	388.127	24	23	1
	Hasidah	361.757	15	12	3
	Al-Feyidah	564.616	19	17	2
	Al-Radifah	155.768	12	12	—
	Ghatty	127.208	10	9	1
	Isawiyah	260.428	12	11	1
	Al-Hasadah	191.098	9	8	1
	Total	4405.168	226	198	28
	Grand Total	10245.346	644	259	293

quantity of water, but sufficient to irrigate the recently farmed and exploited areas. Some settlers, especially in Wadi Sarhan, did change their holdings when the lands allocated developed saline or alkaline soil problems. Some of the early established *Hejar* failed either due to water shortage, for example, Maquouaa and Al-Nabaj *Hejar* in Wadi Sarhan, Al-Jadea and Al-Hamdh in Tabuk area, or due to an increase of salinity of irrigation water, for example, Rashashiyah *Hejrah* in

Wadi Sarhan or because of an increase in soil salinity. Water conditions in the existing *Hejar* as a whole are considered to be sufficient to irrigate the existing cultivated areas except in a few *Hejar* areas, for example, Sudaia *Hejrah* in Wadi Sarhan where water quantity is sufficient to irrigate 500 hectares. The fruits of this trial are remarkable. From the economic point of view, the western coast *Hejar* have become one of the local sources which provide Tabuk and the northern coast towns such as Hakl and Dhuba with vegetables. The Al-Ula *Hejar* have become the areas supplying Wajh town and also Tabuk with vegetables and dates. Wadi Sarhan *Hejar* are the only local sources that provide Qurayyat town with vegetables.

This project has also had social results. At present these *Hejar* are still growing, government facilities and public utilities such as schools, clinics, police offices and water supplies are being established. The *Hejar* are becoming important summer gathering places and modal centres for the relevant nomadic group. (See Chapter Seven pp. 101–102.)

It is worth noting that as well as the *Ikhwan Hejar* and the drought relief *Hejar*, the establishment of such settlements is still continuing. The tribe or group concerned applies to the King to establish individual *Hejar*, and this system was the only way of obtaining relevant assistance and permission until a few years ago. The Government's approval was given very rarely. The indirect cost of maintaining the *Hejar* settlements created by simple demand together with the unplanned nature of exploitation of the land and water resources involved induced the Government to stop authorizing the establishment of new settlements. This remains the case except that, if the Government is satisfied that certain criteria can be met, that is, the area having the permanent essential elements needed for settlement, such as good agricultural potential, then permission may be given. (See the procedures followed in Bedouin settlement pp. 186–187.)

The most recent project for Bedouin settlement was that in Wadi Sahba – the Haradh scheme – but it was also regarded as a prototype scheme for virgin resource exploitation and the reclamation of the Wadi Basin lands. Technically more advanced in design – work commenced in 1385H (1965) – this project is not on a large scale and only one thousand families were to be settled in the plan. A special constitutional status was created, similar to British New Town Corporations. More than 100 millions SR has already been spent for well-drilling, laying irrigation and drainage canals, and the provision of power plant for an area of 4,000 hectares and associated villages. Essentially a special project of limited purpose, it is not really relevant

Table No. (3–3) Facilities and utilities in some *Hejar* in Northern Saudi Arabia.[60]

Area	*Hejrah*	*Population*	*Water Supply*	*Public Utilities*	*Distance from the road (Km)*
Tabuk	Al-Badia	100–500	Enough, good	Police Squad	70
	Damaj	100–500	Enough, good	Police Squad	15
	Mawaileh	100–500	Enough, good	Primary Sch., Clinic, Post Office, Police Squad.	Connected with the road
Al-Ula	Al-Hejer	100–500	Enough, medium quality	none	5
	Mada-in Saleh	5,000–10,000	Enough, good	Boys' Primary School Clinic	Connected with the road
	Al-Azeeb	500–2,000	Enough, good	Boys' Primary School, Post Office	Connected with the road
	Mughaiyra	—	—	—	—
	Abu Zaraib	100	Enough, good	none	Connected
Wadi Sarhan	Tabarjal	500–2,000	Enough; above medium	Boys' Primary School	Connected with the road
	Al-Nasfah	100–500	Enough, good	Boys' Primary School	Connected with the road
	Jamajim	100–500	Enough, good	none	Connected with the road
	Hasidah	100–500	Scanty, bad	none	Connected with the road
	Al-Feyidah	500–2,000	Scanty, bad	Boys' & Girls' Primary School	Connected with the road
	Ghatty	100–500	Scanty, bad	none	Connected with the road

to a study of public land distribution in the way which the *Hejar* schemes are relevant.

The two phases of *Hejar* settlement and the Haradh project, all concerned with Bedouin settlement on Public Land, have had some success but their main importance to present Public Land management and distribution lies in the lessons which can be learnt from experience gained during the last fifty years.

The most important lesson and the one most difficult to apply is that concentration on a single aspect—here the sedentarization of nomads—and subsequent concentration on technical and commercial feasibility, is by no means enough.

When an individual Bedu and his family move into settled cultivation he sells most of his grazing animals. His capital for the first time in the form of money, he enters a new adventure, a settled life, of which he knows nothing and which on entry isolates him from his clan and tribe. Here is a person born in the desert who, with only his natural intelligence, lived for many years far from modern civilization. He believed innately then that his nomadic culture and traditions were right and that modern civilization was the devil's work. He must now completely reverse all the values born of his and his culture's experience. Given this, we have to appreciate that it is easy to erect buildings, pave roads, make technological improvements, generate electricity and create all the facilities that money can make possible, but that it is very difficult to change people's minds and create for them new beliefs. Development involving the kind of change involved in Bedouin settlement must not only be the execution of economic and technical operations but must also be an integrated operation including linked changes reacting with each other. Each stage of development must help people to become accustomed to the new changes it brings.

Production operation is very important, but in order to succeed it is essential to carry out social development simultaneously with economic development in one integrated economic and social scheme. In this chapter we have seen that helping the Bedouin to pass the period of uncertainty and making him understand the importance of agricultural life needs much time and effort, because the Bedouin has a mind saturated with Bedouin traditions and cannot be convinced by the usefulness of modern farming methods in a short period.

This lesson of the past is important today. The Bedouins are inevitably attracted to some of the material aspects of the modernization which they now meet in Saudi Arabia. The lesser hardship of settled life with an abundance of water, electricity and consumer goods is already drawing them into the towns and the strength of tribal nomadism is weakening. At the same time there is ample evidence that what the Bedouins want is to retain their beliefs, values and traditions but also to have the security and some of the attractive elements, such as health facilities, of settled life. This paradox makes any successful sedentarization programme very complex.

It is not difficult to make the Bedouins accept new thoughts, methods, instruments, animal breeds and societies if these can be shown to work satisfactorily. Even if he accepts settled life, however, this life which is new to him creates serious social problems which need to be dealt with very carefully. The rapid change involved totally affects people's way of living and planners must direct their working power to the establishment of acceptable new social structures in order to effect this change with the least possible social damage.

Many developing countries, in efforts to modernize, ignore the human being and leave him discontented or unable to join modern life. Many agricultural land reclamation and development projects face difficulties, although water is available and soil is good, due to lack of understanding of the settler's basic problems.

In the second settlement trial which came to an end in 1390H (1970), one can see a single type of development forced through to meet an emergency and therefore with no prior planning. All over Saudi Arabia similar demands were appearing, demands which could not be met by the existing administrative systems nor be satisfactorily dealt with in the absence of clear concepts of land administration. In this situation the governmental response was to begin a formulation of laws and ordinances in the sector of land administration. One of these, the Public Land Distribution Ordinance, issued in 1388H (1968), was invoked in 1391H (1971) for the Bedouin settlement project in northern Saudi Arabia and provided a new basis for the transfer of land proprietorship to settlers. Table No. 3–2 p. 45, shows that privately owned agricultural land holdings average between one half and five hectares in size. This pattern of holding resulted from the fact that, under the new PLDO, in 1391H (1971), HM the King approved the transfer of proprietorship of the allocated farmed lands to the utilizers on the basis of a special survey carried out under the PLDO. The Courts concerned were then instructed to issue deeds according to maps prepared by the new Public Land Management Department. In fact, after the discontinuation of the financial support and free services given in the first unstructured emergency scheme, settlers faced serious problems. But *Hejar* still existed. We later refer to the Wadi Sarhan region as representative of this project (see Chapter Eight) to examine the measures undertaken by the Government as part of the takeover of responsibility by the new organisation of PLMD to maintain these *Hejar* and make them self-sufficient.

On a completely different basis, a third trial of public land management and allocation can be identified in the period before the issue of the PLDO of 1388H (1968).

Third trial, land distribution through contracting procedures
In 1359H (1939), King Abdul Aziz introduced the system of leasing government land to which the State had assumed a comprehensive title as the owner of such land. Under this system these lands were free from specialization rights and were considered to be inalienable government properties.

The majority of contracting lands made available were in Qatif, Al-Hassa, Jizan and Najran. Lands were leased according to the traditions and customs pertaining in each area, for example, the period of lease generally did not exceed ten years, but in Qatif the period was limited usually to three years, whereas in Al-Hassa it was limited to five years.

Each contracted leased area was generally 36 donums, which was considered enough for a plantation of 1,000 palm-trees, a traditional measure. The lessee was given between one-third to two-thirds of the area as his own personal property after the period agreed upon had passed, but in most of the agreements three-quarters of each holding were recorded to be given to the lessees. The total number of agricultural contracting leases were recorded as 1,120, in Qatif 610, in Umm al-Sahek, in Qatif area 354, in Al-Hassa 9, in Najran 3 and an unrecorded but small number in Jizan. Agreements were dealt with by *Amirs*, approved by the King and registered by local courts. By the end of the use of this procedure, in 1391H (1971), 137 leased properties could be identified as developed and with approved leases. Many of the others had already been regionally approved and developed but still awaited final approval.

Lease registration documents had been issued for areas, but in Umm al-Sahek in Qatif palm-tree areas are still without these documents, and it is the same in many areas in other districts.

Land distribution through the contracting procedure was stopped when the Public Land Ordinance was issued by the Ministry of Agriculture and Water.

The old contracting registration documents were issued and attested by HM King Abdul-Aziz, stating that the lessee should carry out development work for ten years starting from the date of contract attestation, providing that during this period the lessee should at his own expense carry out the reclamation and arrange the planting of the land, provided that one quarter of the land and water concerned would be regarded as "public interest" land according to the old conventions.

After ten years, the lease expired and the lessee had to give one quarter of the production in kind (including dates), after the payment of *Zakat*, to the lessor, that is, three quarters for the lessee and one quarter for the Government. (See Form No. 1, Appendix 1.)

After the era of King Abdul-Aziz, these contracting registration documents were replaced by agreements between the lessee and the Director of the Governmental Properties (Public Domain Department) attached to the Ministry of Finance and National Economy. All agreements continued in force until they were stopped by issue of the Public Land Ordinance.

The practice of defining the duration of leasehold and the area only came into existence during the last phase. The general terms of these agreements were as follows:

1. The period of the agreement is 5 years.
2. The lessee should start agricultural work, digging a well and making irrigation channels.
3. Palm trees, fruit and cereals should be planted especially on the one quarter of the land which belongs to the Government.
4. The lessee has to utilize the land during the first 5 years; however, if he utilized part of the land, the unutilized part will be withdrawn after the determined period is passed.
5. The Government is not responsible for any obligations or expenses.
6. The Government has the right to take back its part (one quarter), of the leased land, but the lessee is not entitled to subdivide the land himself.
7. If the lessee delays in planting one third of the land up to the middle of the first year, the agreement is cancelled and he has not the right to claim any compensation against the expenses incurred by him.
8. The lessee undertakes to pay one quarter of the products of the land to the Government against the part owned by the government, without deducting any costs or expenses for his services from the share of the Government or the *Zakat*. However, if the land is divided between him and the Government, the investing person has to pay the *Zakat* on all the crops of the three quarters of the land and accordingly the three quarters becomes his property.

The government did not in fact take its share of produce or of land from any lessees, even after leases had in many cases expired, as happened particularly in the Eastern Province. The Ministry of Finance and National Economy finally reported to the King by its letter No. 3605 dated 29/11/91H (1971), a proposal to put an end to these contracts. Since there arose a problem of ownership of these cultivated lands after the expiry of leases and of the agreed procedures it was proposed to adopt the following approach:

1. The division of the land already established was confirmed.
2. The physical division could be carried out after obtaining the

lessee's approval; registration would take place in the juridicial registration bureau. If the lessee objected, a juridicial order could be issued to execute the division.

3. A committee with members from the Ministry of Finance and National Economy, Ministry of Justice and the Eastern Province Amirate was established. Members had to contact and deal with the lessees in person and to follow up land division.
4. The committee was authorized to sell the Government part (its one quarter) of contracted leased land if this would be in the Government's interest and if at the same time it did not conflict with the lessee's desire.
5. The committee was authorized in particular to sell the Government portion if it was distant from urban areas, and if it was not expected to be needed within the following ten-year period for public utilities.
6. Land close to urban areas or expected to be needed for public utilities within the following ten years should be kept for these purposes.
7. No claim should be established against the lessee for any non-payment of the Government's production share.

The King approved these proposals in Letter No. 232 dated 9/1/92H (1972) to the Ministry of Finance and National Economy. This letter put an end to land distributed through contracting procedures which had mainly concerned the Eastern Province.

To summarize: in these three trial projects for Land Distribution, land was not granted to a small number of individuals, as in the case of previous land grants, but rather to large groups of individuals. Each system had its own basis and principles but each can be considered as essentially traditional in procedure. The first project started early during the formation of the Saudi Arabian Kingdom and was designed to transform the nomadic life of the Bedouins into a more peaceful settled one. The large number of *Hejar* established was the result of a need to find more than one settlement nucleus for each tribe or group. The second was more directly related to the Bedouin's life and social and economic needs. Bedouin settlement procedure in the North, first an emergency measure, was absorbed in a more general approach. The King Faisal Settlement Scheme in Haradh was part of a transitional policy and in many ways a unique project in land distribution. The third project, the contract lease scheme was directed towards the increase of farm production. It is no longer regarded as a viable long-term policy.

Chapter Four

The Present Transitional Phase

The present administrative organization

In Chapter Three, each of the examples of Government actions which affected the control and distribution of Public Land illustrates attitudes and policies which essentially and inevitably reflect the nature of the early evolution of the Saudi Arabian State. As this evolution has continued, particularly during the period of rapidly increasing oil revenues, the apparatus of government has developed in response to general needs. In the context of Public Land we can see particular changes in governmental organization and in the appearance of Public Land policies. Further changes are still under consideration and we can regard the last twenty years, and the last ten especially, as periods of accelerating transition from a tradition-dominated situation to full bureaucratic and technically equipped government.

The present administrative position is one with a fully developed but young governmental organization. In this chapter we are chiefly concerned with Central Government Organization, the Ministry of Interior and the Ministry of Agriculture and Water.

Other ministries and institutions will be considered in later chapters as their relevance appears (Fig. 4–1).

Progress in economic and social development depends largely on the capacity of the government to plan and execute policies and programmes for development.

First, organization for development. The development process requires planning, decision-making, implementation, operation and evaluation.[20] In the Kingdom, the major elements of Government engaged in this process are His Majesty the King, the Council of Ministers and other Ministries.

His Majesty the King, the President of the Council of Ministers, directs all the affairs of government, especially the financial affairs. He is the Head of State. Economic social development and other related policies, plans, programmes and budgets are authorized by His Majesty and the Council of Ministers. The King has the power to

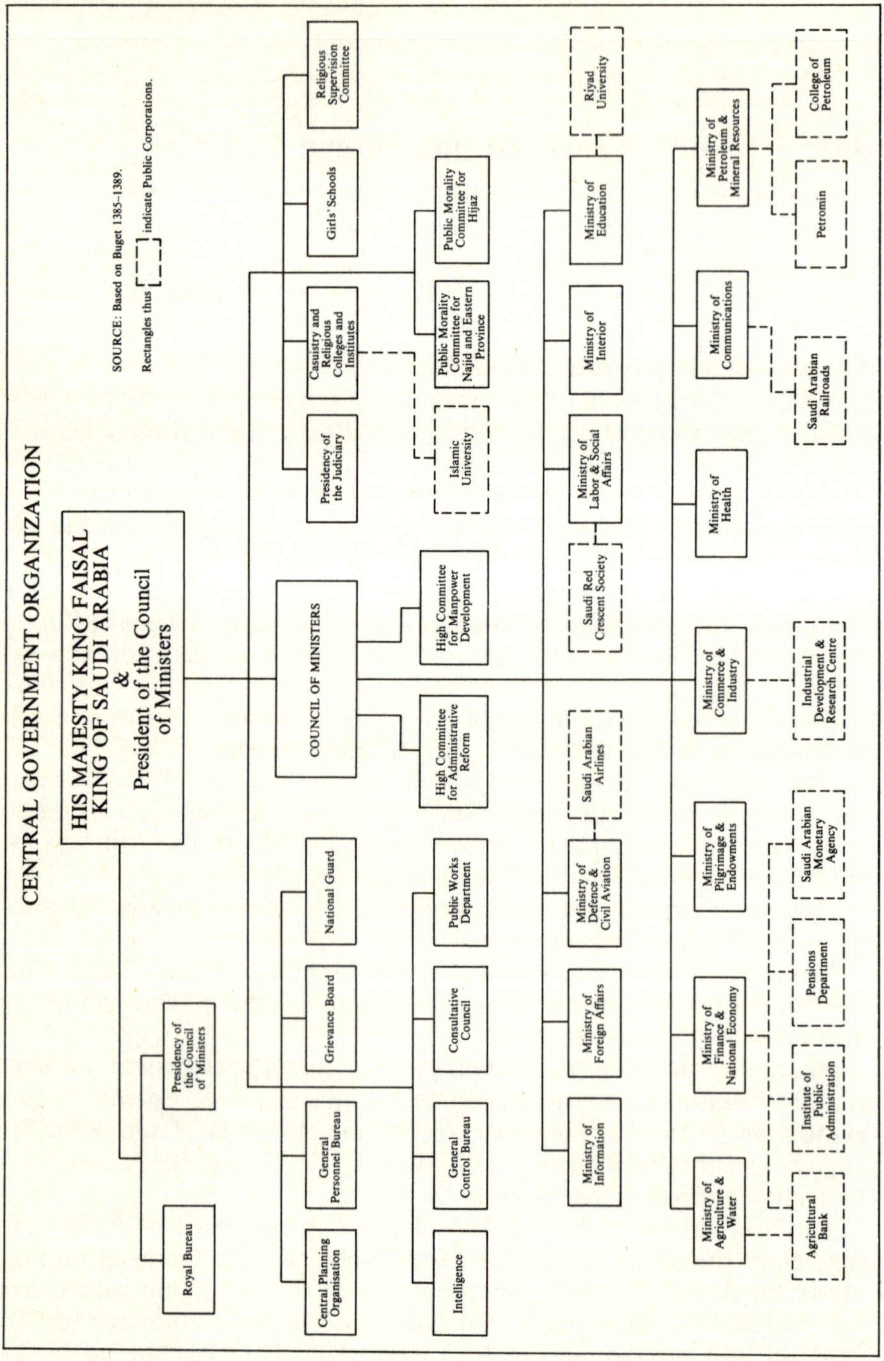
CENTRAL GOVERNMENT ORGANIZATION
HIS MAJESTY KING FAISAL KING OF SAUDI ARABIA & President of the Council of Ministers
SOURCE: Based on Buget 1385–1389.
Rectangles thus [ ] indicate Public Corporations.
Royal Bureau
Presidency of the Council of Ministers
COUNCIL OF MINISTERS
Central Planning Organisation
General Personnel Bureau
Grievance Board
National Guard
Presidency of the Judiciary
Casuistry and Religious Colleges and Institutes
Girls' Schools
Religious Supervision Committee
Intelligence
General Control Bureau
Consultative Council
Public Works Department
High Committee for Administrative Reform
High Committee for Manpower Development
Islamic University
Public Morality Committee for Najid and Eastern Province
Public Morality Committee for Hijaz
Ministry of Information
Ministry of Foreign Affairs
Ministry of Defence & Civil Aviation
Saudi Arabian Airlines
Saudi Red Crescent Society
Ministry of Labor & Social Affairs
Ministry of Interior
Ministry of Education
Riyad University
Ministry of Agriculture & Water
Ministry of Finance & National Economy
Ministry of Pilgrimage & Endowments
Ministry of Commerce & Industry
Ministry of Health
Ministry of Communications
Ministry of Petroleum & Mineral Resources
Agricultural Bank
Institute of Public Administration
Pensions Department
Saudi Arabian Monetary Agency
Industrial Development & Research Centre
Saudi Arabian Railroads
Petromin
College of Petroleum

Fig. 4.1

return to the Council of Ministers any draft decree or order submitted to him for signature.

The Council of Ministers operates under the authority of His Majesty. Each Ministry formulates its policies, programmes and legislations and then proposes them to His Majesty and the Council. The Council has become the direct executive authority and the ultimate authority for jurisdiction.

Planning, Statistics and Research

Concerned members of the Government have for some years recognized the need to improve the planning of economic and social development and to provide the statistical data and other research results for effective planning. A High Committee for Administrative Reform was established in 1383H (1963). Though much remains to be done to improve planning techniques, develop statistical data, and acquire wider knowledge of natural and human resources for effective planning, some fundamental work has been undertaken by the Central Planning Organization which replaced a Higher Council of Planning.

The Ministry of Interior

In reviewing the existing system of regional, district and local government the Economic Report published in 1390H (1970) described the situation as follows:[20] "... they [the local governments] are connected to the Ministry of Interior in several important ways. It is an intricate system with overlapping jurisdictions among local Government units and the Ministry's central operations. In some respects the Ministry exercises highly centralized control of the system, while, in other respects, the local units of Government function autonomously." The main levels of regional and district Government have been determined by the process of political and economic evolution.

The Royal Decree No. 12 dated 1383H (1963) was issued for provincial regulations to provide:

(a) The division of the country into provinces, districts and centres according to its geographical features, population, communications and local circumstances.

(b) The definition of the administrative relationship between different organizations (belonging to Government bodies) and the responsibilities of each.

(c) A note that the need for a system designed to promote and coordinate activities will be highly apparent, but that this has not been implemented.

The Ministry of Interior has two particular responsibilities of importance to this study. Firstly, it is responsible for the Municipalities.

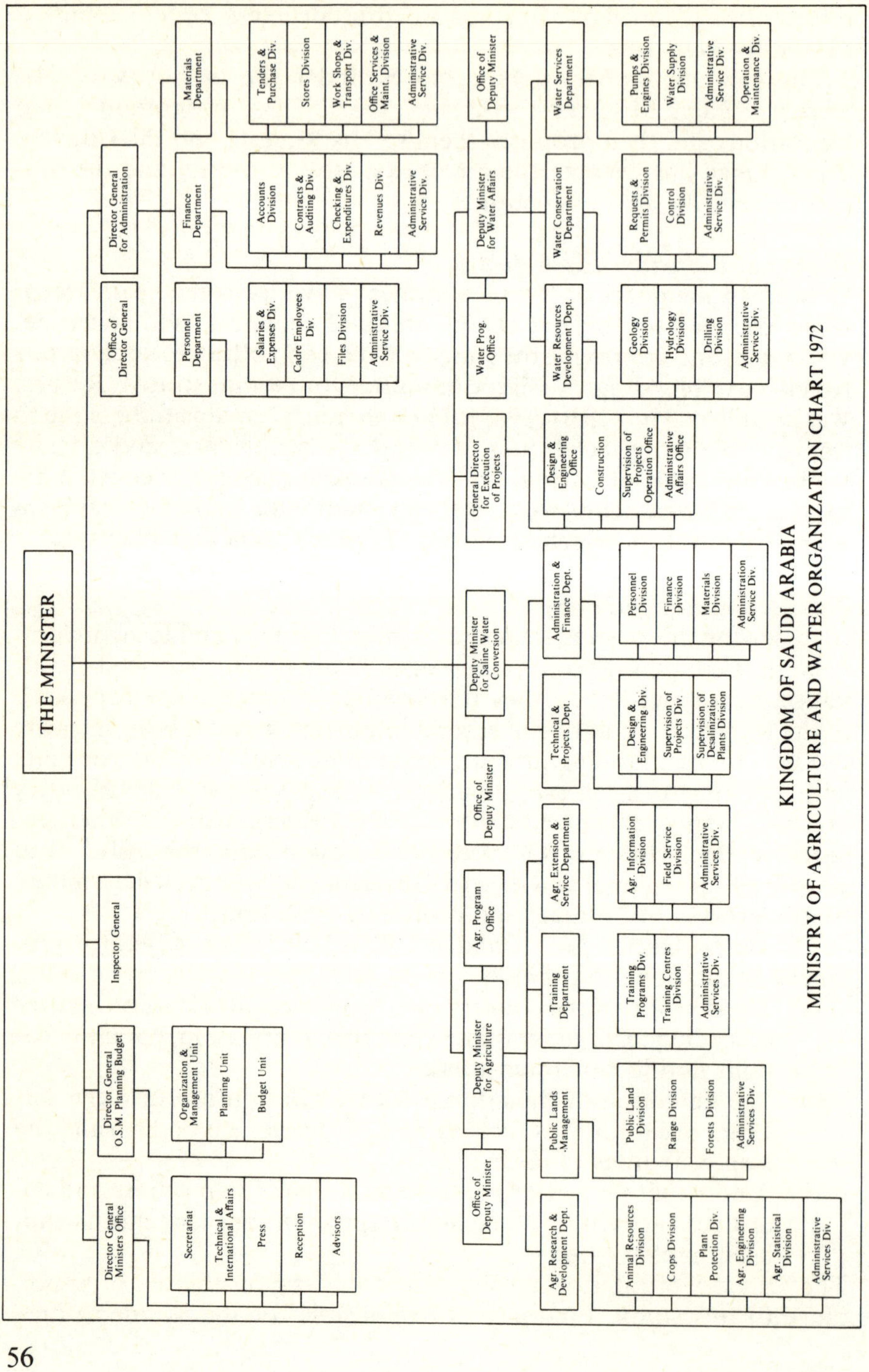

KINGDOM OF SAUDI ARABIA
MINISTRY OF AGRICULTURE AND WATER ORGANIZATION CHART 1972

Fig. 4.2

Municipalities are urban areas of special status derived from size or some special importance. In their cases, since the development of urban planning, the delimitation of land between urban and agricultural categories has become of significance. In this study we are only concerned with agricultural land but the allocation of public land to various, urban uses, present and future, clearly affects all aspects of policy. Secondly, since municipalities have a limited authority over wholesale and retail food marketing, then policies authorized by the Ministry of Interior have considerable influence on agricultural land use. In general, this is a subject where a great deal of improvement could be effected to the benefit of agricultural producers and consumers alike. The Ministry is also responsible for other settlements, that is villages and towns. Some villages are tribal and all the citizens of the tribal village are united under a leader because of his tribal status. In the non-tribal villages the leadership is exercised by the heads of the leading families. Most of the towns are generally extended villages. Some of them are located at the intersection of important communication routes; others are becoming important centres of trade.[13]

The Ministry of Agriculture and Water was established in 1373H (1953). It was first involved mainly with agricultural work but new departments were added to deal with water and other duties. The coordination of the different departments is still being developed. The Minister is supported by one deputy minister for agricultural affairs, another for water affairs and a third for saline water conversion (Fig. 4–2). Strictly, this was the position up to 1392H (1972); since then the second deputy minister post has not been filled. The Minister's office includes consultant, advisory and information offices.

Several General Directorates are attached to the Minister, these being: General Directorate of Administration, which includes Personnel, Finance and Material departments, General Directorate of Organization, Planning and Budgeting units and General Directorate of Inspection.

Under the Deputy Minister for Agricultural Affairs, four departments are attached:

Public Land Management Department which is responsible for the management of 200 million hectares as public range land (grasslands), about 1.6 million hectares of forest land and a sand dune stabilization project, and more than 0.4 million hectares as public land for distribution.

Research and Development Department which is responsible for applied research for crops, plant protection, agricultural engineering, statistics and animal husbandry and fisheries. A number of experimental farms and a locust control station also exist. Due to the lack of highly qualified personnel a number of agreements with foreign universities and institutes to carry out research have been made (See p. 115).

Agricultural Extension and Services Department, responsible for providing tractor services at prices below cost before 1393H (1973), pest control services and veterinary services free of charge, through the field organizations, sixty-three in all, and several demonstration farms.

Training Department which is responsible for in-service personnel, farmers' training and management of the farm engineering centre.

Three technical departments are under Water Affairs, these are:

1. Water Resources Development Department, which is responsible for location and evaluation of water resources and supervises drilling of wells.
2. Water Services Department concerned with supervision operations and maintenance of drinking water supplies.
3. Water Conservation Department which supervises regulations and granting permits for drilling.

These branches of the Ministry of Agriculture and Water (MAW) are mostly relevant to the control, management and distribution of Public Lands.

The importance of agriculture in the Kingdom

Since the distribution of Public Lands with which we are concerned is entirely a non-urban matter, it is important first to outline the main aspects of Saudi Arabian agriculture in the context of land use.

The percentage of persons working in the agricultural sector has dropped from 46 per cent (465,000 persons) of the total male work force in the year 1386H (1966) to about 40 per cent in the year 1390H (1970). The Bedouins form about one-third of this percentage (15 per cent of the total population of the Kingdom). The western and southern region each account for about 30 per cent each of the employed total.[20] The agricultural population density ranges from 5 to 10 persons per hectare in the oases and in the south-west coastal and valley areas to just above zero in large areas of the interior. The agricultural sector contributed about 10 per cent of the Gross Domestic Product income (about 974 million SR) in 1382H (1962) but this percentage has diminished until it reached 6 per cent in the year 1389H (1969) (about 1000 million SR). This sector is now the fifth in importance. The decrease is proportional and not absolute being the result of the increased contribution of other sectors in the local economy, especially the oil sector, which is first and contributed 48 per cent in 1382H (1962) and 54 per cent in 1389H (1969).

Government, commerce and industry, rank second, third and fourth respectively (see pp. 108–109). The annual potential growth in the contribution of the agricultural sector has reached 3.5 per cent, but this increase, which has been achieved by technological development and expansion in the farmed areas, was halved (see Fig. 7–2) resulting from losses due to the progressive salination of some soils, and the decline in farmed areas due to moving sands and the drying out of some surface wells. The conditions and natural factors affecting agriculture are clearly critical. Saudi Arabia is characterized by the vastness of its land of more than 2 million square kilometres which form more than 1.5 per cent of the globe's land surface.[31]

Area	*Km²*	*Hectare*	*Donum*
Total area	2,000,000	200,000,000	2,000,000,000
Utilized area	46,700	4,670,000	46,700,000
a. Forests	68,800	1,680,000	168,000,000
b. Cultivated land	3,690	396,000	3,960,000
c. Range	26,500	2,650,000	26,500,000
Unutilized area	1,953,000	195,300,000	1,953,000,000

The cultivated lands constituted only 0.13 per cent of the total area in 1385H (1965). The total area utilized for agriculture, range and forests, is less than 3 per cent. Examining the above figures, it would appear that efficient use of cultivated land is very important to meet the country's demand for foodstuffs.

We must see this situation in the context of the physical environment's characteristics.

1. *A dominant desert climate.* Climatic conditions, in most parts of Saudi Arabia, change greatly from summer to winter and from day to night. Temperatures might reach on winter nights some degrees below zero, and on summer days more than 50° centigrade. Dry winds carrying soil or desert sand, blow in all desert areas except in the coastal regions.

In general, all regions of Saudi Arabia are considered deserts except for the area of Asir Mountains. About 99 per cent of the country is an arid or semi-arid zone utilized only for grazing when rain falls and grazing plants grow. The annual average rainfall generally does not exceed 100 mm. South-western parts of the country are affected by the monsoons, and the annual rainfall average might reach 500 mm, while Mediterranean rains may affect the northern parts of the Kingdom in winter. In general, rainfall in the Kingdom is characterized by its scarcity, variability, drought for periods of up to seven years, high evaporation ratios (due to high temperatures), low relative humidity, strong wind effects and rapid run-off floods after rain which further reduce precipitation effectiveness.

2. *The presence of saline conditions in most soils.* The accumulation of salts in the soil is one of the permanent problems facing irrigated agriculture. All surface water contains some soluble salts in negligible amounts, but after some years of irrigation a harmful build-up of salts may appear in the soils; salts found in irrigation water remain in the soil, while water itself is lost by evaporation and/or drainage. The presence of salts in the soil in addition to directly damaging some plants may also lessen its permeability to a great degree and make it unfit, physically and chemically, for plant growth.

The most arid zones in the country are (Fig. 4–3):

(a) Ar Rub'Al-Khali (Empty Quarter) the largest sand desert in the world which measures over 1000 Km. from east to west and 500 Km. from north to south.

(b) Nafud which extends to the north west, a red sand desert intersected with broad flat salty stretches.

(c) The Dahna, a long arched strip of sand dunes linking the Nafud and Ar Rub'Al-Khali.

Table No. (4–1) Agricultural expansion over a period of twenty years.

Year	*Cultivated Area in Hectares*	*Way of Estimate*
1370H (1950)	96,000	Estimated by FAO
1377H (1957)	250,000	Estimated by Agriculture Directory
1380H (1960)	300,000	Estimated by IBRD[34]
1385H (1965)	396,467	Statistical Survey by Ministry of Agriculture and Water
1390/91H (1970/71)	385,219*	Consultant survey reports for six areas out of eight

* refer to Table No. 6–4) for details.

Probably the 1370H (1950) estimate was on the low side. One can question whether the cultivated area has expanded almost three times between 1370H (1950) and 1377H (1957) even where agriculture and water equipment were introduced to the country. Between 1377–1380H (1957–1960), the expansion was 12 per cent for the three years, an annual expansion rate of 4 per cent. This expansion could be explained by the improved use of water and agricultural machinery.

Between 1380–1385H (1960–1965) the expansion was 13.2 per cent for five years. The estimate for 1390/91H (1970/71) is not comparable with the earlier figures because it refers only to six areas out of the

LAND USE IN SAUDI ARABIA

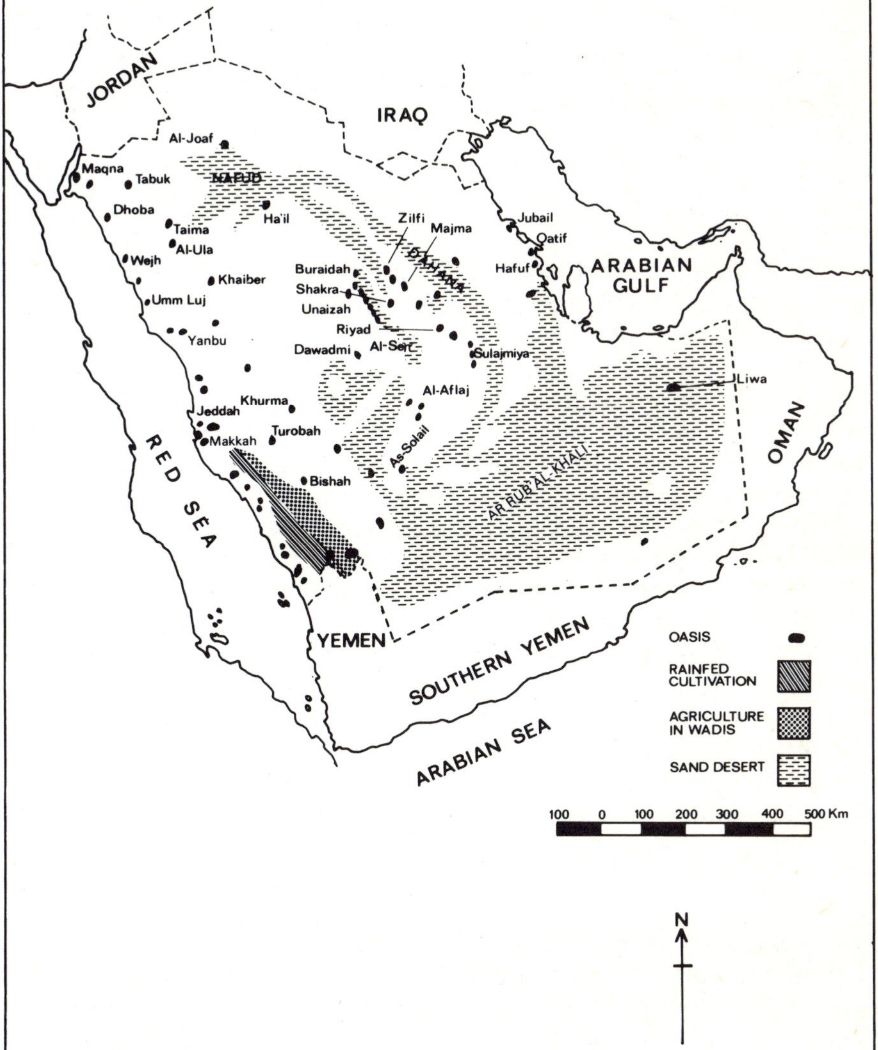

Fig 4·3

eight; the rate of expansion probably continued at the earlier level. Part of this whole expansion resulted from the new utilization of State Land (Public Land), permissable according to *Shari'a.* (See Chapter I.) One can probably infer that the cultivated area in Saudi Arabia has more than doubled since 1370H (1950).

Table No. (4–2) Other changes in agricultural production [42]

Crop	*Area 1369/70H (1949/50) in Hectares*		*Area 1376/77H (1956/7) in Hectares*		*Area 1380/83H (1960/3) in Hectares*	
Field crops	67,838	71%	155,400	79%	175,929	72%
Vegetables	04,128	4%	003,000	1%	033,132	14%
Dates	21,572	23%	023,900	18%	022,281	9%
Fruits	02,226	2%	005,100	2%	011,487	5%
Total	95,764	100%	187,400	100%	242,829	100%

The picture as presented in this table shows that the cropped area has expanded 2.5 times at an annual growth rate of 8 per cent over a period of 12 years.[42] The initial agricultural expansion for field crops occurred between 1369/70H (1949/50) and 1376/77H (1956/57). The field crop area more than doubled but its relative share remained within the range of 70–80 per cent of all cropped areas. The area cultivated by dates was almost stable. The relatively growing importance of vegetables has marked the period between 1376/77H (1956/57) and 1380/83H (1960/63), and also during recent years is explained by changes in the pattern of production. Vegetable and fruit production expanded substantially because of their high profitability (see Table No. 7–7 and Table No. 13–1).

The five-year plan in 1390/1391H (1970/1) noted that the production of vegetables had increased considerably. Production of field crops also increased but less than vegetables. Animal wealth production on the other hand had decreased since 1370H (1950), due to drought in the country, but increased once more after 1390H (1970) due to better rainfall. Poultry production increased considerably.[19] Total animal units of 7.2 millions were estimated by FAO in 1370H (1950).

The Temporary Principles for Land Utilization

Up to this point we have considered three main background elements: firstly: the relationships of the concept of land to Islam and to the State of Saudi Arabia; secondly: the evolution of the structure of government; thirdly: the background of agriculture in the development of concepts of land utilization.

Now we turn to a consideration of Land Distribution Policies with special reference to agriculture, beginning with the recent and present constitutional phase.

The Government began to think seriously in the early 1370s (1950s) about formulating a law of Public Land Distribution. For this purpose, a joint committee from the Ministries of Agriculture and Water, Finance and National Economy, and Interior met in the year 1375H (1955) to consider the principles and conditions of Public Land Distribution and utilization. The details, methods and work programmes were to be designed as soon as the higher authorities authorized the Ministry of Agriculture and Water to initiate a policy of distributing these lands for agricultural and utilization purposes. Traditional land granting in the form of *Iqt'a* had become a heavy burden on the Ruler, due to the huge number of Bedouins and settlers asking for land grants. A new process clearly had to be devised. At the same time the implications of *ad hoc* land granting became clearer and the experience gained during the first phase (see Chapter Three) made necessary a new approach.

The Cabinet Ministers issued a resolution No. 688 dated 25/11/1380H (1960), to the following effect:

"The Cabinet Ministers, after perusal of the documents prepared by the Ministry of Agriculture and Water, comprising Temporary Principles for Land Utilization and since these principles facilitate the distribution of Public Lands among parties willing to utilize them for agricultural and animal purposes, and since the Ministry of Agriculture and Water will carry out all technical studies needed for the establishment of a Department for the utilization of Public Land in accordance with the most modern systems, approve the Temporary Principles for Land Utilization. A Royal Decree No. 113 of 26/11/1380H (1960) promulgated the following main groups of Temporary Principles for Land Utilization.

1. Power given to the Ministry of Agriculture and Water to organize the transformation and distribution of Public Land to utilizers and to supervise land reclamation operations.
2. Authority given to the MAW to defer decisions on ownership and to concentrate solely on the distribution of land for utilization, prohibiting such utilizers from selling or renting their lands and giving them no title to land but only rights to use land.
3. Specified requirements to be met by the utilizers, and orders of priority in land distribution according to specific conditions, such as the utilizers' capability to utilize land, their settlement on the utilized land or on land adjacent to it, their lack of possession of another land. The conditions under which land utilization rights would be lost.

4. Determination of land area allotted to utilizers (1–5 hectares for individuals, 400 hectares as a maximum area for companies).
5. Organization of Regional Committees to supervise the distribution and transformation operation".

The Temporary Principles were based on a still-developing concept of Public Lands. The principal characteristic of this concept is that Public Lands belong to the State represented by the Ruler, and the owner may sell, let, mortgage or give away. The Government, through its administrative system has the right of supervision on behalf of the Ruler. The theory is that the land is given for the purpose of cultivation, and the recipient or occupant must cultivate it. The main categorization of Public Lands is, first *Mawat* or *Mewat* (Dead Land), *Mushaa*, land shared in common by several users, *Mubah*, land open to all and *Al-Ard Al-Bidhah* (White Land), which has no occupants and for which no use has been yet allocated.

These are all unutilized or deserted lands, belonging to no one and noncultivated. They are considered to belong to the public domain of the Muslim community in the form of the State or Government. According to this concept, dead land, barren land, unutilized land, Government land, State land and Public land all have equal meanings. The expression *Public Land* now becomes the most official term used.

During the period 1380H to 1385H (1960 to 1965), potential utilizers from different areas of the Kingdom submitted more than four thousand applications for Public Land ownership. The application forms were provided by the Public Land Division (see p. 68) to collect data as follows (see Form No. 2. Appendix I):

1. Social status of the applicant and other pertinent information including name, family and tribe.
2. Evidence of financial and technical ability to cultivate the land and other types of work which the applicant can do beside farming.
3. Location and area of Public Land concerned.
4. Legal status of the Public Land, especially those aspects pertaining to possible ownership claims by others.

To facilitate checking and deciding on ownership rights and other problems, local committees were formed to inspect the land and make decisions on possible problems and ownership claims of the land. The committee included members from the Ministries of Agriculture and Water and the Interior together with local members.

But these principles were not carried out because they became subject of discussion among the Ministry of Agriculture and Water, the Ministry of Interior and the consultants of the Cabinet Ministers during a period of five years 1380–1385H (1960–1965).

In practice, a series of difficulties and problems arose which led to

Table No (4–3) The numbers of applications filed according to the Temporary Principles for Land Utilization.*

Location	*No. of Applications*
Taima	90
Al-Ula	70
Qasim region	400
Ha'il	955
Bishah	2491
Najran	1
Al-Hassa	189
Shakra	52
Riyad area	133
Ar'ar	76
Abha	2
Taif area	47
Makkah area	121
Total	4,627

* Unpublished departmental memorandum.

the non-implementation of the policy as a whole. Firstly, there was insufficient technical information concerning the actual availability of land and water resources. It is now known that no water potential for agricultural development exists in most of the areas claimed around Riyad, Ar'ar, Abha, Taif and Makkah; in Bishah, there is some water potential but it is not enough to support the huge number of applicants. Even more important was the fact that at that time the Ministry of Agriculture and Water was facing a real shortage of personnel. The General Directorate of Inspection in the Ministry of Agriculture and Water was made responsible for executing the Temporary Principles for Land Utilization (TPLU). The Public Domain Department in the Ministry of Finance and National Economy at that time dealt with land distribution through the contracting procedure system earlier discussed in Chapter Three, pp. 50–52. The Ministry of Agriculture and Water felt that TPLU did not differ all that much from the contracting procedure system and that the Public Domain Department was more capable, from the point of experience and administration, of handling it.

The Ministry of Agriculture and Water also saw its role as limited to the giving of technical advice about the cultivability of the land and availability of water. The Ministry of Agriculture and Water, as a technical Ministry, did not have personnel trained in the non-technical aspects of land distribution and secondly, even the technical facilities provided within the Ministry were not enough to deal with the scale of technical work involved. The Ministry was not in a position to deal with TPLU as an integrated whole and the need for co-ordination with the Ministry of Finance and National Economy, and in particular the Public Domain, was not fully appreciated at the time.

After the Royal Decree which prevented Amirates from granting lands (Chapter Two, p. 31), it was nevertheless necessary to have some method of making land grants through a bureaucratic procedure. TPLU had been established and provided the only available system in spite of the problems.

Therefore it became necessary either to improve the TPLU or to replace them with improved procedures. Meetings and discussions were held between the Ministry of Agriculture and Water and the Ministry of Finance and National Economy which ended with the formation of a consultancy team in which consultants from Cabinet Ministries participated. The Ministry of Agriculture and Water itself took a stand on its belief that if it allotted lands before establishing a tenurial system, it would create problems, while at the same time agricultural resources such as water and soil potential were insufficiently known to justify proceeding with allotment.

The consultant team suggested that modifications to the Royal Decree of TPLU be summarized as follows:

(a) The word *temporary* is to be removed from the resolution because it might suggest the temporariness of the distribution. Such a misunderstanding would defeat the purpose of the Government, because the land utilization desired requires large early investment and no utilizer would commit capital on the scale desired without some guarantee of obtaining a title to the land concerned.

(b) A representative from the Ministry of Finance and National Economy–Public Domain should be included for land survey purposes in the local committee.

(c) The fact that lands within a given area were to be distributed would be announced in local newspapers and on the radio. Applications would be received and allotment made during the following month, after which the distribution decisions were to be submitted to the Prime Minister. The first announcement was to enable anyone with a claim to land to submit his deeds, before any issuing of new ownership deeds for allottees.

(d) New articles were to be added; as follows:

Ownership deeds issued by the Prime Minister, would show location, boundaries and area of the land in addition to all other necessary data.

(e) If the allottee breaks his contract, the Ministry of Agriculture and Water is to report this to the Prime Minister in order to obtain his order for the withdrawing of land and giving it to another allottee.

(f) Lands subject to personal or tribal disputes shall not be allotted until after the Justice Courts give their judgement and prove them to be from the Public Domain.

During this discussion of land legislation, a Royal Order No. 6899 dated 16/3/1383H (1963) addressed to the Minister of Agriculture and Water was issued approving the necessity of land distribution within a short period to enable the utilizers, who were to include the Bedouins, to benefit and earn their living from the land. This was meant to bring some urgency to policy formulation.

While this discussion was taking place to modify TPLU, the Ministry of Agriculture and Water presented in its budget 1384/85H (1964/65) a project called Public Land Utilization. Its purpose was to establish a nucleus of administrative and technical staff and to provide equipment for implementing land distribution, and budgetary provision was agreed for some three years.

Table No. (4-4) The expenditure on the Public Land Utilization project during 1384-1388H (1964-1968)*

Date	*Expenditure SR*	*Kind of Material*
1384–85H (1964–65)	348,578	Salaries & employees
1385H (1965)	71,443	Furniture
1385–88H (1965–68)	207,181	Equipment & machinery
1385–88H (1965–68)	248,837	Soil survey elements
1387–88H (1967–68)	213,293	Soil survey equipment
1388H (1968)	363,975	3 mobile soil laboratories
Total	1,453,307	

*Unpublished departmental data.

Twelve soil surveyor expatriates together with other skilled workers were employed. The purpose was to survey Public Land asked for under the TPLU scheme even though the allotment of land under TPLU was not being carried out. Unexpectedly, it was found that most of the area surveyed had no ground-water available for irrigation, thus emphasizing the fundamental need for scientific survey before any distribution of land.

On 23/5/85H (1965), a legislative committee discussed the consultant team's proposed amendments.

From these discussions it appeared absolutely necessary to re-study the temporary principles for the utilization of Public Land taking into consideration all the different ideas of the Ministry of Interior, Ministry of Finance and National Economy, and the Ministry of

Agriculture and Water. As a result, a new committee was formed from the Ministries concerned consisting of the Minister of Agriculture and Water as Head of the Committee, the Deputy Minister of Finance and National Economy and a *Shari'a* consultant, and the third member was the Deputy Minister of the Interior.

This Committee maintained contact with the Director of the Public Land Division (the author).

The small technical group emerging from the 1384/85H (1964/65) MAW Public Land Project (see p. 67) was strengthened and was established as a Public Land Division in 1385H (1965). Its duties in the first place lay mainly in land survey but it was seen as the nucleus of a specialist department, which, within the Ministry of Agriculture and Water, would assume responsibility for the general sector of Public Land.

In 1387H (1967), a fully fledged Public Land Management Department was formed and a director was assigned. After a short period, a new Public Land Distribution Ordinance was passed by the Council of Ministers (see No. 1005 dated 3/7/88H (1968) and approved by Royal Decree No. M/26 dated 6/7/88H (1968)). When this Public Land Distribution Ordinance was issued it marked a new era of administrative, executive and bureaucratic operation on a national level.

The expression *Public Land*, as stated in the ordinance, means any land wherein the following conditions are fulfilled:

(a) It should be free from existing rights of proprietorship or appropriation.

(b) The economic advantage of its utilization for agricultural or animal production should be clear.

(c) It should be outside the boundaries of the inhabited areas and their related interests in both towns and villages.

To summarize: when the Council of Ministers was set up in 1373H (1953), it was accorded all administrative and executive powers, but the King retained the authority to instruct and direct the Council. The executive power over land control and administration has become the responsibility both of the Ministry of Interior and the Ministry of Agriculture and Water. Land legislation was developed through several stages as Temporary Principles for Land Utilization then as a Public Land Utilization Project. This sequence ended with a Public Land Distribution Ordinance operated by the Ministry of Agriculture and Water and with the formation of a PLMD.

Chapter Five

The Modern Phase

The development philosophy of modern Saudi Arabia, in the context of which we must examine modern Public Land distribution, is exemplified in the following passage from the Development Plan published in 1390H (1970):

> "The commitment of Saudi Arabia to a free economy derives from the teaching of social traditions. It is supported by growing evidence that economic and social change cannot be imposed on the country by the actions of the Government alone but through increasing participation of all elements of Society by continuously encouraging private enterprise – family businesses and individuals – to pursue those activities more effectively than Government agencies."[19]

The Public Land Distribution Ordinance (PLDO), issued by Royal Decree No. M/26 dated 6/7/1388H, could be quoted as one of the measures taken to achieve the goals of the national policy in the spirit of this statement.

Also in the Plan it was said that "Even in agriculture more resources exist than many believed possible before studies were made".[19] These have revealed additional land resources which can be used and subterranean water resources that can be exploited.

Given this philosophy of approach to development and a belief that usable virgin land resources exist then the PLDO's implementation outline is clear: "Development of new lands and enlargement of existing farms by private entrepreneurs will be facilitated by the recent PLDO and will be further encouraged by Government technical assistance and grants."[19]

Under the PLDO the existing Public Land Management Department is to survey public land all over the country to identify and demarcate where:

1. Land would be economically and technically feasible for develop-

ment in that there is enough water for irrigation and the soil is cultivable.

2. There should be no dispute over territory or the possibility of a conflict of interests involving, for example, group rights whether they are rights of ownership or lesser rights such as the right of appropriation or the right of preference or the rights of specifically identified pastures thriving on natural water supply, or the other collective facilities in the utilization and exploitation of which groups of individuals jointly participate.
3. Land is not owned by an individual or group of individuals. In areas of Public Domain Land (see Chapter Four), no action is to be taken before the situation is clarified through contact with local authorities, etc.
4. Land would be outside the boundaries of the inhabited areas (urban areas) and associated town land and village land. Suitable land would not interfere with existing religious status, mineral and petroleum resources' localities.

Before the PLDO was issued, the idea of leaving a distance between urban and arable areas prevailed, and consequently a belt with a width of 10 Km around each town and 5 Km around each village was designated as closed to the distribution of Public Lands. In fact it was found that some village territories (including their farms) did not exceed 1 Km in total width. A report prepared on 21/6/85H (1965) between the Ministry of Agriculture and Water and Municipal and Rural Affairs stated that direct contact between PLMD and the Town Planning Office/Ministry of Interior should be carried out to determine the area needed for towns and village expansion in the future. A reserved belt with a width of 10 Km around the towns and 5 Km around villages for the sake of urban expansion was deemed impractical as it is impossible to forecast the direction where expansion might take place or even the speed of such expansion. A clear need for inter-Ministerial collaboration was established. During the survey of Public Lands, the Ministry of Agriculture and Water had to leave enough distance for public facilities to be used in the future. The Deputy Minister of Interior for Municipal and Rural Affairs should contact the Ministry of Agriculture and Water when the present aerial survey of 37 villages and towns is completed. The MAW should co-operate with the Town Planning Office to get the utmost use of air survey maps as well as having the neighbouring arable lands surveyed.

It became necessary for the Ministry of Agriculture and Water and the Ministry of Interior, represented by Municipal and Rural Affairs, to agree on a basis for determining urban areas and the arable lands.

A minute was prepared on 28/8/1389H (1969), explaining this basis as follows:

1. The arable land located *outside* the urban area: such land which will be also outside the zone of future extension. Growth of the towns will be under the responsibility of MAW after preparing the necessary survey and supplying the Town Planning Office with copies of this survey.
2. The arable land located *near* the urban area, which will be within the zone of future extension. Growth of towns will be under the responsibility of the Town Planning Office. The Ministry of Agriculture and Water and the Town Planning Office will reach an agreement to determine those areas within the growth zone which are likely in practice to be required for urban needs, after which the distribution of any land within the reserved zones will be carried after the MAW has negotiated with the Town Planning Office.
3. The Town Planning Office will supply the Ministry of Agriculture and Water with copies of the general orientation plans prepared for future extension of the towns so that the latter can take the same into consideration while distributing Public Land.
4. The Town Planning Office is to be supplied with the general survey plans of the Public Land which will be distributed for agricultural purposes. Plans for all distribution areas so far surveyed have been submitted to the Town Planning Office and approved by it, that is, Tabuk, Qasim, Al-Joaf, etc.

The Public Land Distribution Ordinance laid down in some detail the basic characteristics of the scheme.

According to the PLDO, a minimum of 5 hectares to a maximum of 10 hectares can be allotted to any single individual (this is considered as a normal economically viable size) and up to 400 hectares for a company (see Chapter Twelve). These areas depend upon the number of applicants and the total area available for distribution.

The basic qualifications of an individual allottee are that: firstly, he should be a Saudi Arabian; secondly, he should be qualified for farming; thirdly, he may not be allotted more than one land grant under this ordinance unless all but the most recently applied-for land is properly used and cultivated.[44] Since competition for distributable lands was expected, fair measures for preferences and priorities were stated in a descending order. The trial period of the utilization of a lot is between 2 to 3 years according to the size of the allotted land and its soil. The allottee in this period has no right of ownership but a right of utilization only. If he proves during this period that he is serious in developing the land and has cultivated at least a quarter of it, then he is given full ownership rights.

The first paragraph of Article No. II of PLDO permitted the distribution of Public Land among non-Saudis after obtaining the approval of the Council of Ministers. An additional non-Saudi proprietorship ordinance was issued by Royal Decree No. 811 dated 15/6/1390H (1970) in which the third item (b), stated that "within the limits of the Public Land Distribution Ordinance, non-Saudis could own agricultural land according to suggestions made by the Minister of Agriculture and Water and discussed with the Minister of Interior".

Of some special importance is the status of Local Committees. Eighteen local committees have been constituted so far to deal with land distribution at a regional level. Article V of the Ordinance states that in addition to the representatives of the Ministry of Agriculture and Water, Ministry of Finance and National Economy, Ministry of Interior, and Ministry of Justice, two members drawn from local people of experience, not employed in any way by Government, should participate in the work of the Land Distribution Committees. These committees are provided with all the necessary data and reports indicating the location of the land, type of soil, water availability and maps of areas proposed for distribution.

The function of these local committees is to interpret and apply the Public Land Ordinance as guided by PLMD, to review the contents of the application forms which are filled in by the applicant, including companies as well as individuals, and assess applicants' ability to develop the land, on the basis of, for example, capital, labour availability, etc. After this the Local Committees will make their recommendations, including the specification of the area to be granted, to the Central Committee, except in the case of applications by companies, recommendations concerning which are made by the Central Committee. Every member is given a special emolument, according to the importance of the work the person contributes, of between 300 to 500 SR. Each member receives his bonus from his employing authority, the rate varying with the regional classification into three groups (Table No. (5–1)). Each Group I region member receives 500 SR, Group II, 400 SR, and Group III, 300 SR.

This classification is based principally on three factors which are:

1. The social and economic standards of the area subject to distribution.
2. The area of Public Land ready for distribution.
3. The volume and difficulty of work expected.

A sum of 400,000 SR has been allotted in MAW budget of 1389/

Table No. (5–1) Groups of Public Land areas classification.*

Group I	*Group II*	*Group III*
Qasim (Buraidah)	Bishah	Wadi Sarhan
(Unaizah)	Al-Zulfi	Al-Serr
Al-Hassa	Shakra	Al-Ula
Al-Kharj	Najran	Taima
Tabuk	Ha'il	As-Sulail
Qatif	Wadi Dawasir	
	Al-Joaf	

* Unpublished departmental data.

90H (1969/70) to pay the bonuses of the two local members with most experience and the representative of the Ministry of Agriculture and Water.

We noted that the Local Committees make their recommendations to a Central Committee of Public Land Distribution in the Ministry of Agriculture and Water. Members of this Committee originally included:

1. Deputy Minister of MAW — Chairman
2. Director General of PLMD
3. A legal adviser for MAW
4. An expert in water affairs
5. Two experts in agriculture

(items 2–5: as members)

More recently these last two experts were replaced by the Head of the Public Land Division of PLMD and a soil technician. The Director General of Agricultural Extension and Service Department also joined this Committee. The main functions and duties of the Central Committee are as follows:

1. To review and check application forms which were reviewed and approved by local committees and to forward these as finally approved to the Minister.
2. To report its general proposals and recommendations from each meeting to the Minister of Agriculture and Water.
3. To review companies' applications and prepare the necessary comments for the Minister to make his decision. It may submit a recommendation to the Minister who, if he agrees, will send it to the Council of Ministers, who are responsible for all allocations to companies.

Since the Central Committee is unable to verify all applications from the regions, this Committee carries out a sample review of individual applications for plots of land. The PLMD, however, has to check every form according to regulations. Other departments participating and assisting in land distribution are Water Resources Development Department, Water Conservation Department which has responsible licences for drilling and the follow-up of drilling requirements and the Agricultural Extension and Services Department which is responsible for field services.

Public Land Distribution procedure

The operational procedure of the ordinance provides in detail specific measures for Public Land Distribution, the maximum and minimum limits of land to be distributed which relate to number of applicants, fertility of lands concerned and ability and capability of the utilizer. It takes into consideration harmony of the rights upon the land, the rights of the utilizers and requirements of the ordinance in reclaiming and developing the land. The procedure can be illustrated by the presentation of a sequence of documents involved in one sample case (see Appendix I).

Under this system the executive procedure by the PLMD is normally as follows:

1. Examination of enquiries and claims received directly or through field organizations. Identification of Public Lands which are not possessed by individuals and are not subject to disputes and determining their approximate area and location (see Form No. 3, Appendix I).
2. Water conditions have to be determined and investigated by the Department of Water Resources Development and reports produced for relevant areas.
3. The survey of Public Lands which on first appraisal have sufficient water and the preparation of necessary maps, for example:
   (a) Physical study: topography, soil texture and structure, erosion, soil profile description and vegetation cover.
   (b) Chemical study: either by a central laboratory in the Ministry or by mobile laboratories, for example, pH in the soil, the salinity of soil (EC), exchangeable sodium percentage (ESP), calcium carbonate percentage ($CaCO_3$ per cent) and calcium and magnesium percentages in the soil (see Form No. 4, Appendix I).
   (c) Classification of lands according to their capability for irrigation.
   (d) Demarcation of blocks of land which has been shown to be of arable capability and its division into suitably sized plots in accordance with PLDO.
4. Announcing in newspapers and sometimes by broadcasting, the

distribution of Public Lands among applicants (see Form No. 5, Appendix I) and issuing instructions to the local land distribution committees concerning application procedure and evaluation. Application forms, available through the field organizations, are of two types, one for applicants claiming specific areas, and another for those who do not ask for specific areas. The forms are designed to give data relevant to the Ordinance or the operational procedure, that is, priorities, capability of utilization, area to be allotted and the period criterion for development (see Form No. 6, Appendix I).

5. Studying applications sent by the local distribution committees before submitting them to the central committee for action. Also, preparing the documentation of Public Land decisions which will be signed by the Minister of Agriculture and Water, and submitted to allottees through the Ministry's field organizations (see Form No. 7, Appendix I).
6. Sending technicians (mostly soil specialists) on tours to the distribution regions to inspect the capability of allottees and guide them how to manage their lands properly. This type of work is carried out in co-operation with the field organization.
7. Studying all other land claims deeds which come to the Ministry from courts or sub-offices of the Ministry of Finance and National Economy, and giving an opinion, (see Form No. 8, Appendix I). Other claims, for example, for well-drilling in Public Lands are managed jointly by the Water Conservation Department and PLMD.

Finally, to apply the rules and regulations of the PLDO judiciously, a judge is appointed by the Ministry of Justice who, having his seat in the Ministry, decides the disputes or the disputed issues. His judgement should be enforced by order of the Minister of Agriculture and Water.

The Public Land Distribution Ordinance and its relationship to previous land grant practices

As examined in Chapters One to Three, before the issuing of the PLDO of 6/7/1388H (1968) several different land distribution systems had been adopted and these schemes and the land to which they referred had now to be taken over under the new arrangements following the issue of the PLDO. Fundamentally, no problem of principle appeared because all the phases of land distribution policy were based on the acceptance of Islamic concepts of land proprietorship and interpreted by *Shari'a*. From the operational point of view the changes implied by PLDO were essentially administrative and organizational. However, by 1388H (1968) the growing wealth of Saudi Arabia and, in particular, a greatly increasing urbanization and demand for land for building was producing a new market for land. Many of the applicants for land allocations were eager to obtain land now, not for its traditional utilization value but for its negotiable cash value and rapidly increasing capital value over a period of time. The implementation of the PLDO therefore had to take into account existing processes of allocation and, as a matter of urgency, limit the extent of speculation in land transferred from public ownership to private hands.

After the Public Lands Utilization Project had been agreed (see p. 67), all regions were advised that nobody was allowed to touch Public Land without having, in advance, an official permit for the use of Public Land for planting trees or a land investment contract with the technical and administrative organization of a Public Lands Utilization Project.

A Royal Order circulated to all regions in 1386H (1966) laid down the basic rules for the private land properties of individuals and gave rights equivalent to private ownership to small settlements (normally inhabited by a blood-group community) over a surrounding "reserved zone".

In the case of private properties (whether farms or urban areas) local customs were to be applied thereto.

Concerning small settlements' or hamlets' lands not already utilized, and over which ownership was requested, the same was to remain as governmental Public Lands under the supervision of the Ministry of Agriculture and Water. If an individual from the settlement concerned requested an extra piece of land or a new piece, then he should request this from the Ministry of Agriculture and Water (as is done in other larger towns and villages) since the Ministry of Agriculture and Water is responsible for Public Lands Distribution according to TPLU and the Public Land Utilization Project.

As for the claims of some hamlets in which the motive for their requests to fix the boundaries of their hamlets is the fear of aggression or encroachment by some other tribes whom they think threaten their interests, such claims should be referred to the Government (normally the Ministry of Interior); nobody would be allowed to plant or dwell on unutilized land within the hamlet's boundaries unless he obtained a governmental permit in advance.

Another Royal Order instructed all regions as well as field organizations to supervise Public Lands and to ensure that no occupation or utilization of land (except under the TPLU or the Utilization Project) likely to give rise to a claim to ownership, should be allowed to occur.

Since the Ministry of Interior, as the executive power in the Kingdom, could devolve its responsibilities to the regional governors, according to executive authority the Governors had the right to impose penalties on intruders on Public Land. These responsibilities were confirmed later after the issue of the PLDO.

Under previous procedures, agricultural machinery could be obtained from the Ministry of Agriculture and Water in order to till and otherwise prepare land for cultivation. In a special circular the MAW emphasized the illegality of the use of such machinery on any unutilized Public Land for which there was no authorized allocation for development.

The power of the Ordinance

It was stated in Article VIII of the ordinance that: "The Ministry of Agriculture and Water shall supervise the allotted land from the technical point of view and check as to the effectiveness of its utilization by the party to whom it is given".[44]

Land development henceforward would be supervised and inspected. The local agricultural field staff should once every six months tour the area to check the progress of work and report to the PLMD accordingly. The technical staff of the PLMD would undertake similar tours for spot checking and verifying the previous records once every year. The head of each field organization was to accompany the nominee of the General Directorate of Inspection of PLMD on these inspection trips.

The State has the right to remove the land from the allottee if an unsatisfactory position is observed. Criteria for this removal are stated in the same Article VIII as follows:

> "The Minister of Agriculture and Water may, by an order, cancel the right of appropriation of a party after serving two months' advance notice when it is confirmed that the party failed to utilize even the minimum limits of acreage within the fixed period of time, or the party's lack of interest to develop these lands is proven otherwise. He (the Minister) may then allot this land to another person, who shall utilize it after having paid the actual expenses already incurred by his predecessor for the exploitation of these lands".[44]

Here again we see the *Sharīʿa* principle that the allotment shall be owned only when it is developed. Following this concept, any allotment that is not developed is considered free from appropriation by the allottee. Under Article VII the allottee was required to develop land within three years. After this period and after formal announcement (see Form No. 4, Appendix I) for example, by radio, TV and other information facilities (according to Article VI), if the allottee has failed to develop it, two procedures may be taken:

(a) Cancelling the utilization after serving two months' advance notice since the period of development is overdue, or,

(b) The allottee may be given another period for development.

In case of subsequent failure, cancellation may take place.

The reason for providing an alternative to automatic cancellation, is that to cancel the right of utilization given (see Form No. 9, Appendix I) is difficult in democratic countries without giving rise to claims and problems. In theory the State has these powers to take action but in practice the special characteristics of the Saudi Kingdom produce flexibility.

During the application of the PLDO, it is expected that claims or complaints will arise, so the Ordinance gave the Minister of Agriculture and Water the final authority to interpret the regulations and execute the procedures.

According to Article IX, "If the allottee fulfils the land requirement as regards to the minimum area and time given for its development, he will be handed over the final ownership deed by the Minister of Agriculture and Water, or any other to whom the King delegates this authority."[44] This article is also applicable to lands granted by the Ruler before the issue of the PLDO with regard to the period of utilization.

Nevertheless, traditional granting of land is still practised by the Ruler of the State, although diminishing rapidly during the last ten years and now very rare. Large areas had been granted by the Ruler, before the issue of the PLDO, through verbal or written orders, many of which have not been centrally recorded. There is no available data, especially for those issued in the early years of King Abdul Aziz and King Sa'ūd.

Table No. (5–2) indicates the extent of known land grants made before and after the issue of PLDO but, even with the latter, falling outside PLMD operations.

The PLMD has no responsibility for lands granted in this way except as covered in Article XI of the Ordinance which indicates that the Ordinance shall be applicable on Public Lands granted by the Ruler before the issue of the Ordinance and where the ownership of such Lands had not yet been fixed at the time of issue of the Ordinance.

The Islamic principle is maintained which indicates that unused land, granted by the Ruler, remains "Government property" or "Public Land" if the allottee fails to invest in and utilize it during the period

Table No. (5-2) Areas in donums granted according to Royal Orders, from 8/1/1384 to 8/7/91 (1964-71).

Area	*No. of Utilizers (Beneficiaries)*	*Area Distributed*	*No. of Royal Order*	*Date of Royal Order*
Madinah	55	8,518.7	624	8/1/1384 (1964)
Taif	1	27.1	20,399	26/8/1384 (1964)
Ha'il	1	2,880	15,032	15/7/1384 (1964)
Bishah	115	3,828	17,447	14/8/1385 (1965)
Qasim	1	250	17,719	19/8/1385 (1965)
Qasim	1	1,000	16,677	20/8/1385 (1965)
Al-Howta	1	708	24,879	29/10/1386 (1966)
Unaizah	1	100	936	21/11/1386 (1966)
Al-Hassa	1	75	27,647	4/12/1386 (1966)
Al-Hassa	6	400	3,909	24/2/1387 (1967)
Yanbo'a	1	10	12,285	22/6/1387 (1967)
As-Salsalah	69	5,199	10,668	18/5/1388 (1968)
Tarabah	206	2,238.2	11,808	2/6/1388 (1968)
Tathlith	42	652.2	19,172	10/9/1388 (1968)
Qasim	5	500	5,194	8/3/1391 (1971)
Qasim	2	3,250	9,550	29/4/1391 (1971)
Qasim	1	100	14,654	8/7/1391 (1971)
Total	509	29,736.2		

of three years. Such land is subject to the other principles and rules of the Ordinance for distribution among companies or individuals according to areas, priorities and period of appropriation.

The rules of the Public Land Distribution Ordinance are not applicable on lands granted by the Ruler before the issue of the same where investment and utilization had been actually realized. In the case of land which has not been wholly or partially invested or utilized, but for which legal ownership documents exist, in accordance with applicable regulations the matter lies with the courts according to Items No. 85 and 86 (see p. 20). These items indicate that the competent Government Departments concerned have to be consulted and also other interested parties through advertising in local newspapers, etc., before the ownership of such lands is considered ultimate or fixed.

The Ministry, in the application of the Ordinance and the operational procedures thereof, may face objections from individuals. They may consider some land as their property because of various other grants which they claim have been made and consequently have a claim to appropriation for having held these lands for either short or long periods. In some cases they claim an inability to fulfil the time requirement due to lack of financial facilities or due to a shortage of time given for utilization in particular circumstances.

Other examples of disputes and claims are:

(a) Lands sold or granted on an uncertain basis;

(b) Lands subject to individual or group disputes, even if apparently ended with friendly agreements supported with legal documents;
(c) Land units exceeding the maximum area stated in the Ordinance;
(d) Land without defined boundaries according to registration documents issued in this regard.

To solve such difficult cases and to achieve the objective of the Ordinance which primarily aims at the utilization of land and increasing the cultivated area as well as arranging the flexibility in the application of the Ordinance, the following procedures were laid down:

1. Lands grants by the Ruler before the issue of the Ordinance and not yet utilized, regardless of whether relevant documents of ownership were actually obtained or not in full compliance with the procedure of the judicial courts according to Articles No. 85 and 86 (see p. 20), will be subject to Articles 9 and 11 of the Ordinance. These lands, regardless of the area, will be treated by giving every person who was granted land an additional period of three years from the date of consideration of the case (the maximum period mentioned in the Ordinance) in order to prove utilization. If during this fresh period he does not utilize it according to Article VII, then Article VIII will be applied. In case of utilization, ownership will be confirmed.
2. In this procedure it will be necessary to identify cases where non-utilization has been the result of the land offering special difficulties to utilization or where the grant has been of an area so large that significant use could not be expected within three years. In such cases the fresh period of allotment may be for a minimum rather than a maximum of three years. If, however, even after a longer term has expired utilization cannot be shown, then the grant can be withdrawn.
3. In the case of land granting in areas where there is little economic feasibility and/or inadequate availability of water and soil (according to MAW survey and study), or in areas where increased water extraction would adversely affect existing agricultural areas, MAW will neither give permission for well-drilling nor will withdraw such areas after three years have passed even if there is no utilization.
4. If any of the lands mentioned in Item 1 are not clearly defined by boundaries, that is, if the border is imaginary or vague as with track routes or mountains, and so on, then the land in question has to be measured and ownership documents checked on site by a committee formed from MAW, Ministry of Interior, Ministry of Finance and National Economy and the Ministry of Justice.
5. If lack of water or other social considerations should raise difficulty

the matter would be left for the Ministry's evaluation, and MAW would determine the beginning of the trial period relevant to any previously granted lands. Special procedures as illustrated by Forms 10 and 11, Appendix I will be utilized.

When the Public Land Ordinance was issued and the Ministry started distribution of land accordingly, all previously completed application forms under the TPLU were disregarded. Consequently, some individuals who were expecting grants did not receive any land.

In order not to deprive these individuals of their earlier rights the Ordinance was held to apply to the plots for which the TPLU forms had been filed and approved. Taking into consideration economic feasibility, distributable area, etc., these individuals were given priority in distribution according to the PLD Ordinance. In the advertisements of land distribution, the local committee not only must announce that certain lands are Public and available for distribution but also that in some cases prior distribution rights are held by former TPLU applicants.

In these ways the PLDO was made applicable not only to land allotments made under the new policies but also, through special procedures, applicable to all previous land grants. From 1388H (1968) onwards, the machinery for a co-ordinated approach to Public Land management and distribution has existed.

To summarize: MAW in applying PLDO is naturally following the executive procedure in setting up implementation procedure and committees at the same time complying with relevant rules, explanations and Islamic teaching pertaining to ownership rights. PLMD has to undertake the field steps in the application of PLD. It starts by allocating Public Land located outside urban areas; this it will fix in collaboration with governmental bodies within and outside the Ministry.

Chapter Six

Agricultural Land and Resource Development

Agricultural holdings and ownership

The tenurial characteristics of agricultural land holding in the Kingdom are most distinctive when compared with those of other Middle Eastern countries. There is, in particular, no concentration of land ownership in a few hands and the cultivated lands are remarkably evenly distributed. Owner-occupied agricultural holdings cover 96.7 per cent of the cultivated area.

Table No. (6–1) Distribution of holdings in the Kingdom according to size and type of tenure.

Size of Holding	*Owned Holdings*		*Rented Holdings*		*Mixed Holdings*		*Total*	
(Donums – 0.1 ha)	*Number*	%	*Number*	%	*Number*	%	*Number*	%
Less than 10	75,333	56.10	1,362	42.70	368	30.82	77,063	55.57
From 10 to less than 30	27,235	20.28	654	20.50	309	25.88	28,198	20.34
From 30 to less than 100	21,370	15.92	553	17.34	270	22.61	22,193	16.00
More than 100	10,345	7.70	621	19.46	247	20.69	11,213	8.09
	134,283	100.00	3,190	100.00	1,194	100.00	138,667	100.00

It also appears clearly that most holdings are small in size. More than half the number of holdings (55.6 per cent) do not exceed 10 donums per holding in area, an uneconomically small area for full-time farming (see also pp. 183–185).

Holdings of less than 30 donums amount to 75.9 per cent; holdings of less than 100 donums amount to 91.9 per cent; holdings in excess of 100 donums (10 has.) constitute only 8 per cent. There is no landlord–peasant problem in Saudi Arabian agriculture but there is a problem of fragmentation, or more accurately "morcellement".

The processes encouraging this dominance of small holdings may be said to be legal in that inheritance, customary and *Shari'a* law reflect the traditional needs of subsistence communities. The forces making for the traditional dominance of small holdings are all bound up with the nature of traditional agriculture. With simple technology it was difficult to serve a large-sized farm, due, for example, to the primitive methods of well drilling and of agricultural operations. Agricultural mechanization which has lessened the effectiveness of this constraint has been introduced only recently. Farmers were used to cultivating areas only sufficient for domestic consumption because of a general absence of market possibilities.

Primitive methods of water extraction and the scarcity of water restricted agricultural expansion and therefore further strengthened the demand for land in the few most easily exploited places.

With modern technology and that agricultural mechanization already existing, it is now practical in some cases to utilize large agricultural holdings. This type of change might be one of the outcomes of the implementation of the PLDO.

Table No. (6–2) Agricultural properties distributed in different areas of the Kingdom, 1380–1386H[31] (1960–1966) (area in donums).

Location	*Agricultural Area, Total*	*Productive Area*	*No. of Owners*	*Average Property/ Person Total*	*Productive Area/Person*	*Rented Area %*
Northern	326,507	104,682	11,510	28.4	9.1	0.1
Eastern	126,136	101,593	9,098	13.9	11.2	18.6
Western	339,648	252,098	19,518	17.4	12.9	1.6
Qasim	2,695,748	319,635	9,071	297.2	35.2	4.3
Southern						
Inner South	457,833	381,963	38,816	11.8	9.8	9.3
Middle South	680,274	515,128	8,540	79.7	60.3	16.4
Qunfidah	905,927	752,439	43,312	20.9	17.4	3.3
Jizan	3,113,376	1,537,136	48,188	43.9	31.9	0.4
Total	8,645,449	3,964,674	188,053	64.15	23.5	6.75

The estimated area under agricultural ownership in the Kingdom is about 7.65 million donums, of which 3.96 million donums are productive (usually under cultivation). Of the holdings in the Kingdom 94.2 per cent are operated directly by the owners or operated by a hired manager or through contractors. The product resulting from the utilization of these lands represents the product from about 4.5 million donums because a part of this land carries more than one crop in any one year.

There are other statistics available only for field crops. The area planted for winter field crops is 956,238 donums, and the area of summer field crops is 2,807,191 donums. No information exists about vegetable crops according to season (Fig. 6–1).

Since the PLDO was issued the changes in the position of agriculture in Saudi Arabia have accelerated. Traditionally, farming was mainly a local response to local demand. Today, overall national policies, social and economic, together with commercial market forces are of great importance. The dynamic spatial patterns of production and of marketing have now to be appreciated if Public Land Distribution is to be effectively productive.

With field crops, cereals (wheat, maize, barley, millet, sorghum) are widespread in the Kingdom. Wheat and barley are grown in all the regions, but especially in Qasim, the north and the centre of the country; sorghum, millet and maize are also grown in the southern region (Asir, Jizan, Najran and some other territories). The most widespread single crop is alfalfa, especially dominant under palm trees where other crops or vegetables are not grown. As a cash crop, its market value always exceeds that of local wheat varieties. Alfalfa withstands different conditions of soil and salinity ratios; moreover it improves soil characteristics.[30] The total area planted with field crops is 3,920,018 donums.

Vegetable crops are becoming very popular in those villages close

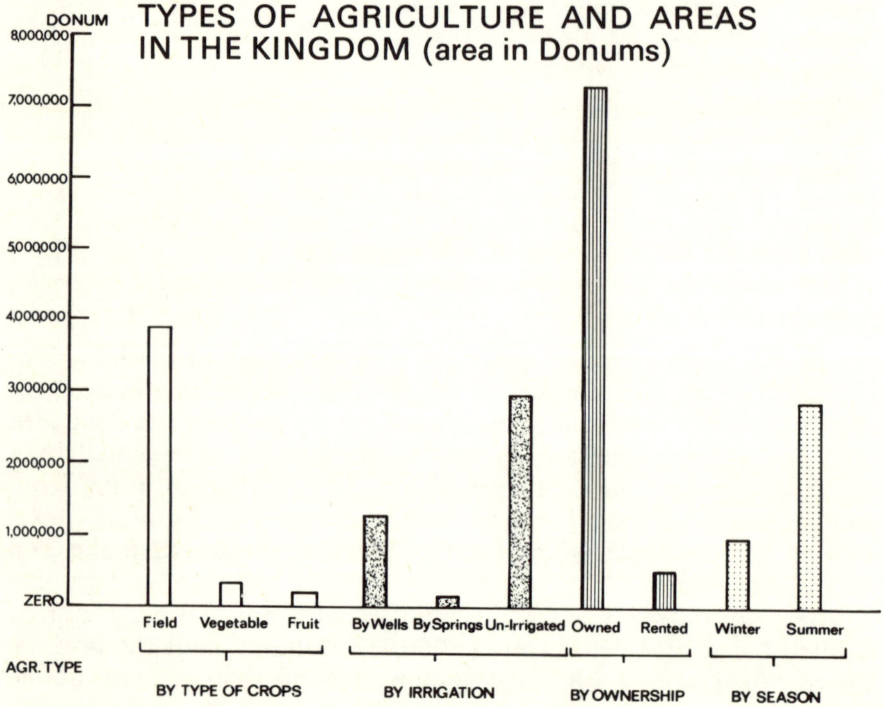

Fig 6·1

Table No. (6–3) The type of agricultural land in the Kingdom.

By Type of Crop			*By Irrigation*			*By Ownership*		*By Season*	
Field	Vegetable	Fruit	Irrigated by wells	Irrigated by springs	Non-irrigated	Owned	Rented	Winter	Summer
3,920.018	309,013	223,539	1,275,026	38,345	2,882,518	7,238,107	445,152	956,238	2,807,191

to urban markets where transportation facilities are most available for marketing. Almost all varieties of vegetables have been introduced into the Kingdom because of the increase in population and its wealth, an increase in health and nutritional understanding and the growth of towns and villages. Some regions (such as the central and eastern Regions) export their vegetable crops to Arabian Gulf states because of transportation advantages. The total area planted with vegetable crops in the regions of the Kingdom is 309,013 donums.[30]

The non-date tree-fruit crops have increased in importance. These are affected by the same factors as those which influence vegetable crops. The total tree-crop planted area (including palm) in all regions of the Kingdom is 223,539 donums. In Saudi Arabia there are between 7 and 9 million mature palm dates (10 per cent of the world palms) distributed in nearly all territories (except Asir) and covering 60–70 per cent of the present cultivated area. In the past the date was a staple food, the palms supplied many by-products; as a crop it does not require high skill and is the hardiest crop in the country to withstand adverse conditions, for example, desert climate, sandy soil, high salinity and poor drainage. However, there is a low demand for dates at the present time due to changes in food habits, availability of other fruits and a relatively poor market presentation.

The basis for the expansion of cultivation

Cultivation expansion can be achieved in regions where the following possibilities are available:

1. Arable land with good natural characteristics of terrain and soil.
2. Economical water resources for agricultural use.
3. Locational accessibility.

Table No. (6–4) The locations and areas of cultivated, arable and non-arable lands in the six areas of the Kingdom according to consultants' reports (area in hectares) (see also Fig. 6–2.)

Area	*Cultivated Area*	%	*Cultivable Area*	%	*Non-cultivable Area*	%	*Desert and other un-utilizable Area*	%
I	14,514	0.003	117,197	0.310	2,000,000	5.333	35,368,289	94.354
II & III	108,000	0.45	909,000	3.75	4,169,000	17.23	19,014,000	78.57
IV	20,000	0.06	2,962,000	8.20	5,411,000	14.98	27,732,000	76.76
V	9,705	0.10	42,860	0.43	311,130	0.31	9,916,305	99.16
VI	233,000	1.16	150,000	0.76	101,000	0.50	19,940,000	97.58
Total	385,219	0.3	4,181,057	2.24	11,992,130	6.39	111,970,594	74.4

These are the fundamental factors now always kept in mind when dealing with land distribution. Land and water are the two factors which are directly considered by the Ministry of Agriculture and Water in ascertaining the availability of arable land. Area studies and resource inventories made by Ministry technicians and entrusted international firms reveal that Saudi Arabia has additional land resources which can be used for increasing output.

By examining the above table it is clear that there is a huge area of unused cultivable land which exceeds by more than ten times the cultivated land (see Fig. 13–3). There was no reliable information existing for land use before 1384H (1964). The Kingdom was divided at that time into eight survey areas based on geological formation boundaries. Six of these areas covering 1,273,000 square kilometres were contracted to three consulting firms to make the following surveys:

1. General survey of all ground-water resources.
2. General survey for soil classification and land use.

AREAS OF WATER AND AGRICULTURAL RESOURCE INVESTIGATION

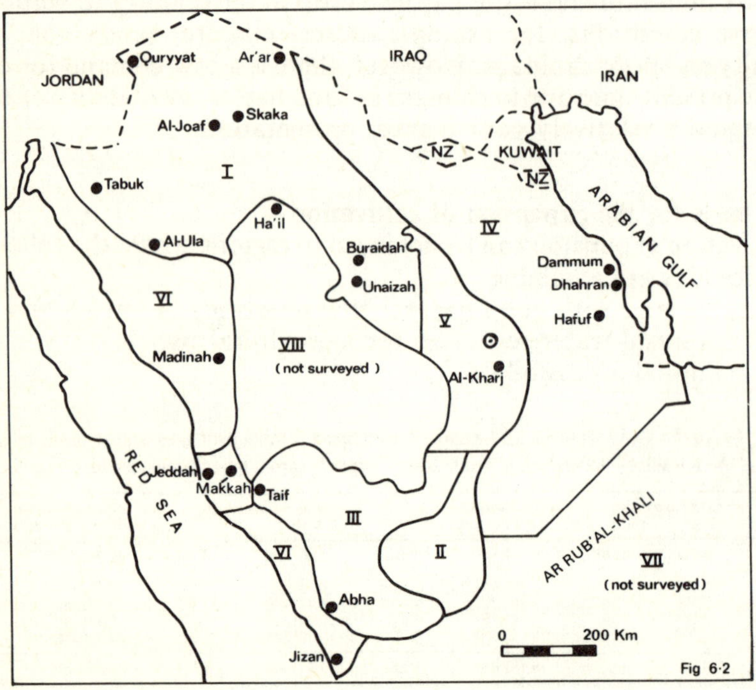

Fig 6·2

3. General survey of all agricultural potentialities existing and the possibility of their development.

These surveys were completed in 1390H (1970) (Fig. 6–2).

Area I represents almost all the Northern Province and Qasim. Area II and III represent wadi regions watered from Hijaz and Asir mountains. Area IV represents Eastern Province. Area V covers the centre of the Central Province and finally Area VI coincides almost with the Western Province.

As a result of the above-mentioned studies, the following facts appeared: due to the availability of ground-water, there are good opportunities in Saudi Arabia for utilizing much of the Public arable Lands which have not been previously cultivated. It is possible to raise the productivity of present cultivated areas through the application of chemicals, improved seeds, machinery, agricultural methods and development of agricultural production facilities.

Area VII (Ar Rub'Al-Khali) is one of the largest areas in Saudi Arabia and is covered by enormous moving sand dunes. This area has not been studied and so far is only used for grazing.

As for Area VIII (The Arabian Shield), hydrological studies only are being carried out. It appears that water potentiality as well as agricultural capacity in this area is poor. However, the use of such lands of poor water potentiality will remain confined to grazing (Fig. 6–2).

By reviewing Table No. (6–4), it would appear that the proportion of the total area under cultivation is exaggerated. This is due to the fact that this Table represents only the six areas of the Kingdom which have already been studied. When Areas VII and VIII are added the proportion falls to 0.13 per cent approximately.

Table No. (6–5) indicates that, in view of the available amount of water, it is possible to increase the cultivated area in Al-Joaf, Tabuk and the whole of *Qasim* (Buraidah and Unaizah) by utilizing 15,940 hectares of now uncultivated land. This is equivalent to 50 per cent of the present cultivated lands in the aforesaid areas. Greater Qasim includes beside the Qasim itself, Shakra, Az-Zulfi and As-Serr.

According to the availability of water in the Wadis Area, especially in Ranyah, Bishah, Najran and Wadi Dawasir (and As-Solail), it is possible to increase the cultivated area there, by more than 10,000 hectares.

In the Eastern Province, there is water potentiality to develop and cultivate a new area of 33,530 hectares which is equivalent to three times the present cultivated area. It is also possible to develop areas not previously cultivated as Haradh area. Jibrin Oasis and Wadi Al-Miyah in which 4,000, 5,000 and 9,650 hectares respectively may be developed. Moreover, it seems possible to increase the cultivated lands

Table No. (6–5) The possibility of agricultural expansion according to water availability (area in hectares)[31].

Area	Region	Cultivated in 1968	Maximum Cultivable	Could be Developed
I	1. Al-Joaf-Skaka	2,920	5,000	2,080
	2. Tabuk	400	3,460	3,060
	3. Greater Qasim	29,200	40,000	10,800
II & III	4. Wadi Ranyah	530	620	90
	5. Wadi Bishah	3,000	3,550	550
	6. Wadi Najran	2,565	3,365	800
	7. Wadi Dawasir	2,050	10,800	8,750
IV	8. Jibrin		5,000	5,000
	9. Haradh		4,000	4,000
	10. Al-Hassa	7,070	20,250	13,180
	11. Coastal Belt (Qatif)	4,300	6,000	1,700
	12. Wadi Al-Miyah & others	350	10,000	9,650
V	13. Al-Kharj & Dilam	7,605	11,195	3,590
	14. South-Al-Aflaj	2,405	2,570	165
VI	15. Dhoba	380	445	65
	16. (Taima & Al-Ula)	1,450	1,540	90
	17. Rabigh-Yanbu	1,480	1,860	380
	18. Qunfidah	23,000	36,000	13,000
	19. Southern Mountains	55,200	60,800	5,600
	Total			82,550

in Al-Hassa Oasis by three-fold, that is, by adding more than 13,000 hectares to the present cultivated area. Regarding Qatif, the cultivated lands may be increased by more than 1,700 hectares.

In Najd, water is available to add new agricultural lands of 3,755 hectares in the Al-Kharj, Dilam and Al-Aflaj areas.

In the Western and South-western Provinces, new areas of more than 19,000 hectares may be cultivated in Dhoba, Taima and Al-Ula, Yanbu, Qunfidah area and the southern mountains close to Jizan.

The total area which could be developed on the basis of apparent water availability comes to 82,550 hectares. Since the cultivated area was 3,964,674 hectares in 1385H (1965) (Table No. (6–2)), the agricultural area could be expanded by approximately 20 per cent (Fig. 6–3).

In addition to water, soil suitability must be considered. There is a wide range of soils in Saudi Arabia, but most of the soils exist under desert conditions. The major limiting factors for cultivation are: salinity, alkalinity, shallow depth, gravel, hard pans and high water-table. Drainage limitation is a common feature of almost all the arable lands; similarly, low fertility is a common characteristic. Topographic extremes, that is, very flat countryside or extreme dissected terrain, are not conducive to irrigated farming.

Soil characteristics are directly linked to the nature of the geological

ZONES FOR AGRICULTURAL EXPANSION

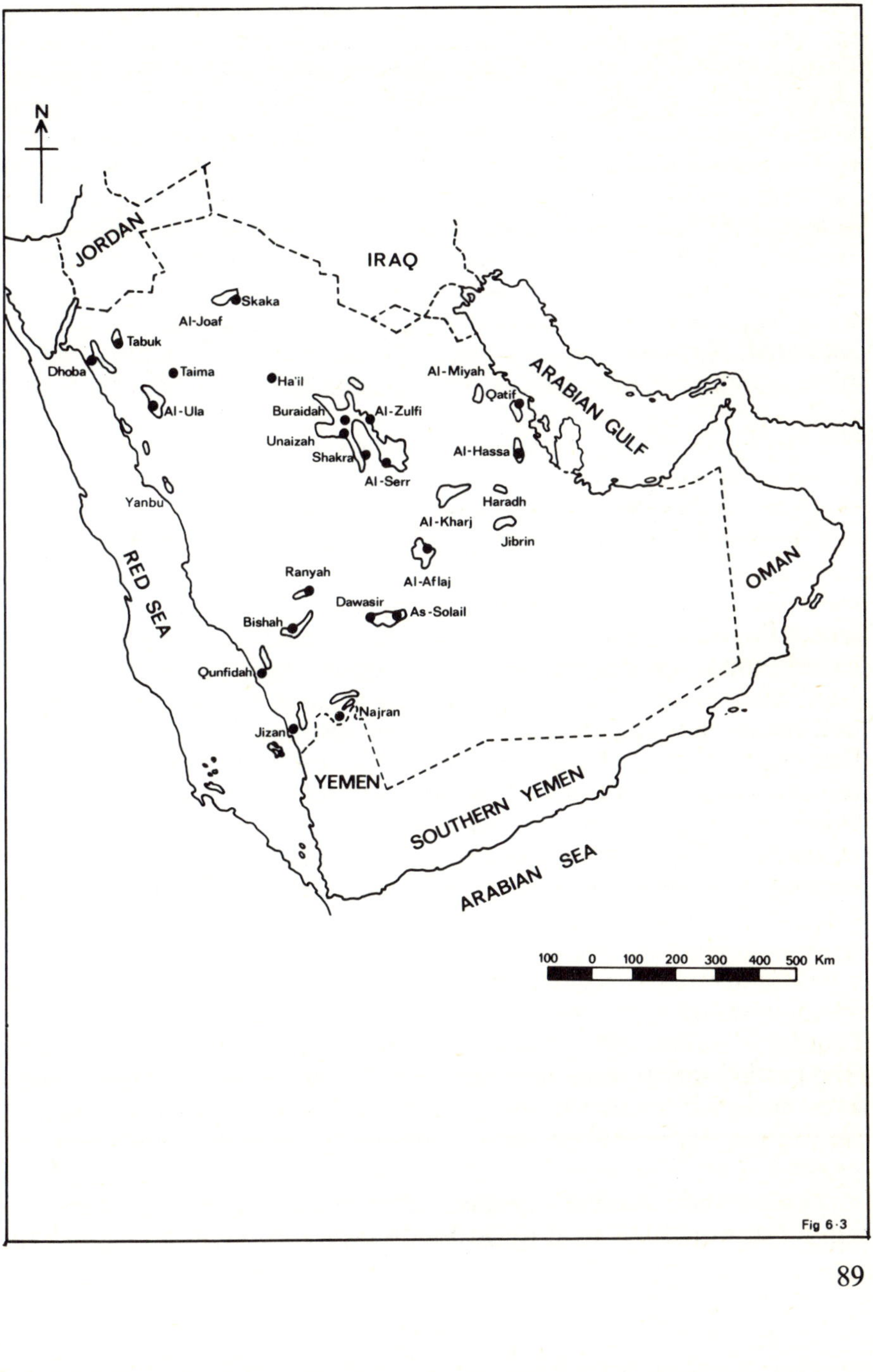

Fig 6·3

material from which they are formed. Soil formation in the Kingdom is greatly affected by high temperature, scarcity of water, and wind erosion. Arable lands are mainly found on alluvial soils formed by the deposition of weathered quartz, limestone, sandstone, siltstone or shale materials, thoroughly mixed by the action of wind or water and showing all the textural combinations from sand to clay. The best arable lands are met in wadi bottoms, old river beds, closed basins below rock escarpments and in basins within sand dune zones.

The central and northern regions of the country generally consist of lithosols (desert soils), usually covered with desert pavement. The coastal area land seems to have developed from loose, deep, saline marine sands with poor drainage. The intermediate depressions, and those on the east coast are characterized by areas of sabkhas (saline flats) which appear as very flat and have solonchak (sodic) soils with salt crust. Sabkhas are non-arable because of their shallow water-table, absence of drainage outlets, high salts content, or hard pan presence at 40 to 50 cm depth.

Even so, vast tracts of land with soils suitable for cultivation are found in Al-Aflaj, Al-Kharj, Bishah, Haradh, Qasim, Wadi Dawasir, Wadi Al-Miyah, Wadi Hali, Jizan and Qunfidah (see Fig. 13–3).

The general availability of water in areas of cultivable soil is of course insufficient; the nature of the water resources and the implications for their exploitation must be examined. Before a systematic search for water resources in the Kingdom began, it was believed that the Kingdom was one of the driest countries in the world. But studies conducted by the Ministry of Agriculture and Water have revealed that the quantity of underground water resource is now much more than was believed five years earlier. Comparison of known water resources with the recent water consumption rates shows that these water resources, nationally, are sufficient for tens or even hundreds of years. This does not mean that water extraction may be vastly increased in all areas but it does mean that underground water resources found in vast areas of the Kingdom are sufficient for many years' use without exhausting the capital supply.

Ground-water is related very closely to the geology. It was found that the eastern, northern and central parts of the Kingdom are formed of sedimentary rocks containing water-bearing formations varying in quality and quantity. Such sedimentary deposits cover two-thirds of the country. Most of these deposits are represented by sandstones or limestones which contain a considerable amount of ground-water (Fig. 6–4).

Most of these aquifers contain water more than 29,000 years old. Some formations are near the ground surface and some are very deep,

GENERAL GEOLOGICAL MAP OF SAUDI ARABIA

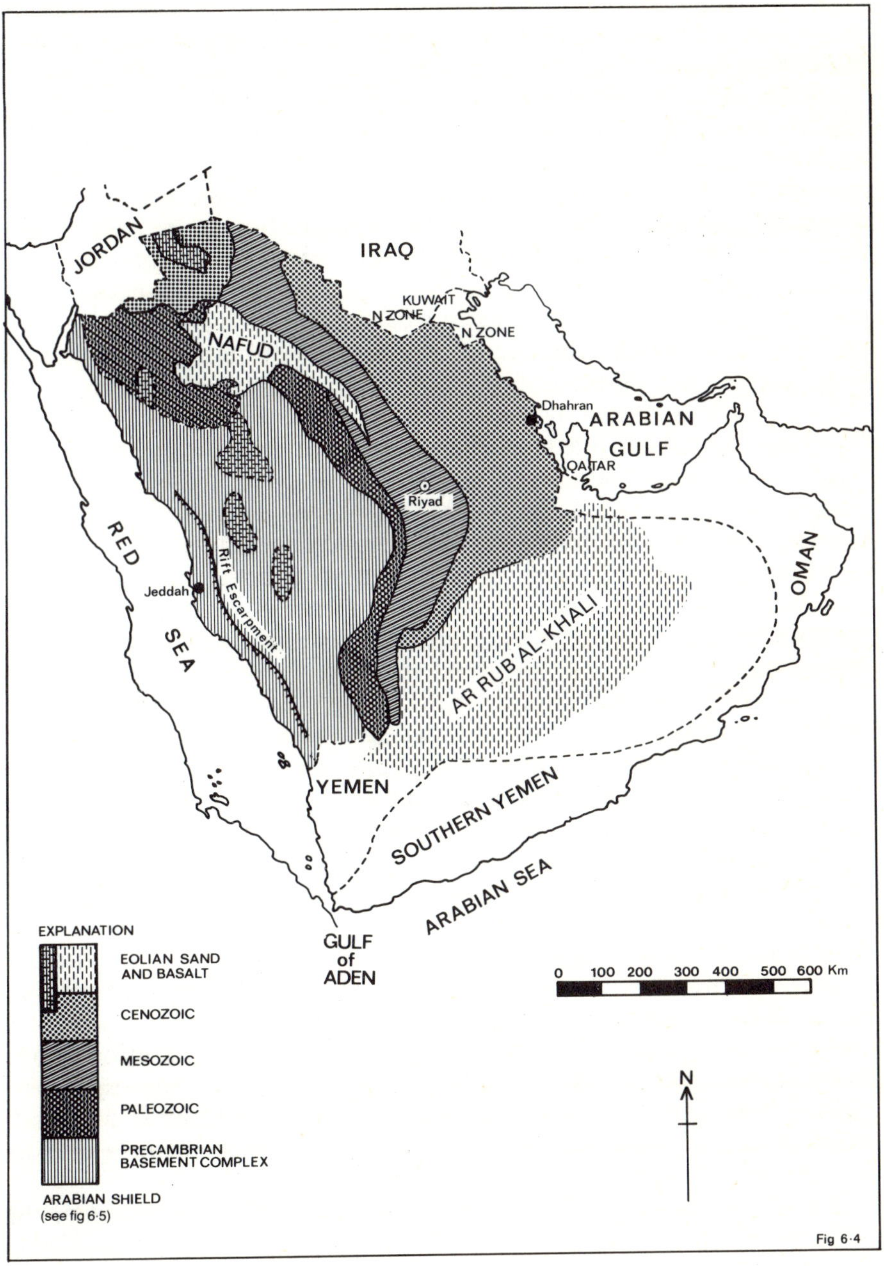

so, when thinking of extracting water, drilling and pumping costs should be taken into consideration. Some of these formations are not rechargeable, so water resources in some areas are diminishing as in the case of oil resources. Up till now and according to studies made by consultants, twenty-eight important sedimentary aquifers have been discovered.

As far as surface water is concerned, Saudi Arabia is the largest country without rivers. That rainfall which does occur is sporadic and variable, so there are periods of precipitation associated with rapid run-off, high evaporation and percolation into surface sediments and lower formations. As noted on p. 59, precipitation is greatest on the western mountains and any current recharging of aquifers depends on the percolation of water into the eastward dipping sedimentary beds. Where these beds are poorly represented, such as in the western part of the Kingdom which is known as the Arabian Shield, surface water alone is available and then only in small amounts (Fig. 6–5).

The Arabian Shield is composed of igneous rocks of the pre-Cambrian basement. Parts of these rocks are covered by an alluvial mantle varying in thickness from place to place but the water storage in these rocks is in most cases very meagre. The wadifills (aeolian surface deposits) are not thick and, therefore, do not allow the storage of quantities of water sufficiently reliable for any economical agricultural project in most wadi areas. Most of the existing wells have failed to produce prolific water and water quality deteriorates after periods of drought.

Considering the above-mentioned facts, all the Ministry experts and water technicians have concluded that the water resources in this area, covering some one-third of the Kingdom, are unreliable for agricultural utilization while at the same time existing general demands and growing urban demands place considerable strains on the regional water resources (Fig. 6–5).

However, there are cultivated areas in the Arabian Shield with slowly increasing agricultural demands for water. The balance now between demand and supply is in a state of equilibrium and any further increase of water withdrawal from these areas will adversely affect the existing agricultural areas, as in the case of Bishah.

Also in the Shield, there are areas where drilling operations have to be prohibited to ensure the safety of the supply of domestic water. This is applicable to the north-east of Madinah, Khamis Moshait, Wadi Abha, Sir Al-Assan and Wadi Turabah which is considered as a future reserve water resource for Taif in the future.

The Ministry of Agriculture and Water has been convinced of the economic insignificance of cultivating the lands of the Arabian Shield

ARABIAN SHIELD AREA

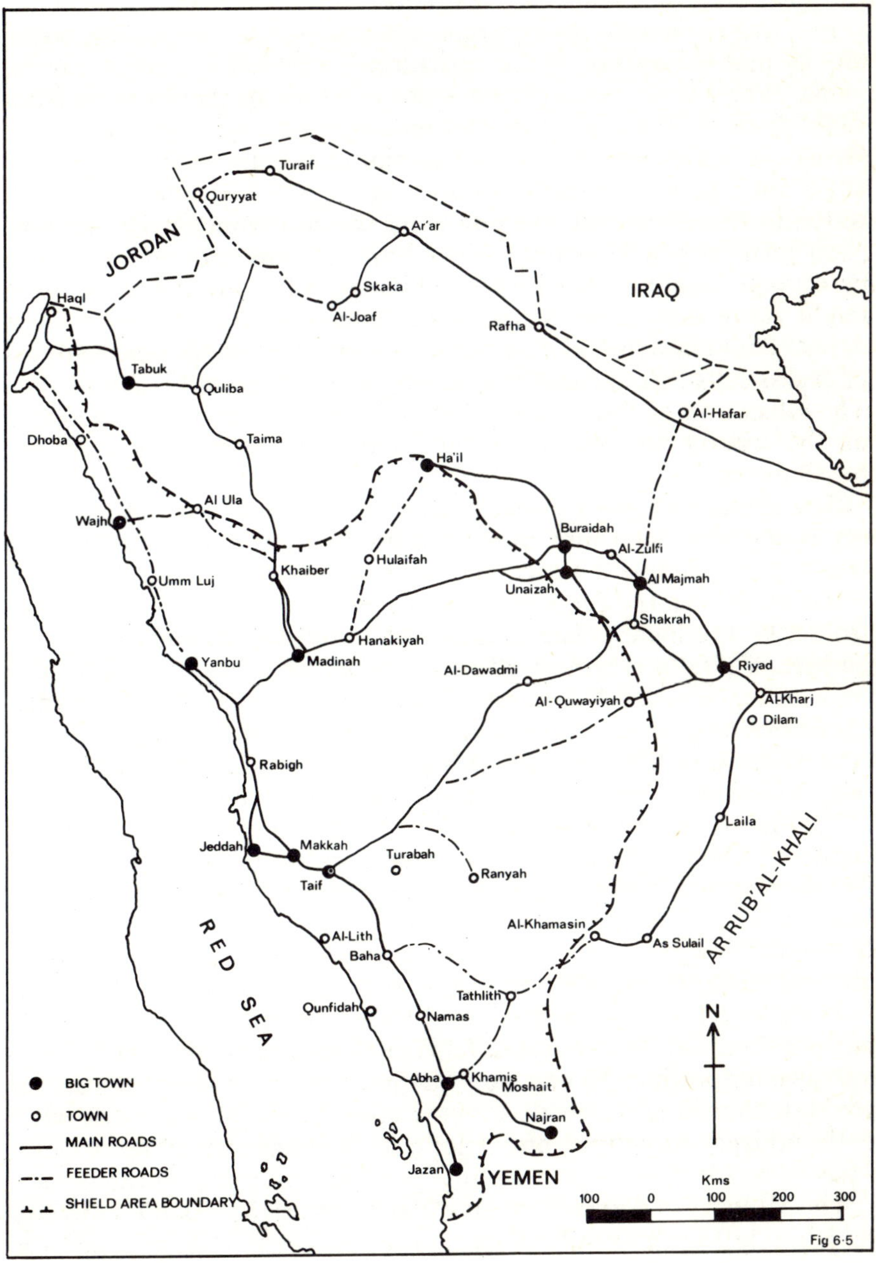

Fig 6·5

under these conditions and considers that these lands should be left as pasture areas. Moreover, if there is any pressure for the distribution of land, it should be allowed only if circumstances make it unavoidable and then only on a most limited scope.

For the remaining areas, some general points concerning water quality and the nature of the agricultural demand for water can be made. Water quality: irrigation water in Saudi Arabia ranging from 1,000 to more than 4,000 parts per million (ppm) salt content is used. Generally 3,150 ppm is near the maximum for the safe watering of any plant and in such instances drainage must be excellent and each watering should permit leaching from the root zone.[30] The present problem in irrigated farming is the salinity of underground water. The percentage of salts in the water might be small, but continuous farming might result after some years in an increase of harmful salts. This danger could be avoided, to a limited extent, by the periodic removal of excess salts through increase of irrigation, if the soil is permeable. The allocation of Public Land for farming must be based therefore on the criteria not only of water quality but also of the drainage possibilities.

The demands made by agriculture on water resources reflect crop needs and also determine minimum production and maximum cost levels. For example a Research Department letter dated 21/10/89H (1969) states that the demand for water by alfalfa during a year ranges from 100–112 inches. The quantity of water needed to irrigate one hectare of alfalfa is almost 60 g/m (gallons per minute). This is also in accordance with FAO desert climate data established in California. (*Sprinkler Irrigation*, UN Publication, Rome, 1969.) Assuming 30 per cent irrigation efficiency in the Kingdom, wells which fail to produce 60g/m have to be considered unproductive and uneconomic for use.

The depth of ground-water in the Kingdom varies from several metres to 1,000. According to the criteria set by the Water Resources Development Department, if the static water level is 100 metres, or less, and the water production is 60 g/m, such water is considered economic for agricultural use, although a 500 metres depth is still permissible for agriculture if the well is sufficiently free-flowing.

These criteria now adopted by MAW are not only quantitative but also financial. Water cost differs from one area to another according to water production and water depth. If costs of water extraction are high, then land is only distributed after the position is made clear to the utilizers, sometimes only after having obtained their agreement, so as to be on the safe side against complaints arising in the future.

The Ministry of Agriculture and Water, under the PLDO is directly responsible for the physical feasibility survey of Public Lands for

ROAD NETWORK & POPULATION CENTRES 1971

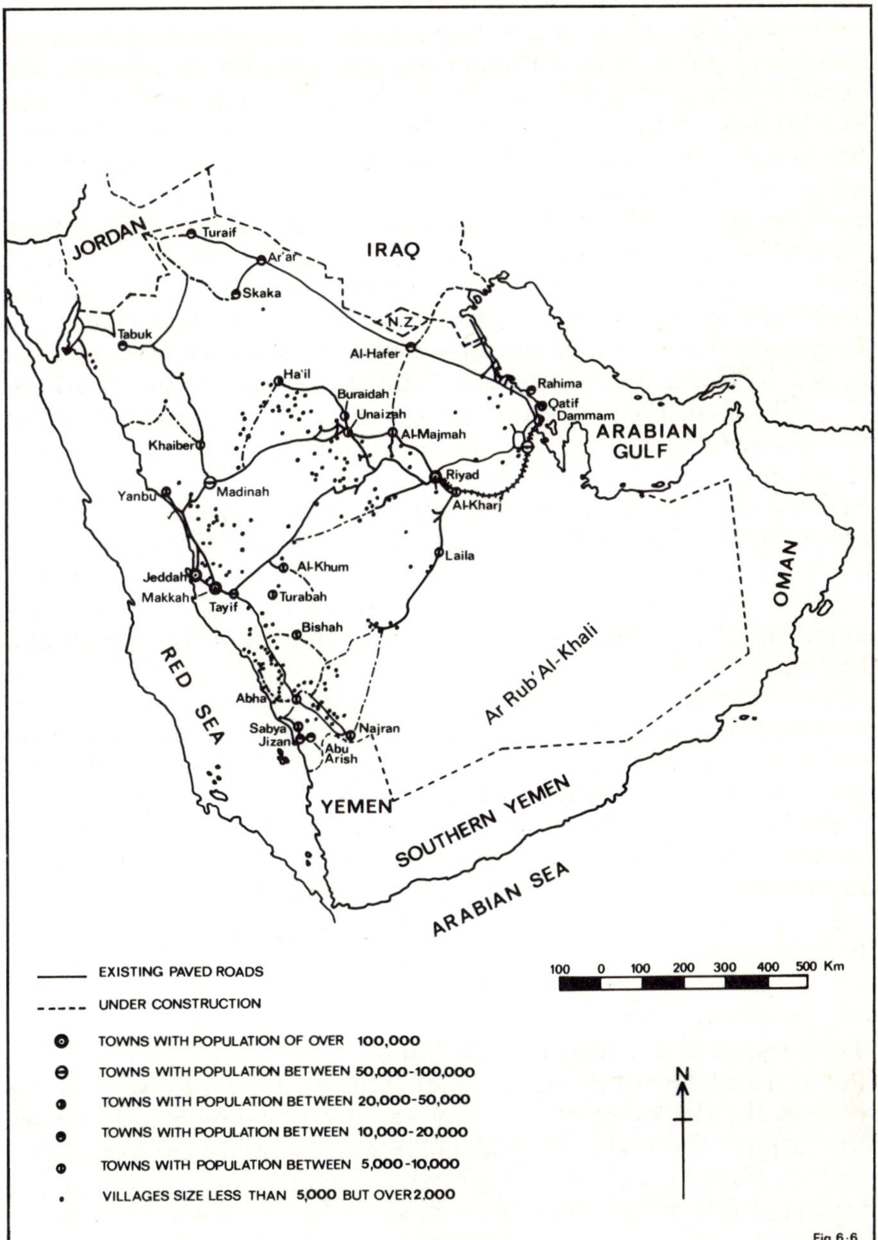

Fig 6·6

distribution but other infrastructural considerations, in particular those concerned with the effects of location are obviously of great importance. Communications must be available if effective agricultural development of new lands is to be carried out.

The Ministry of Communication provides the vitally important services linking the agricultural areas with consuming centres. The Ministry of Agriculture and Water therefore collaborates closely with this Ministry in the design of an integrated transport system to serve the marketing needs of the major areas of agricultural production adequately.

As far as the arterial communication system is concerned there are only 440 kilometres of railway, connecting Riyad with the Eastern Province. There are also eighteen airfields located in the principal towns and almost 11,000 kilometres of asphalted roads (Fig. 6–6). Location in respect of these arterial networks is clearly important but so are the feeder links connecting farms to arterial communications.

Until 1384H (1964), it was the work of the Ministry of Agriculture and Water to open country roads to the important agricultural areas, for example, Al-Hassa and Asir mountain areas; but since then the Ministry of Communication has undertaken responsibility for feeder roads. Information analyses of the state of agriculture in Saudi Arabia are utilized by the Ministry of Communication in this work. For this purpose, the country is divided into several agricultural provinces almost similar to the division used by the Ministry of Agriculture and Water.

Two main factors are taken into consideration in the regions surveyed, (a) feeder roads to existing agricultural areas and (b) feeder roads to potential agricultural areas. (See Fig. 3–4 and Fig. 8–4 for proposed feeder roads and primary roads.)

The communications network not only directly affects the value of land but through its transport has markedly changed the rural outlook and capability concerning land use. Nowadays, desert cars and trucks owned by Bedouins replace the traditional caravan transportation used in the past.

The location of distributed Public Land

Public Land Distribution in Saudi Arabia, more precisely, is the organized distribution of that land regarded as cultivable and owned by the State. PLD is based on actual resource appraisal and economic facts and aims at developing agricultural production; in having this central aim it differs from previous distribution practice. Once the soil and water facts are established, the total area of distributable

LOCATION OF PUBLIC LANDS SUBJECT FOR DISTRIBUTION

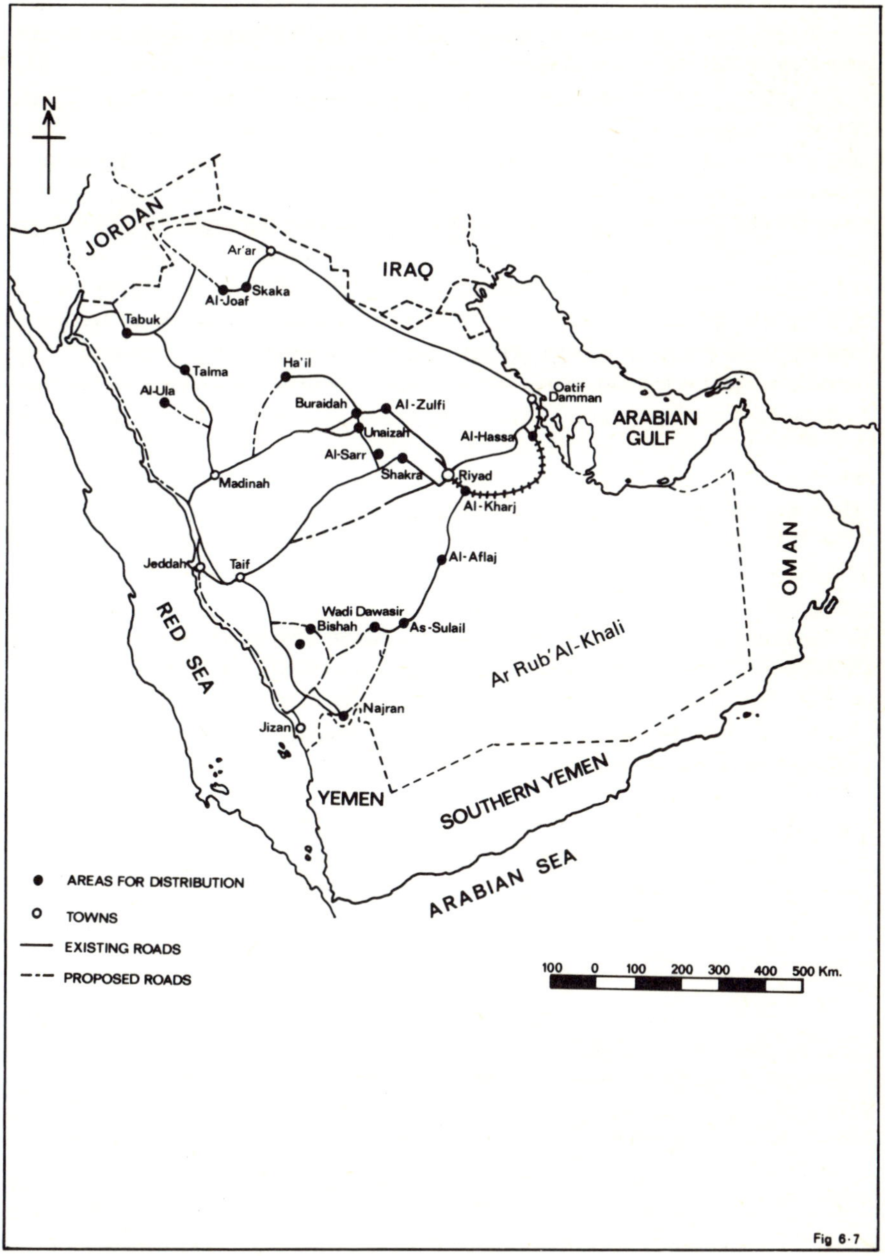

Fig 6·7

land is demarcated for each region and the plots of land defined and classified.

In each area prepared for distribution, the whole Public Land distribution procedure exemplified in Chapter Five (pp. 74–75) is then followed. Land is now being distributed in eighteen separate areas (see Fig. 6–7).

The identification of land suitable for distribution follows the elimination of unsuitable land. When the PLDO was put into action, huge areas in the country were surveyed and a great deal of land was announced as available for distribution. Following the build-up of work by the PLMD, areas which have no water potential or in which water had to be reserved for non-agricultural purposes were identified.

Table No. (6–6) illustrates how survey work during the early stages affected the position. In twelve different areas, in response to local demand, the PLMD mounted land and water potential surveys. The areas are shown in column 2. At the same time it was announced that in these areas there would be land made available for distribution. Following detailed survey work it was found that in none of these areas was there sufficient water either to supply both agricultural and other needs or to maintain significant expansion of cultivation.

In this first phase, the PLMD was forced by reasons of urgency to survey land potential before accurate hydrological information was available. Most of the areas named in Table No. (6–6) were located in Arabian Shield territory, and the Water Resources Development Department recommended, following a hydrological survey, that no increased water extraction should take place in those areas in order to protect the existing farmers therein. Consequently the lands could not be made available for distribution (except Bishah, Riyad, Hariq

Table No. (6–6)* Areas in donums prepared for distribution before water was divined.

S. No.	*Name of the Area*	*Areas already Surveyed (Donums)*	*Areas Declared for Distribution*
1.	Bishah	216,580	72,000
2.	Riyad	8,050	824
3.	Madinah & suburbs	98,363	
4.	Baha	1,003	
5.	Afif	1,726	
6.	Al-Quwayiyah	120,000	
7.	Dawadmi	29,459	
8.	Ranyah	37,486	
9.	Turabah	51,033	
10.	Hariq	95,030	50,000
11.	Al-Hawtab	113,949	50,832
12.	Abha, Asir	15,270	

* Unpublished departmental data.

and Al-Hawtah). The Department thought at first that water was available in these latter areas, but later informed the Public Land Management Department that this was not so.

Table No. (6–7) Areas (in hectares) prepared for distribution according to PLDO and having water potential.*

Area	*Land Announced for Distribution*	*Land to be Announced for Distribution*	*Area Delivered to Utilizers*	*No. of Utilizers*	*Proposed Distribution Programme over 3 Years*
Al-Joaf	1,700.0	1,317.1	1,921.9	260	1,000.0
Tabuk	44,904.7	—	16,399.4	2,972	13,365.7
Taima	336.0	—	—	—	336.0
Al-Ula	1,434.0	—	1,002.0	41	3,143.9
Qasim-Buraidah	84,590.0	7,991.7	2,199.5	358	8,459.0
Qasim-Unaizah	9,575.4	—	165.9	28	3,191.8
Ha'il	62,895.7	52,526.4	1,536.0	340	6,289.5
Bishah	7,270.0	426.9	—	—	727.0
Najran	2,000.0	—	194.2	48	2,000.0
Wadi Dawasir	3,600.0	4,550.0	360.0	73	1,200.0
As-Sulail	13,205.0	191.8	109.0	14	4,401.6
Al-Hassa	37,840.0	4,416.0	1,076.7	187	974.7
Qatif	12,485.0	50.1	918.7	25	4,161.6
Al-Kharj	8,120.0	582.1	1,956.8	377	1,956.7
Shakra	800.0	—	—	—	700.0
Al-Aflaj	1,200.0	—	300.0	27	1,200.0
Az-Zulfi	400.0	—	—	—	400.0
As-Serr	9,430.7	—	—	—	3,143.5
Total	301,786.5	72,052.1	28,140.1	4,750	56,651.0

* Unpublished departmental memorandum at 14/11/1392H (1972).

As the PLMD developed and as both land potential and water resource surveys cumulatively produced more information, the whole picture slowly became clearer. By 1392H (1972), as shown in Table No. (6–7), it was possible, first, to announce within the context of the Development Plan the general availability of land for distribution; secondly, the PLMD was able to formulate a three-year programme identifying specific lands within eighteen areas for distribution. The period of three years brought the programme into phase with the last three years of the Five-Year Plan.

On the basis of water availability only, the total area of Public Land regarded as suitable for development totalled 82,550 hectares (Table No. (6–5)). From this total, one could then exclude from basic PLMD responsibility those lands utilized in specific investment projects, for example, King Faisal Settlement Project (Haradh), Al-Hassa irrigation and drainage project and Jibrin and Wadi Al-Miyah. These four areas covered 31,730 hectares. There are also other areas noted in Table

No. (6–5) which for various reasons are not yet prepared for distribution, those mostly located near the Red Sea, such as Jizan and Qunfidah. The remaining areas to be distributed and developed under the PLMD totalled 48,010 hectares. This represents 12 per cent of the area under cultivation in the Kingdom (see Table No. (6–2)) and 32 per cent of the irrigated area (see Table No. (6–3)). Thus the potential expansion is on any basis a very large-scale effort.

If Table No. (6–5), representing the combined consultants' first reports on water resource availability and the area distinguished above as coming under the PLMD, is compared with the PLMD programme as shown in Table No. (6–7), then a clear discrepancy arises. Basically this is because the evaluation of water resources at a preliminary survey level cannot be of a high order of accuracy and there is a difference in scale between hydro-geological assessments of major water resources and the agricultural assessment of water resources sufficient for limited development. This whole question of water resource potential is continuously under review and more detailed surveys are being carried out. The decisions of the PLMD have to be based on the balanced and varied information in the possession of MAW at any one time.

To summarize: we can note that the agricultural area of Saudi Arabia is very small compared with the size of the country. Agriculture is dominant, traditional in character and organized in small-size holdings. According to recent soil, water and agricultural surveys, there is no shortage of land for the present level of demand but water remains the limiting factor for agricultural expansion. Even so, it is possible to increase the existing agricultural area by up to 20 per cent. The Government is in favour of mobilizing the agricultural resources and the rural population and it is willing to participate in the agricultural sectors, even though oil is the main backbone of the economy. What then becomes significant is the actual implementation of land distribution and the effective utilization of these new productive resources.

Chapter Seven

The Positive Social and Economic Results of Land Distribution

Important changes have already occurred in the life of the Bedouins in Saudi Arabia. A process of sedentarization with accompanying differentiation in status has occurred over the centuries, particularly throughout much of the Central Province wherever tribal villages (*Hejar*) exist. (See Chapter Three.)

Because the settlers frequently could not support themselves alone by their primitive and half-hearted attempts at agriculture, some of these new settlements rapidly became disused; others contain a whole range of building types from brick dwellings to temporary shelters. Success or failure depended on many factors and a study of these has yet to be made. The settlements that survived and became small oases are inhabited nowadays on a large scale. Government schools have been established in all of them along with other public facilities (see Table No. 3–3) and they are becoming important summer gathering places for those members of the various sub-tribes who have gone away to work and who come back for the summer periods.[21]

Many groups of nomads throughout the country attempted to establish such *Hejar* settlements mostly by asking the Government's permission for their establishment. The economic interdependence growing between the remaining nomads and these settled villagers could then easily be seen as a natural continuation of the tribal relationships. It can, in fact, be shown that this process is taking place at present in many of the recently developing small oases in the desert outside the areas of the major urban complexes. Other tribal groups, remaining nomads, have switched to large-scale sheep herding. Sheep herding is a much more sedentary activity than camel herding. Sheep herders move much less often and less regularly, sometimes not moving their tents for a year or more.[21] The use of trucks, the development of service towns and governmental support has resulted in a major change in pastoral activities for the majority of Saudi Arabian Bedouins.

The final form that any settlement takes is of course a function of socio-economic relationships on the one hand and location on the other. What we see in Saudi Arabia is accelerating change both in relationships and in locational functions and forces. One sequence in this change is a progression from nomad, semi-nomad and semi-settled, to fully urbanized life. In this sedentarization and settlement of the nomadic and semi-nomadic population, two types of processes may be distinguished: the first is spontaneous sedentarization as an unguided process; the second is induced sedentarization as an intended, purposeful measure.

Since about 1380H (1960), one special form of spontaneous Bedouin sedentarization has begun to take place in and around the major towns of Saudi Arabia as well as near some of the major sites of the oil industry. Within the Eastern Province of Saudi Arabia, there have appeared shanty town complexes which either belong to or are inhabited by tribal individuals who are only partially integrated into town life.

Most of the adult males resident in these settlements either work or have worked for the Government in the army and national guard, for oil companies, as truck drivers or general labourers. In these shanty-towns or urban fringe areas some pastoral element often survives and the women and younger sons move out to graze their sheep and goats in the desert during the grazing period. Oil wealth has attracted the migrations of many tribes to Al-Hassa such as the Bani Khalid, Bani Hajeer, Ojman and even the Motir tribe from the central region. All this has been one aspect of non-rural sedentarization.

In rural areas, on the debit side, the harmful effects of the oil industry's impact on tribal life, on cultivation and grazing are considerable. The land now suffers greatly from a shortage of workers and this has made it impossible to cultivate existing utilized areas adequately and therefore a shrinkage of the extent of agriculture has occurred. This is not only true of cultivation but also of livestock and pastoralism. Oil and its associated wealth have introduced modern motorized vehicles. Lorries and trucks have replaced camels and people prefer modern transport even in the desert.

As far as the agricultural cultivators are concerned, Public Land Distribution is relatively simple, concerned with matching a supply of land with demand from already experienced cultivators. With the Bedouins, however, the position is more complicated. The virtual disappearance of the animal caravan trade and the devaluation of the camel together with the strengthening of the vaguely-formed desire of many Bedouins to obtain some of the attractions of settled life: all this produces the problem of how to bring the Bedouin into effective participation in the national society. The settling of nomads on public

Table No. (7–1) Professions of utilization applicants in different distribution areas, up to the end of 1392H (1972)

Professions	Tabuk	Al-Kharj	Qasim Unaiah	Qasim Buraidah	Ha'il	Al-Aflag	Wadi Dawasir	As-Solail	Najran	Al-Ula	Al-Hassa	Qatif	Al-Joaf	*Total*
Employee	1350	62	7	102	222	12	36	1	19	10	52	9	134	2016
Unspecified labourer	658	170	17	176	110	4	17	10	0	2	14	3	20	1201
Housekeeper	599	—	—	—	—	—	—	—	—	—	—	—	—	599
Merchant	307	3	—	—	—	—	—	—	8	—	31	3	53	405
Driver	54	44	—	6	—	—	3	—	5	—	1	—	5	118
Guard	60	39	—	—	1	—	—	—	5	2	3	—	2	112
Farmer	4	24	3	53	4	8	11	—	2	2	69	6	38	224
Artisan	7	4	1	21	—	—	—	3	1	—	5	—	—	42
Contractor	3	—	—	—	—	1	—	—	—	—	2	1	—	7
Unemployed	17	—	—	—	3	—	—	—	1	—	9	1	10	41
Student	9	—	—	—	—	—	5	—	—	—	—	1	1	16
Labourer	—	31	—	—	—	1	—	—	1	—	—	—	36	69
Sheikh	4	—	—	—	—	1	1	—	—	—	—	1	—	7
Amir	—	—	—	—	—	—	—	—	—	—	3	—	1	4
Total	3072	377	28	358	340	27	73	14	42	16	189	25	300	4861

land therefore involves more fundamental changes. Nomads have always been a part of our society and now it is necessary to provide means for them to adjust and modernize themselves without losing the basic social and spiritual well-being which is so prominent a feature of their lives.

We must now look more closely at the people to whom Public Land is allocated, their own and the national background, the purposes for which the land is to be used and how PLD operates in this general situation.

Table No. (7–1) lists the occupations of applicants for Public Land to the end of 1392H (1972). The Bedouins are in the main represented as unspecified labourers, guards, drivers and agricultural labourers. The applicants as a whole include many who have had no previous experience in agriculture, people of different professions, simple peasants as well as employees and others. Therefore, it is important to formulate methods and practices, using simple modern agricultural techniques, to match the applicant's capabilities. Of course, this is not as easy as it seems, especially as many potential land utilizers have no idea of the simplest scientific methods used in land conservation or utilization or needed for the achievement of maximum productivity.

According to consultant surveys, 66 per cent of the population of Saudi Arabia are working in agriculture (including those working in forests, fisheries, animal wealth and crop production), but under this heading also come the Bedouin groups. If we wish to analyse the pool of human experience from which the applicants are drawn, the most recent available information concerning the population is only for six survey areas out of the total of eight.

If we now assume that the urban population will not provide a significant number of applicants for Public Land in areas and that the rural settled cultivators will only apply for extra land for agricultural expansion we then see that the Bedouin population constitutes the single largest pool from which applicants can be drawn.

Consultants have indicated that severe economic and sociological problems are associated with nomads adjusting themselves to the rapid changes taking place in the Kingdom. They tend to lose their proud status when moving to urban centres and become more dependent on a money economy. Gradual or partial rural settlement of nomads could, by means of the Land Distribution Programme, make the change in the Bedouin's way of living occur gradually.

While this would mean a change from livestock keeping to "dirt-farming" with many consequences, the importance of livestock has already declined considerably and is continuing to do so.

Table No. (7–2) A summary of human population number estimates* (1385–1390H = 1965–1970 survey) in six areas.

Areas	*Total Numbers*	*Urban*	%	*Rural Settled*	%	*Bedouin Including Semi-Nomads*	%
I.	400,000	176,000	44.0	72,000	18.0	152,000	38.0
II. & III.	772,000	131,000	17.0	457,000	60.0	184,000	23.0
IV.	590,000	320,000	54.3	150,000	25.4	120,000	20.3
V.	390,000	278,860	71.5	61,140	15.7	50,000	12.8
VI.	1,216,000	243,200	20.0	712,800	58.6	260,000	21.4
Totals	3,368,000	1,149,060	34.5	1,452,940	29.6	766,000	19.25

* Estimates at time of Survey, 1965–1970

Table No. (7–2) shows the position in 1390H (1970); in Chapter Four we noted that the total number of animal units estimated in 1370H (1950) was 7.2 million. This shows a very large decrease which has particularly weakened the Bedouin communities who dominate livestock keeping.

Table No. (7–3) A summary of current livestock population (animal units) in six areas.[37]

Area	*Total Animal Units*	*Total No. Controlled by Bedouin*	*% Controlled by Bedouin*
I.	421,964	270,064	64
II. & III.	354,000	215,000	61
IV.	400,000	380,000	95
V.	69,680	32,760	47
VI.	663,040	237,000	36
Total	1,908,684	1,134,824	50.5

As for other economic factors, there are indirect elements which help to increase the attractiveness of the areas suitable for cultivation. Firstly, the low return to small-sized agricultural holdings can be adjusted by PLD and the holding sizes enlarged by the fringing of new land into cultivation. Secondly, asphalting and paving roads, both long-distance and feeder, to ensure good communication for marketing, not only in the local area of the villages but also to consumers in towns, form a great inducement to commercial farming. Thirdly, no restrictions exist for the exportation of surplus agricultural products and this is important at a time when the Arabian Gulf countries have become large importers of agricultural products.

Nonetheless, there are other factors which severely limit the area of utilizable land such as the vast areas of sandy soil, the shallow depth of soils, wind erosion and rapid rain run-off. Poor fertility soils are common as organic matter is reduced by the prevailing high temperatures and insulation. Excessive salts in soils result from a shortage of rain and absence of leaching. Limited water resources and topographic and structural factors adversely affect drainage.

PLD therefore cannot merely be a general policy but has to deal with specific land, water, social and economic factors. In examining PLD from an economic point of view several factors have to be taken into consideration in fixing the final area to be allotted. First, the total available areas to be distributed and the number of applicants form the primary factor. Second, there is the capacity of land: for example, water availability, fertility. Third, the capability of the applicant for land, as regards capital and work, has to be considered. An FAO commission noted that an economic holding size is 4 to 7 hectares for Middle Eastern countries. From Saudi Arabian experience, the areas stipulated in the PLDO were from 5 to 10 hectares.

As a rule, encouragement was given for Public Land Distribution of the maximum area permissible rather than the minimum, other things being equal. The Central Committee agreed to avoid the restrictions which would follow a keeping to the minimum[44] and the plans of distribution submitted to local committees allow the handing over of two neighbouring plots in case the area of both does not exceed the maximum limit explained in the Ordinance.

For land distribution, the executive procedure of the Ordinance advises utilizers in the same location to collaborate in the achievement of common tasks, such as the drilling of a well. Land utilizers are encouraged to have joint ownership of wells and to share the initial and maintenance costs in accordance with their share of irrigation water-use according to their farm size. Also, in the executive procedure, in the case of several persons developing their allotted land jointly, it is accepted that these lands as a whole and neighbouring plots of land distributed to the members of one family be considered as one unit. Thus the utilization of 25 per cent of the total area during the period of appropriation may be considered quite enough for establishing individual ownership just as if each person had fulfilled his part of the requirement after the period of appropriation had passed.[44]

Individuals collaborating in agricultural work can in some circumstances be considered as "one body"; this principle can be applied to those who show real participation in agricultural work. Brothers or sons of the owner who jointly participate are consequently considered as "one body". Whereas the Public Land Ordinance and the relevant operational procedures normally consider more than one individual as a "company" which would receive different treatment from an individual, in this case and in order to facilitate distribution of land, joint family participants are considered as one person and consequently given one piece of land for agriculture and animal investment. They are treated in all other ways as one person. This system is particularly important in Al-Hassa.

Public Land is distributed free of cost by the State, and the State therefore makes no financial demands on the utilizer. On the contrary, it provides him with every possible technical assistance which he may need to utilize the land distributed to him successfully. Later on in this chapter, pp. 116–119, we consider financial assistance. These are some of the principal factors encouraging cultivation expansion and land utilization which have begun to affect the Saudi Arabian scene.

Modern agriculture requires large areas of land to enable the fullest use of machinery which cannot be employed on traditional smaller holdings. This in turn requires new planning in irrigation and agricultural methods from the beginning. For example, plots used for wheat growing should have a minimum size of 18 m length and 6 m breadth.

The use of machinery for many purposes – for example, tractors, levelling machines, digging machines, fertilizer machines and spraying and dusting machines for pest control – is essential for agricultural development and the raising of production and productivity but its application is difficult except in new areas or those reorganized by agricultural planning. Moreover, the use of machines is very valuable and becomes more critical as wages are rapidly increasing and it becomes more difficult to obtain necessary labour inputs.

Variation of agricultural practice and the change of traditional methods require a new approach and this becomes easier to apply on new lands. Palm trees, for example, traditionally are planted in high densities common on all those farms where inter-cropping is not normal. New-style production requires the inter-planting of various fruit trees as well as various kinds of vegetables, and therefore it is deemed necessary for new land to be added on which new husbandry practices can be introduced.

Modern animal husbandry competes for land to a great extent with agricultural production. Poultry farms are now spreading all over the country as well as in areas given over to livestock and cattle farming. All these farms impose demands which can most easily be met by the utilization of new lands.

The identification of the economic effects of land distribution

Land distribution and agriculture exist in the context of particular national characteristics and assumptions. Briefly the situation is as follows.

The leaders of the country are completely committed to the process of development along with the maintenance of political stability. There is a growing readiness of public opinion to accept change and to desire participation in the process of Nation building. A continual effort to build up the national infrastructure and to develop all sectors is now being made. The high national income remains dependent on oil but diversification is desired. The commitment to a free economy runs throughout all planning.

The factors which serve to obstruct these positive movements are mainly shortages in trained manpower and the difficulty of creating an efficient administrative machinery when this is passing through a period of reform and reorganization.

Saudi Arabia displays features of both developed and developing economies. Oil and its economic consequences identify the country as a developed country due to its high income, high saving rates and favourable balance of payments.

Table No. (7–4) Balance of payments estimated by million US Dollars.*

Year	*Total Receipts "A"*	*Total Payments "B"*	*A – B*
1389 (1969)	2072	2182	−110
1390 (1970)	2438	2376	+62
1391 (1971)	3918	3023	+895
1392 (1972)	5668	4262	+1406

* Saudi Arabian Monetary Agency, Annual Report 1390–91H (1970–71) and 1391–92H (1971–72).

But on the other hand – and this affects the majority of the population – the Kingdom has a dominant traditional agricultural sector, a very small industrial sector, a severe shortage of indigenous skilled labour and entrepreneurs, and an unbalanced trade structure, all of which identify Saudi Arabia as a developing country.

Table No. (7–5) The trade situation (excluding oil) in Saudi Arabia by million SR.[4]

Year	*Exports*	*Imports*
1382/83 (1962/63)	397.2	1,266.0
1383/84 (1963/64)	885.7	1,557.7
1384/85 (1964/65)	777.9	1,695.7
1386/87 (1966/67)	576.4	2,288.2

The Gross Domestic Product of Saudi Arabia increased from 8.6 billion SR in 1382/83H (1962/63) to 15.2 billion SR in 1388/89H (1968/69) (Fig. 7–1). There is a large outflow of investment earnings and wages due to the heavy investment of foreign oil companies and the number of other foreign companies and non-resident workers in Saudi Arabia; this outflow in 1388/89H stood at 3.5 billion SR, over one-fifth of the Gross Domestic Product (GDP). After subtracting these net foreign payments, the remainder forms the Gross National Product (GNP).

Sectoral balance

The major source of revenue in Saudi Arabia is oil, a non-reproducible resource which must be mobilized as a means to develop other sectors. The industrial and service sectors, including the provision of public utilities and social welfare are receiving most attention from the Government. As yet, agricultural growth is seen mainly as a response to demands created by growth in other sectors. However, ultimately, agriculture could not only reduce the overdependence of the entire economy on oil, but the development of rural areas would increase the purchasing power of farmers to buy non-agricultural products. The integration of a prosperous agriculture into the whole economy will be of vital importance.

Over the period from 1382/83H (1962/63) to 1388/89H (1968/69) the private sector oil companies contributed directly about 54 per cent of GDP, the non-oil private sector about 30 per cent and the public sector 16 per cent. All three sectors have grown but have remained nearly constant in relative proportion (see Fig. 7–1). The average growth rates of sub-sectors, however, have varied. Between 1385/86H (1965/66) and 1388/89H (1968/69), it was only 1.7 per cent for agriculture, the lowest growth compared to others (Fig. 7–2). The services other than education show the next lowest growth rates, while construction, finance, transportation and utilities are all higher.

In the economic plan period, 1389/90–1394/95H (1969/70–1974/75), it was expected to achieve 4.6 per cent growth in agriculture.

The contribution of agriculture and objectives can be summarized thus: Increased agricultural production leads to increased employment in other sectors such as transportation and marketing. Local production of crops and animal wealth minimize importation. The prices of local products are less than those imported and self-sufficiency saves foreign currency.

How then can agriculture be developed? First, is the utilization of the available resources of land and water now not being developed? Second, can the productivity of the existing farmed area be raised by

Table No. (7–6) The percentage distribution of persons employed in 1386H (1966) and total demand in 1390H (1970) and 1395H (1975) by sectors.[20]

Sector	*1386H*	*1390H*	*1395H*
Private	89.03	88.13	87.24
Nomads	15.02	12.30	9.02
Settled agriculture	31.16	28.07	23.34
Petroleum and Mining	2.50	2.42	2.43
Manufacturing	4.07	4.39	4.72
Construction	10.33	11.99	13.74
Electricity, Gas	0.83	1.03	1.31
Commerce	9.51	11.03	13.24
Transportation	4.37	5.26	6.58
Services	10.83	11.64	12.86
Other	0.41		
Public	10.93	11.69	12.36
Petromin	0.04	0.18	0.40

modern techniques? Third, can the production be adjusted to meet changing consumer demands? To increase production by the expansion of the area farmed is easier and faster than by raising the productivity of existing farmed lands.

Introducing modern techniques can be another important factor for raising productivity, but it will take a long time before farmers become familiar with and accept these new techniques. This is why extending

GROSS DOMESTIC PRODUCT
BY MAJOR SOURCE

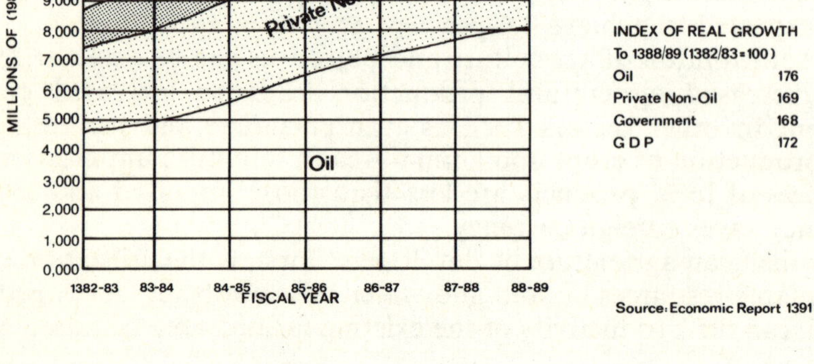

Source: Economic Report 1391H (1971)

Fig 7·1

AVERAGE ANNUAL GROWTH RATES OF VALUE ADDED BY SECTORS

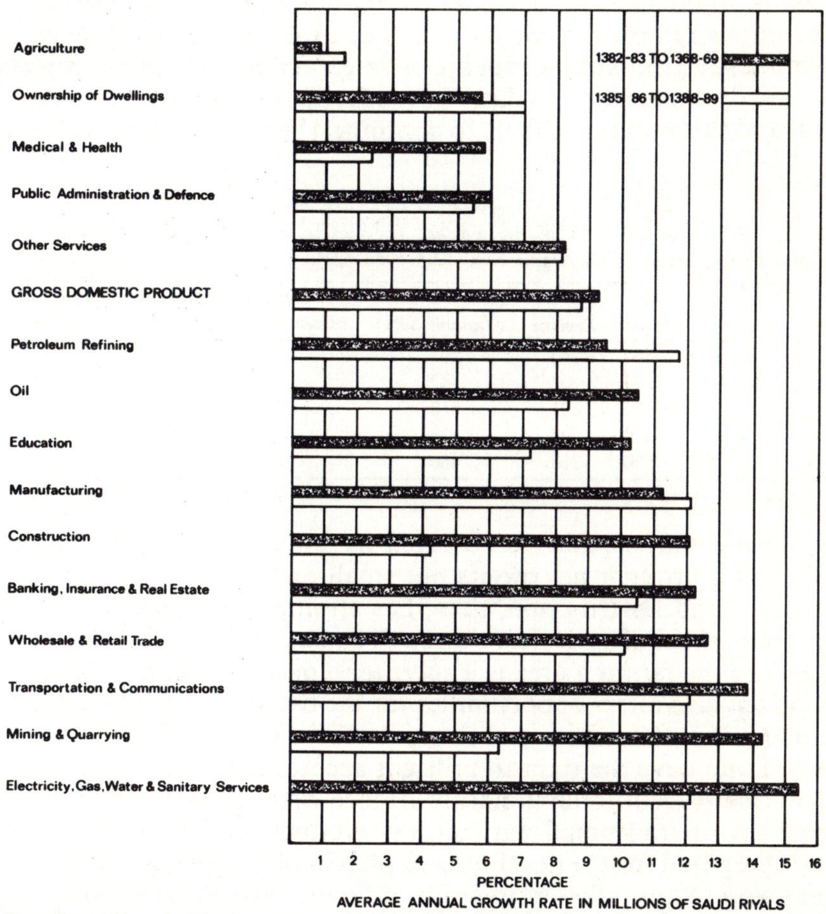

Source: Economic Report 1391H

Fig 7·2

the farming area through land reclamation is an attractive *short term* measure with obvious implications for Land Distribution Programmes.

The raising of productivity by simple modern techniques such as by using improved seeds, fertilizers, insecticides, etc, remains important for long term development and also because effective modern techniques have to be introduced on the new lands brought into cultivation.

Lastly, to change agricultural production by adapting the production pattern according to market requirements both could increase farm income and decrease reliance on imports; in this sense it represents an improved use of land. For example, the production of vegetables and fruits at the expense of dates, and to some extent cereals, has already taken place, as dates have lost their importance as a staple food, and this process is likely to continue. (See Tables No. (4–2) and No. (7–7))

Table No. (7–7) The estimates of the average production, cost and prices for the main agricultural products in Saudi Arabia 1380–83H (1960–63)[4].

Products	*Kg/ Donum*	*Cost/ Donum*	*Gross Revenue /Donum SR*	*Net Revenue /Donum SR*	*Cost/Kg SR*	*Price SR /Kg*
Dates	560	140	201	+ 61	0.26	0.36
Wheat	100	68	42	− 26	0.68	0.42
Tomatoes	1,350	231	810	+579	0.17	0.60
Vegetables	600	205	324	+119	0.34	0.54
Fruits	500	365	480	+115	0.61	0.96

It is clear that cereals (represented by wheat) brought net losses, whilst dates brought net profits but small ones.

Public Land Distribution, then, has an important part to play in the development of agriculture through extension of the farming area. Extending the farming area is a *short term* measure but new land development also offers opportunities for the use of new techniques and methods, thus introducing change. At the moment, the utilizers of Public Land have the right to utilize it according to their own thinking, normally traditional in nature. Hence what we may expect is the expansion of traditional agricultural production. The outline proposals prepared for the development plan in themselves go no further than being quantitative estimation of lands to be distributed.

What is meant here by land utilization is any type of investment in agriculture or animal production, any types of crop and any types of methods used. This would mean that the utilized Public Land at the end of the five-year programme would be typically traditional agriculture in type and technique. The long-term measures needed to raise productivity are clearly vital.

Table No. (7–8) The distribution of Public Land according to the Five Years' Development Plan (area in hectares)*.

Subject	*1389/90H (1969/70)*	*1390/91H (1970/71)*	*1391/92H (1971/72)*	*1392/93H (1972/73)*	*1393/94H (1973/74)*	*1394/95H (1974/75)*	*Total*	*Remarks*
Public Lands Identification and location	B	—	E	—	—	—	—	370,000 area expected
Period of distribution	—	B	—	—	—	E	—	Distribution of total area expected during plan period
Supervision of land investment already distributed	—	—	B	—	—	E	—	—
Total area distributable	—	740,000	148,000	222,000	296,000	370,000	370,000	Distribution of surveyed lands with equal annual increment during plan period.
Number of plots subject to distribution	—	7,400	14,800	22,200	29,600	37,000	37,000	Assumed 10 Ha plot for each individual

B means beginning and E means end.

* From unpublished departmental data.

How can we achieve a final goal of improved and more productive agriculture over a larger utilized area? The problems and obstacles faced in previous land distribution could be avoided. This would help but it does not satisfy the need. A contribution by government bodies from several related sectors is needed to develop proper land utilization. The solution is to diversify land utilization through a co-ordinated and harmonious development approach.

Since, however, the agriculture sector is a private sector, our prevailing economic philosophy cannot allow the imposition on the country of purely Government action; it only allows the encouragement of private enterprise. Applying this philosophy to agriculture, it appears that the necessary changes in production could be made through two main channels, firstly, by extension of other services and, secondly, by financial subsidies and supports. This in turn begins to define the areas of responsibility of the Ministry of Agriculture and Water.

The Ministry to which these responsibilities have fallen is faced with a great variety of demands at a time when it itself is in an early stage of development. A study of Saudi manpower calibre for the Ministry of Agriculture and Water was conducted by the Training Department in Spring 1390H (1970).

Table No. (7-9) The number of Saudi MAW employees according to academic qualifications.

Academic qualifications	*Number*	%
Without academic qualifications	2,344	45.2
Less than Elementary Certificate	1,086	21.0
Elementary Certificate or equivalent	1,124	21.6
Intermediate Certificate or equivalent	271	5.2
High School Diploma or equivalent	57	1.1
Less than Agriculture Diploma	45	0.9
Intermediate Agriculture Diploma	125	2.4
Intermediate Industrial Diploma	13	0.2
Intermediate Commercial Diploma	14	0.2
University Degrees (not agriculture)	61	1.1
University Degrees (agriculture)	66	1.1
Total	5,206	100.0

This table reflects the scarcity of academically qualified personnel employed by the Ministry of Agriculture and Water. It is also important to note that out of 127 Saudi university graduates, only 66 are graduates from agricultural colleges.

Table No. (7–10) The field specializations and academic qualifications of the agricultural college graduates in MAW in 1390H (1970).

Field of Specialization	*Qualification*	
	Bachelor's Degree	*Master's Degree*
General Agriculture	30	—
Agricultural Economics	9	2
Soils	4	1
Agronomy	3	2
Food Technology	4	—
Animal Production	3	—
Entomology	2	—
Plant Physiology	2	—
Horticulture	2	—
Plant Pathology	1	—
Extension & Rural Sociology	1	—
Total	61	5
Grand Total	66	

High level experts and specialist consultants from abroad are similarly not available in sufficient numbers (see Table No. (11–3)). At the same time fresh college graduates can only be mobilized according to their capacity and experience.

The Public Land Management Department with specific Public Land Department responsibilities is even more under strain. The manpower available in 1392H (1972) was as follows:

Saudi Citizens	*Non-Saudi Citizens*
One MSc Soils (USA)	Three MSc Soils
Four BSc Soils (USA)	Four BSc Soils
Two BSc Riyadh University	
Three Secondary School Level	Two Cartographers
Two Land Surveyors for Cadastral Survey	22 Land Surveyors for Cadastral Survey

The PLMD not only has technical duties to perform but a programme which has vast social, economic and commercial implications. Much of the routine volume of work is therefore carried out by the agricultural field organizations and the PLMD concentrates on central activities and technical operation through the local committees and field organizations. Extension work, one of the essentials for success, is not therefore carried out extensively or directly by the PLMD. This aspect will be further considered in later chapters.

The other main channel of action, financial supports and subsidies to encourage agricultural expansion is much more a matter of central policy concern to PLMD, MAW, and of course other Ministries, although the detailed financial requirements associated with land reclamation and exploitation by individuals can only come from technical field evaluations.

A subsidy is essentially a control mechanism of production and consumption and in Saudi Arabia the Economic Development Plan has adopted four types of subsidy for the agricultural sector.[19] These are:

1. Subsidy for fertilizer.
2. Subsidy for machinery and farm modernization.
3. Subsidy for price for a limited number of agricultural commodities.
4. Farm development subsidy for development of new land and water resources.

Consumer food subsidies have been given but up to the end of 1392H (1972) no production subsidy was given for any commodity production. Further consideration of subsidy practices is made in Chapter Nine but here it is important to note, in the context of PLD, that only subsidizing of costs of agricultural inputs has hitherto been practised.

The fourth type of subsidy noted above, that is, grants and loans towards the costs of developing new land and water resources, is most significant at this point. In the Development Plan, general financial provision was made for one aspect of this – small-scale private irrigation projects – even before the PLMD was able to carry out surveys and design its programme. For Plan purposes it was assumed that in such projects for each 20 hectares served by one well subsidy, loan or grant provision would be provided up to a total of 300,000 SR.

Table No. (7–11) Development costs of small scale private irrigation projects[19] (in thousand SR).

Item of Expense	Suggested Source of Funds: Loan	Subsidy or Grant	Total	Cost per Hectare (a)
Drilling, pump, engine, etc	100	100	200	10
Associated services, facilities and equipment	60	20	80	4
farm planning	0	20	20	1
Total cost of development (b)	160	140	300	15

(a) Based on 20 hectares per well.
(b) Operation and maintenance charges are included in cost of production estimates.

The proposed programme as quoted from the Development Plan read: "Under this programme, Ministry of Agriculture and Water technicians would prepare specifications for wells, irrigation and drainage systems, machinery requirements, and initial operation of land parcels allocated by PLMD. These specifications would support the owner's application to the agricultural bank for a loan for well drilling and installation, land preparation, equipment and similar expenses. A subsidy or grant could be given for some predetermined proportion of development costs; payment would be conditional on adherence to specifications for well location and installation."

It was also indicated that "further land development will require additional well drilling contractors, distributors and repair men for pumping machinery, land levelling technicians and contractors and the like". Bearing in mind that PLMD is responsible for projects to facilitate optimal use of grazing range, experimental work in range improvement, sand dunes stabilization programmes, national parks, forest conservation and reafforestation, the total work load to be carried by PLMD is enormous.

State expenditure in subsidizing or paying outright for inputs into agriculture can be evaluated from Table No. (7–12).

Of these items, PLMD has the responsibility for items 3, 4 and 11, all of which (excluding forestry) are directly associated with PLD.

This programme as a whole was intended to assist all the agriculturalists and utilizers who were given Public Land through the Public Land Distribution Programmes. In order to encourage development of these lands as rapidly as possible and therefore add to the irrigated

Table No. (7–12) Financial allocations for agriculture[19] (in million SR).

MINISTRY OF AGRICULTURE AND WATER	*Recurrent*	*Project*	*Total*
1. Administration & Planning	61.6	—	61.6
2. General Services	71.3	—	71.3
3. Water Resource Development & Conservation of Forests	20.5	—	20.5
4. Public Lands Administration	5.6	—	5.6
5. Research & Development	51.6	—	51.6
6. Extension & Agricultural Services	331.1	—	331.1
7. Training & Manpower Development	5.0	—	5.0
8. Price Support Subsidies	23.0	—	23.0
9. Fertilizer Subsidies	73.8	—	73.8
10. Farm Mechanization & Modernization Subsidies	75.0	—	75.0
11. Farm Development Subsidies	105.0	—	105.0
12. Existing Major Projects	—	178.9	178.9
13. Other Projects [(a)]	—	315.0	315.0
Ministry of Agriculture & Water Sub-Total	823.5	493.9	1,317.4
AGRICULTURAL BANK			
Operating expenses	33.4	—	33.4
Expansion Programmes and building	8.1	—	8.1
Increase of capital	108.7	—	108.7
Agricultural Bank Sub-total	150.2		150.2
GRAND TOTAL	973.7	493.9	1,467.6

[a] Projects related to supporting services.

land area in the Kingdom, 105 million SR were allocated in the Development Plan for this purpose. The fact that these lands have hitherto been undeveloped implies either a lack of knowledge of the existing land and water resources or that the cost involved in their development exceeds the benefit at current discount rates, or both.

Even with the general knowledge from resource surveys that ground-water in particular exists below these lands, the risks and uncertainties of land development are so great that the large capital investments required for wells, pumps, engines, land levelling and drainage may not be voluntarily forthcoming. Therefore the development subsidy can be viewed as a grant to reduce the risks of development and to make new and possibly higher cost producing areas ultimately competitive with older producing areas.

The problem of land distribution and development is complicated by the wide regional variations in the cost of developing a water supply for irrigation and in the access and distance to consuming centres or markets. The cost of well development is a function of the depth to ground-water and the depth of pumping. Well depths can vary from a few metres up to over 1,000 metres. As a rough guide, well drilling costs for irrigation (including casing) are in the neighbourhood of 120 SR per metre. At the same time, pump lifts vary from zero for

INITIAL INVESTMENT IN PUMP AND ENGINE 200–400 gpm DISCHARGE

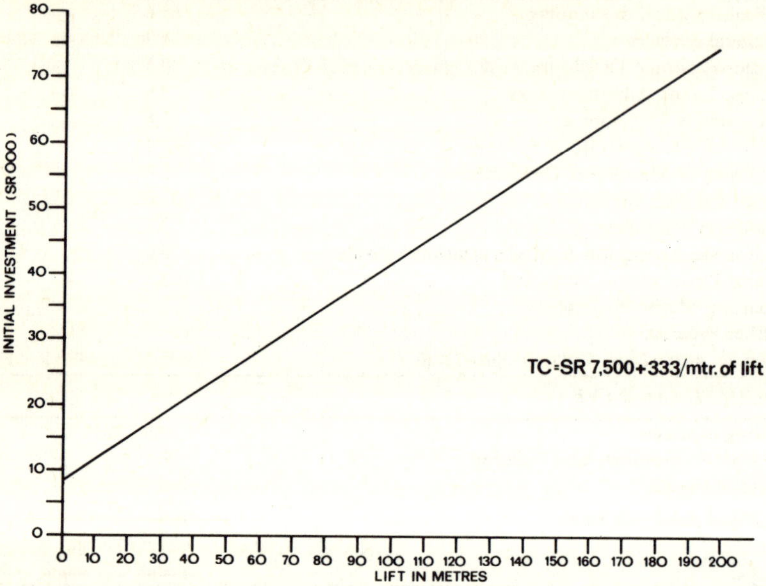

Source: Riyad Pump Dealers (Prepared by Dr. More)

Fig 7·3

free-flowing wells to several hundred metres in certain areas. Fig. 7–3 gives a rough estimation of total cost for initial investment in pump and engine.

In the short run, the most important variable controlling the crop pattern in these new areas will be access and distance to markets. Transportation costs where no paved roads exist are two to three times the rate in areas where access is available. The ease of getting produce to market, especially highly valued perishable vegetables, limits the crops a farmer can grow to the less profitable storable commodities.

Although modern farming operations require extensive investment in equipment, labour, seeds and fertilizer, the development subsidy should be limited to those items required to make new land ready for irrigated production. These fall into three categories:

1. Water resource exploitation: well-drilling, pump and engine or motor.
2. Water distribution: reservoirs for storage and irrigation channels.
3. Land levelling and drainage.

Using the criteria of simplicity and reliability in distributing the subsidy, several methods of subsidy-giving are possible: according to the area allotted to the utilizers; according to the actual cost for land development; or according to the cost of production.

It is thought advisable to distribute the subsidy as a flat rate for each area zone and according to a constant percentage, for example, one half or less of the actual cost for the items mentioned. Therefore it has been recommended that the subsidy be paid, adjusted for water cost, in stages making a fifty per cent payment after the well has been developed and the pump and engine installed, and the second half paid when the entire farm has been properly levelled and appropriate water distribution devices have been installed.

The distribution programme was itself designed for the last three years of the first national development plan (see Chapter Six). The proposed areas (see Table No. (6–7)), were delimited according to water potential and the capacity of PLMD personnel. By using well, pump and engine costs ascertained for each area, and assuming 13,000 SR as the cost of land levelling, irrigation distribution system and water reservoir for each five-hectare unit (see Table No. (7–13)), it was then possible to arrive at a working system of financial assistance to the new land utilizers.

During this most recent phase of Public Land Distribution, one can therefore say that a whole range of financial support and other assumptions had to be made at central planning level long before there could be much feedback of information from actual distribution and the establishment of cultivation on the new lands. At the same time the collaborative machinery involving several interested governmental Ministries and departments had to be created as the PLD policy was actually being carried out.

So far as subsidies were concerned several Departments were involved: the Water Resources Development Department dealt with the estimation of all actual costs of well drilling, pump and engine installation, for each area subject for distribution, as well as technical specifications: the General Directorate Project for Execution was concerned with the specification of water reservoirs and the Research Department for canal specifications. The PLMD was responsible for land levelling, soil and topographical survey.

Since PLD subsidy requirements, while large, are part of a more general scheme it has been recommended that a joint committee should be assigned for subsidy payment control. This consists of one member from the Ministry of Finance and National Economy; two members from MAW, that is, PLMD and Planning Unit and one member from the Central Planning Organization.

While 105 millions SR was allocated in the economic plan, three years have passed since the development plan was adopted and no

Table No. (7–13) Cost of land preparation for development.

	Criteria (m)				Cost SR/m			Cost (000 SR)			
Area	Well Depth	Casing Depth	Static Water Level	Pump Level	Drilling	Casing	Drilling + Casing	Well	Pump + Engine*	Well + Pump + Engine	5 Ha Development†
Al-Joaf	100	10	flow	—	40	100	50	5	—	05	18
Skaka:‡											
Tabuk F	150–200	5–10	10	35	45	55	46,4–48,7	8,3	18,6	26,9	39,6
Saq. F	700	5–10	flow	—	45	55	45,4–45,8	31,9	—	31,9	44,9
Tabuk	300–350	80–100	10 flow	35	70	60	83,7–90	28,2	18,6	46,8	59,8
Taima	120–150	10	35–40	38	60	60	64–65	8,7	20,8	29,5	42,5
Al-Ula	100	10	20	25	60	60	66	6,6	15,8	22,4	35,4
Qasim:											
N. Buraidah Saq.F.	650–950	550–600	15 flow	15	45	55	77–97	69	12,5	81,5	94,5
Buraidah											
1.Saq.F.	700	530–550	flow	15	45	55	86,3–88	60	12,5	72,5	85,5
2.Tabj. F	240	180	flow	15	45	55	86	20,6	12,6	33,2	46,2
Unaizah											
W-side Tabuk F.	150–200	50–80	20–30	35	45	45	58,7–74,4	11,6	18,6	31,2	43,2
E-side Tabuk F.	150–200	5–10	20–30	35	45	45	46,4–48,5	8,3	18,6	26,9	39,9
W-side Saq.F.	700	50–80	20–30	35	45	45	48,9—51,3	32	18,6	50,6	63,6
E-side Saw.F.	700	5–10	flow	—	45	45	45,5—45,8	31,9	—	31,9	44,9
Ha'il	170	25	100	100	70	70	80,3	13,6	41,2	54,8	67,8
Bishah	60–70	20	10	15	—	—	214–286	17,5	12,5	30	43
Najran	40	40	20–25	30	100	80	180	7,2	17,5	24,7	37,7
Wadi-Dawasir	250	100–120	10 flow	10–15	80	75	110–116	32,5	12,5	45	58
As-Sulail	250	100–120	5 flow	5	80	75	110–116	32,5	09	41,5	54
Al-Hassa	137	36–48	flow 10 m	10	—	—	109	15	10,8	25,8	38,8
Qatif	100–121	58–69	flow	—	—	—	132–160	16	—	16	29
Al-Kharj	120	120	10–20	20	70	60	130	15,6	14,1	29,7	42,7
Shakra, lower Khurmah	150	100	30	30	60	55	110–120	14,5	17,5	32	45
Al-Aflaj	120	60–80	15–30	35	60	55	87,5–96,6	11	18,6	29,6	42,6
Al-Zulfi	120	120	30 flow	30	90	60	150	18	17,5	35,5	48,5
As-Serr	400–450	330–350	30 flow	35	45	55	85,5–93	38	18,6	56,6	69,6

* From Fig. 7–3.

† Assuming that:- (a) Land levelling cost 100 SR/ha (500 SR/5 ha)
(b) Irrigation distribution system cost 2000 SR/ha (11,000 SR/5 ha)
(c) Water reservoir cost 2500 SR
(d) Areas used as proposed distribution programme over 3 years from Table No. 6–7

‡ Formation.

money has yet been disbursed under items 3, 4 and 11. However, other subsidies and loans are being implemented, and these will be discussed in Chapter Nine. The point essentially is this: PLD is a large and complicated programme and more time has been required for the build-up of the programme than was envisaged in the first place.

To summarize: the oil sector as the major but non-reproducible resource in Saudi Arabia must be mobilized to develop other sectors through revenue. Service sectors serve as tools for national development, whereas the agriculture sectors offer the main production possibilities. The Government in its development plan has adopted as a national policy, in order to expand this production sector, the distribution of Public Land where sufficient water and soil can be made available to those people who meet specified criteria. Development of Public Land in Saudi Arabia contains many risks and technical difficulties. Funds have been generally allocated as farm development subsidies to aid the utilizers of these lands in realizing their expectations and contributing to the national agricultural output.

Chapter Eight

Case Studies of Public Land Distribution in Saudi Arabia

Physical and human appraisal

Peppelenbosch in his introductory statement notices that society in the Arabian Peninsula forms a trilogy consisting of urbanites, farmers and Bedouins,[49] each operating in a different setting and contributing to the support of the other two. If we apply this concept to Area I, (see Fig. 6–2 and Fig. 8–1) we can identify three appropriate communities, the town, the village and the tribe, all located in the Great Nafud sedimentary basin. Since Area I is characteristic in this sense of Saudi Arabia as a whole, we shall concentrate our case-studies on this region. The total estimates of population in Area I, according to Basil Parsons' reconnaissance survey in 1388H (1968) was 400,000, classified as 44 per cent Urban, 18 per cent Rural settled and 38 per cent Bedouin.

Area I includes four regions: Tabuk, Wadi Sarhan, Qasim and Al-Joaf covering 37 million hectares. Less than 100,000 hectares are privately owned and over 99 per cent of the area has been classified as Public Land. However, water resource surveys indicate that the water resource potential in the whole of Area I is sufficient for maintaining irrigated cultivation only on less than 20,000 hectares. A part of this potential is already utilized on privately owned land (see also p. 125).

In Area I, Tabuk represents an urban-dominated area in which Tabuk is located without any village settlement in the surrounding hinterland. In Wadi Sarhan we find purely nomadic Bedouins. Buraidah in Qasim is a representative rural settled area. Whilst Tabuk characterizes one type of open situation in which a rural sector can, hypothetically at least, be added to the urban module, and whilst Wadi Sarhan characterizes another type of "openness" in that the range of resource use, settlement and economic activity can be expanded from the single element of Bedu pastoralism, the Buraidah situation is less open to change. Here, as we shall see, cultivation and sedentary settlement are already present, surrounded by non-nomadic pastoral zones. Al-Joaf exemplifies oases settlement, based on date gardens, of Bedu who retain a nomadic element in their lives.

LOCATION OF STUDY AREAS

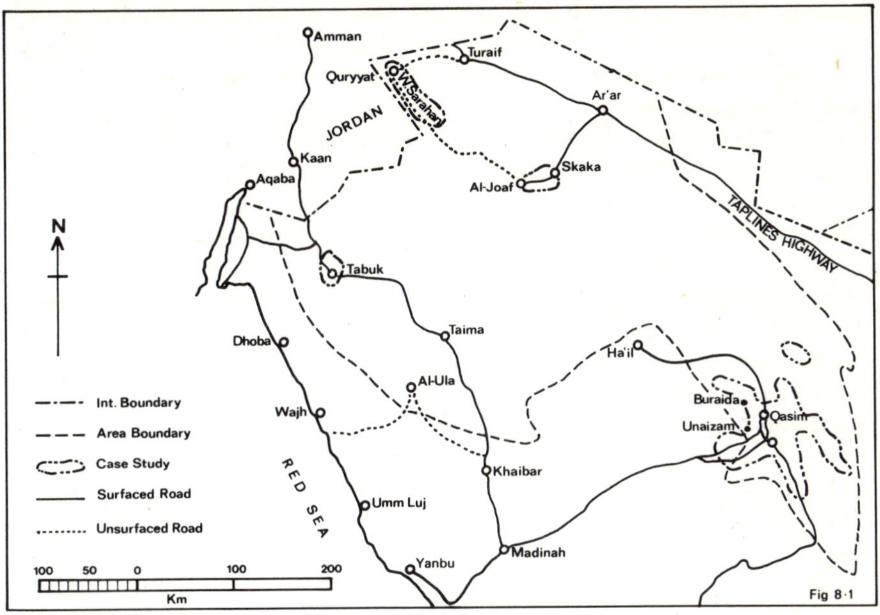

Fig 8·1

In these four cases, sufficient ground water is available to allow the expansion of agriculture in Tabuk, Qasim (Buraidah) and Al-Joaf but in Wadi Sarhan water potential is limited.

From west to east, along the Saudi Arabian–Jordanian frontier, tribal territories are occupied by the Howaitat, Bani Atiyah and Shararat. The characteristic features of pure nomadism are evident in all these tribal groups in the case studies' area. These features are:[49]

1. Non-sedentary animal husbandry is dominated by the search for natural pastures.
2. Entire human groups accompany the flocks and herds in their migrations.
3. The nomads roam seasonally over winter and summer grazing grounds following more or less fixed routes on tribal land.
4. An active trade exists between the nomads and the villagers and town-dwellers, mutually supporting and maintaining the three elements of the total society.

Public Land was distributed in Tabuk for the first time according to the PLDO; none of the previous systems affected this zone. There were only five farms associated with Tabuk; this is why it is considered as a clear case. In Qasim (Buraidah) land distribution has taken place over a long period and large areas were granted by the State Ruler or by local Governors. Public Land Distribution by the

PLDO is paralleled by land grants still being made by the State Ruler. Finally, a Bedouin settlement project was started in Wadi Sarhan as a temporary relief for nomads and has been cultivated in a sedentarization programme giving full property rights over the land according to PLDO (see Chapter Three). In Al-Joaf the PLMD is faced with land demand and very little free potential.

These case studies cover most of the utilizable part of Area I, but because the data available considering climate, human population, animal population, land classification, etc., are mostly found for the whole of Area I, then, for purposes of the first preliminary survey, we shall consider Area I as a whole rather than only the case study zones. Area I is characterized by a hot, dry and windy climate. Rainfall occurs normally in winter time, ranging from 30–60 mm. per annum. In these arid conditions the Bedouins and their livestock are supreme. As regards the animal population:

Table No. (8-1) Livestock population and type of ownership in Area I.[32]

Animals	*Bedouin Livestock (2 yr average)*	*Other Livestock*	*Total Numbers*
Camels	138,400	43,000	201,400 (Camels and Cattle)
Cattle		20,000	
Goats and Sheep	658,270	444,500	1,102,770
Total Animal Units	270,054	151,900	421,954

(1 Animal unit: = 1 camel, 1 cow, 5 sheep or 5 goats)

These data show that 64 per cent of the total livestock is controlled by the Bedouins. About 50 per cent of Bedouin animal unit equivalents were camels.

In any land distribution programme aimed at maximizing resource use, essential data on the land considered in the context of water, human resources, government policy and institutions, are a pre-requisite to the evolution of any plan for reducing the dominance of nomadic pastoralism. A general land capability classification of Saudi Arabia has been carried out using US Bureau of Reclamation standards. This Land Capability is an interpretation of the soil surveys and relates environmental characteristics to the capability of the land to maintain irrigated crop production. Class I land is land that will give the greatest economic return as it has the minimum of deficiencies and is capable of the widest cropping range. At the other end of the scale, Class VI land is wholly unsuited to irrigated agriculture. In Area I, areas of Class I land are too small to be mapped on this scale. There are, however, larger areas of Class II and III land also suited to irrigated agriculture though with lower capacity to repay investment costs and annual charges, but again areas are widely scattered. Class II and III land is subdivided on the basis of characteristics detrimental to development – *s* (soil), *t* (topography), and *d* (drainage). In the US Bureau of Reclamation scheme, Class IV land (not mapped) is regarded as only being suitable for limited arable purposes whilst Class V (also not mapped) is non-arable under existing conditions, though they may have some potential value.

Table No. (8–2) Arable land classes and subclasses in Area I case study zones (in hectares).[46]

Area	*2s*	*2d*	*3s*	*3d*	*3st*	*3sd*	*3td*	*3s+d*	*Total*
Tabuk	—	—	287	—	—	6,307	—	—	6,594
Qasim (Buraidah)	707	1,258	5,788	461	663	6,873	—	77	15,827
Wadi Sarhan	—	—	5,650	404	—	9,335	—	—	15,389
Al-Joaf	—	1,158	—	—	—	926	—	—	2,084
Total									39,894

It is worthwhile to mention here that the total cultivable land in Great Qasim is estimated as 70,552 hectares, and other equivalent scattered areas total 22,578 hectares. This makes the total cultivable land in Area I come to 117,197 hectares (see Table No. (6–4)). These figures confirm the fact that there is no shortage of suitable land, but available ground-water is believed to be sufficient to develop only 15,940 hectares (2,080, 3,060 and 10,800 hectares for Al-Joaf, Tabuk and Qasim respectively); see Table No. (6–5).

Here are land type characteristics of each case study zone.[36]

Tabuk

Clear surface drainage pattern, sand accumulated in sandstone wadi bottoms, soil surface mostly covered by gravel. Wadi bottoms make up about 20% of the site and are the main areas of production.

Al-Joaf

Nearly level basin depressions. Gentle sloping to areas near Al-Joaf. Soils are alluvial with textures mostly of sandy loam and silt loam.

Sarhan

Occupies a long strip extending from Al-Joaf to Jordan, a low gradient wadi with a wide flat bottom. Soil accumulations but mainly gravel with patches of sand and silt.

(Qasim) Buraidah

Flat plains characterized by gravelly materials often cemented together and crusted, with sand dunes in depressions. Soil profile seldom exceeds 2 metres. The underlying material has low permeability.

As can be seen, the topsoils generally tend to be of light texture though heavier textured horizons occur at depth (2 m) particularly in the Buraidah area. The soils are alkaline (pH 7.5–8.5) and are deficient in organic matter and nitrogen. Because they are calcareous, these soils have a marked deficiency in available phosphate. Some areas suffer from salinity but, provided internal soil drainage is good, these soluble salts can be removed by leaching. Other areas suffer from high exchangeable sodium and, because there is insufficient gypsum present in the soil in some areas, reclamation of these soils requires the application of additional gypsum. (See Table No. 2 and Table No. 3, Appendix II.)

Such information, prepared by a consultant for Area I Survey purposes and not specifically obtained for PLD purposes, is useful as a broad outline for understanding the case study zones, but cannot be mobilized directly for land distribution. To be more specific, the consultant described the land and water potential in general terms whereas the PLMD needs more detailed information for specific areas, for example, one of the major areas set aside for allocation in Qasim (Al-Mostawy) is outside the area covered by the general survey. (See Figs. 8–2 and 8–5.) Since PLMD has to survey the specific areas required for distribution, it has had to obtain from the Water Resources Development Department much more space-specific data about water potential, its location and permissible area for distribution, as well as to carry out more detailed soil and land evaluation surveys by itself.

PLMD have decided on some general technical principles. Thus lands in Classes II, III and IV can be distributed if sufficient irrigation water for leaching out excessive salinity is available. Since poor drainage is not uncommon and drainage is handicapped by the poor permeabilities of layers at various depths and by the existence of some salts, deliberate leaching may not always be feasible. Surface topography may require levelling.

Some lands under Class V can be distributed if the following problems can be resolved. Drainage systems are required for the removal of the harmful salts, but sodium removal causes a problem because the physical structure deteriorates unless gypsum is added. Enhancement of fertility is essential. Since most of the land is sandy and there is almost no vegetation or humus cover on the surface, it would be necessary to add manures, nitrogen and phosphorous fertilizers at the beginning. Cultivating the lands with leguminous crops such as alfalfa or beans would also be advantageous.

Distribution of Class VI lands should be avoided because the lands are unsuited to irrigation.

Sequence of events and timing

Tabuk: this is an area very close to the north-west boundary of Saudi Arabia. Much of its importance derives from its strategic location as a minor frontier zone point.

The north-west district of Saudi Arabia has a location of some strategic importance, and, as a result, it has the highest regional measure of road mileage in relation to the population. This fact, despite its insignificant population size, is mainly because the area overlooks the Gulf of Aqaba. This is of especial importance since 1366H (1946). Even before this time, Tabuk lay in a sensitive area adjacent to the Trans-Jordan Amirate established in 1339H (1920). The political history of north-west Arabia during this early Hashemite period emphasized its locational importance to Saudi Arabia; for a period Trans-Jordan even laid claim to Al-Joaf and Wadi Sarhan which lie well within Saudi territory.[13] Not until 1380H (1960) was this frontier open to trade and travel.

Tabuk therefore was partly at the end of a route, partly a potential frontier exchange post (and actually so since 1380H (1960)), and partly a centre receiving special attention from Riyad.

The Tabuk-Madinah route started to be built even before the completion of the Jeddah-Madinah route which, expanded to the north, reached Tabuk in 1382H (1962). The first objective in building the Madinah-Tabuk road was for military purposes[3] and this remained valid up to 1378H (1958). Nevertheless, since that date, while the trade factor was added to Tabuk's locational value, the need for military preparation in this region of Saudi Arabia remained, due to the fact of the closeness of the Israeli frontier, which has increased in importance since 1385H (1965).

Owing to this strategic location, roads were also built to link the inland town of Tabuk with both Haql and Ash-Sheikh Humayd on the coast of the Gulf of Aqaba.[10] Tabuk is the largest military town in the north-west frontier where a new army township is being built. Haql is the nearest Saudi seaport to Ilat (the only Israeli port on the Red Sea). Freight traffic is more associated with economic growth than military importance. Trucks are increasingly used for freight transport through Tabuk mainly carrying imported materials from Beirut to the inland towns. The first linking paved road with the surrounding countries was the Tabuk–Trans-Jordan road and this is still the only paved connection with the north.

Abdo[3] pointed out in his 1382H (1962) survey that traffic was limited to connections with some neighbouring countries in the north, particularly those with Lebanon, Syria and Jordan, then with an average of forty vehicles daily on the Madinah–Tabuk road, these supplying a part of the Western Province and a part of Qasim with imported goods. The quantities of commodities (mostly vegetables and foodstuffs) reached 250 tons per day. This is why Tabuk has become a significant controlled customs entry point. For the sake of comparison, forty-four vehicles used the Tapline road (east–north-west road) daily.

Generally in Saudi Arabia the road network is closely correlated to the pattern of major urban settlement. In the Tabuk region, however, the roads built for non-economic reasons have preceded the growth of settlement. In particular, the entrepreneurs have seized the trading opportunities offered by the location and communication facilities of Tabuk and have contributed to urban growth. Tabuk was the traditional homeland (*Derah*) for the Bani Atuyah tribe, of which a large number have become settlers at the growing urban centre of Tabuk, but, unlike Qasim, no indigenous sedentary farming community existed. Tabuk developed without indigenous roots and it is remarkable how social integration between the incoming people from various parts of the country in this garrison and trading town grew through the spread of social services and in the modernizing of the way of life.

Why do not small traditional farms exist in the district? Here strict control of land in the military zone surrounding Tabuk prohibited this, while normally in Saudi Arabia all areas surrounding towns and villages are grazed and offer urban fringe attractions to the nomads. Bedouins therefore have either to find jobs in Tabuk or else have to go far away to find grazing areas; there are no water points or shallow wells to attract Bedouins to settle temporarily in summer periods.

Tabuk is also located on one of the three main foreign pilgrim roads. An estimated number of 37,000 pilgrims[3] travelled along the Tabuk–Madinah road in 1381H (1961). The number of Muslim pilgrims coming by road has continually increased, particularly from Turkey and Syria. During the season of 1388H (1968), 49,191 pilgrims crossed the Saudi–Jordan boundary into Saudi Arabia and 15,272 followed the Tapline road.[10] The Town Planning Office in Jeddah has estimated the population of Tabuk to be 32,000 in 1383H (1963). There are two hotels, a bank, a civil hospital, a military hospital, and an airport (see p. 211 for other public and private facilities.

To sum up, Tabuk is the result of the existence of a military base, a customs post and transport. The development of communications has also been accompanied by the appearance of a considerable number of new settlements outside the town.

Wadi Sarhan: is a part of a Bedouin settlement project in the north.

It is a broad depression 2 to 20 miles wide and 200 miles long, extending in a north-west and south-east direction from Al-Joaf in the south up to the north of Qurayyat. The wadi has no outlet; it lies 1,000 feet below the adjoining plateau and the whole area around it drains into it.[9]

It is considered a rich valley in surface water which permits some oases and a few settlements to exist, and this richness is marked in comparison with the surrounding area of flat, lifeless land covered with small black lava fragments. Between Wadi Sarhan and Turaif another lava flow exists which makes the land barren and very difficult to cross (see Fig. 3–2). Khof was the largest ancient settlement of the Oases of Qurayyat at the northern end of Wadi Sarhan.[10]

"For thousands of years one of the most important trade routes connecting the Mediterranean and Central Arabia passed through Wadi Sarhan".[9] Now the situation is different. The Tapline and its highway cross the boundary with Jordan which gives this area economic and political significance.[10]

The discovery of phosphate in commercial quantity recently gave the area a new face. Phosphates were discovered in 1389H (1969) on the boundary line between Saudi Arabia and Jordan, east of Tobaik mountain and near Turaif; in the eastern part of this section lies Wadi Sarhan. Nevertheless in spite of Tapline and its highway, and the border importance of the area, Wadi Sarhan has become remote and, unlike Tabuk, it has gained no privileges in the age of modern transport and communication. However, the southern end of the long wadi is being better linked with the interior in every respect.[10]

Wadi Sarhan is dominated by the Shararat tribe. These Bedouins and others of the north were very badly affected in 1381H (1961) due to a drought period and this produced Government intervention (see Chapter Three, pp. 41–42). The financial expenditure on the project continued for nine years, until it was seen that the Bedouins have become accustomed to cultivation. It was felt that it was possible to stop financial aid of the rescue type and increase technical development involving PLD.

Qasim: Before 1370H (1950), the Qasim area, which was located in the middle of the barren heart of Arabia, an isolated region surrounded by huge bodies of sand dunes, had a lack of paved roads to connect it with the rest of the Kingdom. Subsistence agriculture was the only type of farming and a severe shortage of water was noticeable. In this harsh region a tradition had developed of undertaking commercial activity in other areas but still regarding Qasim as the homeland.

After 1370H (1950), as a result of the rising national income from oil, commercial business of this type, both in Saudi Arabia and especially outside, with the surrounding countries has grown considerably. This increase in wealth has enabled land-holders and farmers to be expansionary and in particular to seek for more water. They started by deepening their original hand-dug wells by drilling and one of these attempts hit the water-rich Tabuk aquifer formation in 1373H (May 1953). This produced real wealth and marks the start of a new and very promising era in the history of Qasim. It has lost its geographical isolation. Water discovery urged the Government into detailed investigation of this new source of prosperity and to link Qasim by highways to the main markets in the Central Najd and Hijaz regions.

Al Joaf: This is the oldest settlement area in northern Saudi Arabia. East of the Jordan frontier and Wadi Sarhan, Al-Joaf is structurally a deep part of a great basin.[34] Irrigated farming has been practised since early days in the Al-Joaf–Skaka Oases with natural and hand-dug wells. Shallow flowing wells have been drilled recently. The remainder of the area has only a few date-palms around isolated water wells and is inhabited by Bedouins dependent upon grazing. Al-Joaf area has little agricultural development potential because there is so little suitable land left for further development.[46]

Specific regional policies of land distribution

Tabuk: The growth of settlements in Tabuk over two decades has been rapid. Most of the houses are of a new and concrete type and almost all new houses are supplied with water and electricity. The expansion of Tabuk market has been very significant, relying entirely on imported goods and food-stuffs from the northern surrounding countries. There were no farms but there were several existing private gardens (*bustan* type) belonging to *Sheikhs* and notable people in Tabuk. This is a type of land use of traditional status rather than for purposes of profit; such land is used by the permission of higher authority. The part of the Northern Bedouin Settlement Project in the Tabuk and Western Coast area (*Hejar*) provides Tabuk town with a modest quantity of fresh vegetables (see p. 46).

The new population and the movement into Tabuk is paralleled by the steady increases in real incomes which in turn have resulted in new and increased demand.

The process of land settlement in Tabuk typifies a change from nomadism to commerce, originating in non-agricultural activities (see pp. 101–102). The town is a prosperous commercial centre in which financial operations are carried out. It is an area developing by normal unplanned colonization, similar to the situation of Makkah, as a commercial, non-agricultural district, having exchanged products of Syria and the Mediterranean from pre-Islamic times.

The energy for this process comes from the change from traditional to the modern monetary values of the new entrepreneur population. As a result, merchants have established a money-making system and have made great fortunes from their trading enterprises. Once such capital is formed there can appear a demand for outlets in new fields of what Watt described was happening at Makkah at the beginning of the seventh century by saying, "The merchant living in a town dealing in luxury goods of small bulk is able to increase his wealth almost without limit."[56] In respect of economic change, Islam has fully accepted commerce and business, and in respect of social changes, Islam also allows the movement away from tribal solidarity towards a large measure of individualism.

Here recently has appeared the opportunity of Tabuk. It is unlike Qasim. Tabuk is an open area with no existing community or social rigidities and no existing land use rigidities. The appearance of new linkages through commercial interest has produced a possibility of modest to highly profitable enterprise development.

The life of the nomad is always hard. There, from the need to seize all possible opportunities comes a general motivation which causes spontaneous "natural" settlement and occupation of new territory. There has always been a steady process of urbanization, and this has meant the growth of commerce. This process is continued and accelerated in modern Saudi Arabia by public expenditure. In the case of Tabuk, individuals joined the army, the State gave them monthly stipends and provided a garrison town for them to live in. People can also gain their livelihood by commerce instead of stock-breeding.

Now a new factor is emerging, the possibility of sedentary agriculture and of more sedentary settlement. This settlement now has to be executed in a manner consistent with Public Land Distribution systems. In the Tabuk area, Public Land Distribution has become the means for an adaptation of the nomadic system to more modern ways of living. As shown in Table No. (7–1) the unspecified labourers, drivers and guards are mostly Bedouin, numbering 772 out of the 3,072 enumerated as the utilizers in Tabuk up to the end of 1392H (1972).

Public Land is also a new field for outlet and profit. 1,350 utilizers are employees and 599 are housekeepers; in all 307 merchants applied for Public Land. Bedouins, employees, housekeepers and merchants make up 98 per cent of the total utilizers in Tabuk.

In *Wadi Sarhan* and other areas of the Bedouin Settlement Project in Northern Saudi Arabia, after the discontinuing of the first financial aid programmes PLD policies had to face particular and consequential problems (see Chapter Three).

The sudden cessation of financial aid would bring shortages in the financing of agricultural work, since a bonus was given to each pump-operator in addition to free fuel, plough and seeds. The unavailability of a substitute financing source would arise from an inability to obtain loans from the Agricultural Bank, due to the absence of ownership deeds, resulting in turn from delays in land allocation procedure and the nature of the *Hejar* schemes. Difficulties in marketing, due to the distance and remoteness of *Hejar* from the major marketing centres, were in any case considerable. On *Hejar* land the essential water-pumps were Government property and without financial and technical assistance it was clear that repairs and maintenance could not be carried out and a great number of pumps would become non-operative. Other machinery services, as also with extension work, could not be supported by the new *Hejar* settlers who were short of capital and agricultural experience.

In Wadi Sarhan, therefore, the application of the PLDO had to take into account some special circumstances. First, this meant giving the Bedouins ownership title to the lands they worked and bringing many of the holdings up to PLDO area standards by adding adjacent lands to the existing farms. Since neither the *Hejar* farms nor adjoining land are strictly Public Land, it was necessary to have approval of HM The King to distribute the project's agricultural lands according to PLDO (see p. 49) and issue ownership deeds through the Courts. In addition, special aids offered by MAW were made available to the project settlers. The Government's pumps were left with the utilizers for a maximum of three years as an encouragement for them to continue agricultural work. The free distribution of seeds and fertilizers according to existing project practice was maintained. The extension services were taken over through the preparation of a technical programme for the Project Area – a programme related to plant protection, extension fields and the use of modern agricultural methods.

MAW also undertook to negotiate with other Ministries and agencies so that the transition from a settlement project scheme to a PLDO-based development programme would be safeguarded. The Agricultural Bank was requested to help with credits and the Ministry of Labour and Social Affairs to assist with the establishment of agricultural societies Petromin (The General Petroleum Establishment) was approached over the supply of fuel for agricultural use at cost price. Lastly, the Ministry of Communications was asked to level agricultural roads linking the *Hejar* of Wadi Sarhan with Qurayyat and the *Hejar* of the Coastal area with Dhoba town so that market centres were accessible to the new farmers.

The application of PLDO in this case has resulted in several direct benefits. Settlers were encouraged to settle and build houses instead of using the black hair tents. The greater emphasis on technical services instead of financial aid helped towards real viability. The encouragement of perennial agriculture instead of the previous reliance on seasonal crops, by planting different kinds of trees and perennials, has lifted the ecological and economic standards of farming. The PLD approach has more completely assisted in the lessening of dependence on pastoralism than did the *Hejar* scheme and by concentrating on cultivation has enabled the establishment of new and, in time, viable production units. Improved market facilities as well as production have resulted in higher incomes.

In *Al-Joaf* Bedouin livestock herds are numerous but many of the pastoralists wish to settle and practise cultivation. Ground-water is available from sandstone aquifers;[46] Al-Joaf formation is at 48–146 metres' depth with moderate water quality and quantity, Tabuk formation at 48–256 metres' depth mostly free-flowing with excellent water quality. Al-Joaf and Skaka Oases however need improved drainage for any expansion of irrigated land. The limitation here is land with suitable terrain and soil within the scattered small areas earlier used for cash-crop dry farming. Since these areas are widely scattered in a desert region, it is expected that the allocable areas for distribution will be utilized ultimately by Bedouins in small-scale reclaimed areas, and commercial markets for part of the production will grow with the further development of Tapline settlements.

In *Qasim* application and utilization of ground-water without control and firm policy in the past brought complex problems – waterlogging, soil salinity and drainage problems as well as economic and organizational difficulties. There is, therefore, an urgent need of prevention of further water misuse. Further artesian drilling has to be controlled and any new expansion has to be planned, this to be achieved through the Public Land Distribution programme.

Qasim is divided into three main agricultural administrative districts: Buraidah, Unaizah and Ar-Rass (Fig. 8–2). As we see in Table No. (6–2), in these districts, according to the 1380–1386H (1960–66) agricultural survey 2,695,748 donums of land were enumerated as being held by agricultural land utilizers but it was noted that of this only 319,635 donums were productively worked. On the other hand,

LAND CLASSIFICATION & AGRICULTURAL DISTRICTS IN QASIM REGION

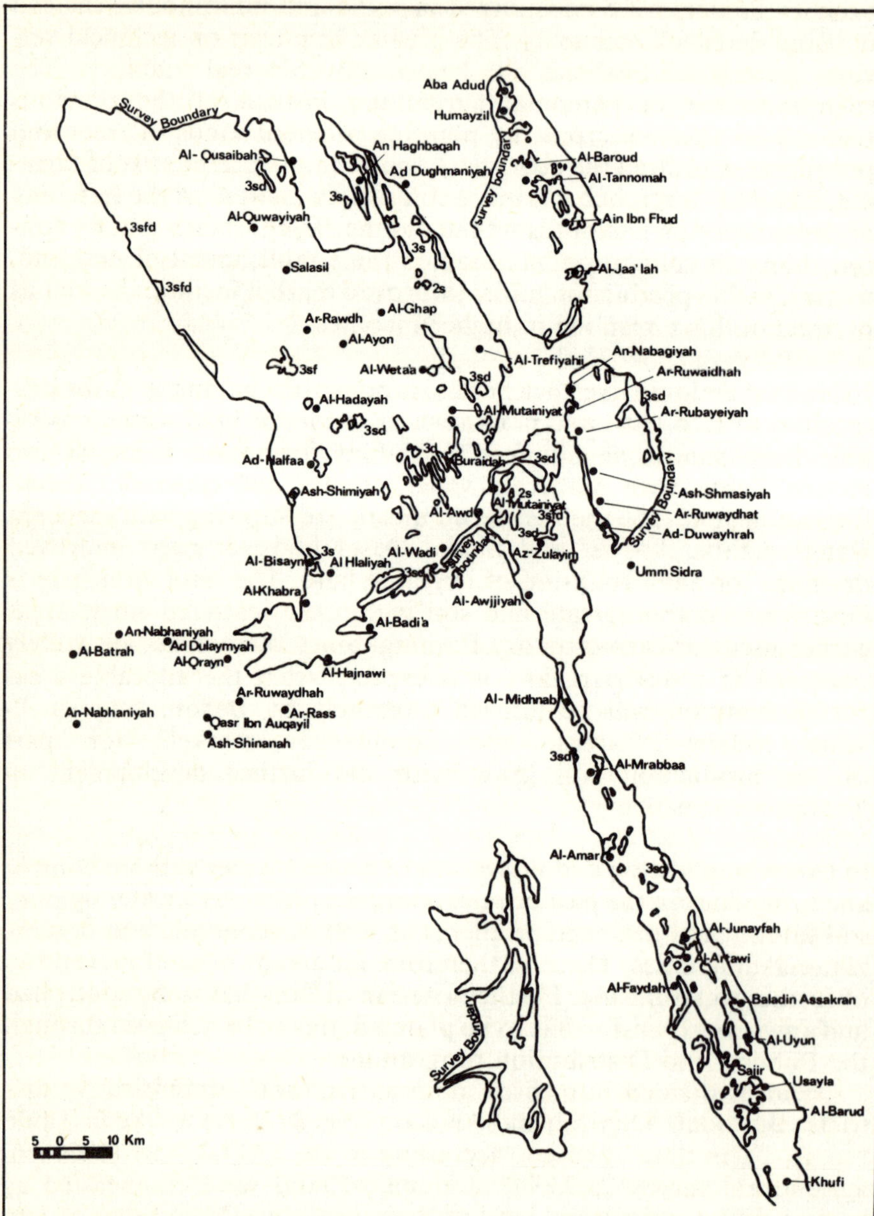

Fig 8·2

taking the figures prepared by the regional consultant in 1387H (1967) it seems that the total potential arable land (excluding the water availability factor) in Greater Qasim is 831,180 donums; this consultant study enumerated only 292,000 donums as under cultivation. The maximum cultivable area which is now believed can be supplied with water, is 40,000 hectares (Table No. (6–5)).

There is clearly a great difference between these estimations. In the 1380–1386H (1960–66) survey the sizes of holdings were recorded according to the farmers' statements; most of the region's farmers do not know the exact area of their holdings and have a tendency to exaggerate their size. As for farm size we have seen in Table No. (6–1) that the average farm size in Saudi Arabia for 55.5 per cent of holdings is less than 10 donums; 75.9 per cent of farms had areas less than 30 donums. This represents the dominant picture in the country and such small farms employ the largest proportion of the rural population.

If we take these latter figures as our criteria, the first preliminary agricultural census suggests that Qasim is typical of the established agricultural areas of Saudi Arabia from the point of view of land holding. If we then take the 1387H (1967) Consultant figure of 292,000 donums under cultivation and the Ministry of Agriculture and Water's estimate of the number of agricultural properties in 1381–82H (1961–62), *viz*, 9,071, then we have a mean figure of 30 donums of cultivated property. Since this last mean figure shows a reasonable correspondence with the national estimations, we can perhaps use as a reasonably accurate approximation the first two figures, that is 292,000 donums cultivated in 9,071 farms.

Since 1386H (1966) a number of new properties were established. This has been achieved by the unplanned taking of land and by the subdivision of existing holdings. The basic process in this situation is associated with the existence of a modified traditional farming society which has new technical and economical opportunities but which retains old-established attitudes to land.

With the prevalent small size of farm holding it becomes questionable as to whether or not mechanization is the right approach, especially if social disturbance is to be avoided. The obvious alternative is distribution of Public Land which has water potential in a controlled programme, using simple modern techniques for its utilization.

Farmers are in great need of information related to soil properties, farming practice and the importance of water conservation in this changing situation. The preliminary findings of early surveys can never be adequate for detailed development plans but will at least serve as a starting point. Many agricultural practices in the region at the present time are necessarily based on traditional knowledge passed down from generation to generation, but new farmers are introducing machinery, sometimes of a heavy type. Monitoring and surveying structural changes, patterns and trends in the agriculture of Qasim become vitally important if bad effects are to be avoided (for example, an imbalance of heavy machinery at the expense of hand tools).

In general, therefore, we have in Qasim a situation not uncommon in developing regions of a non-technologically trained farming population with traditional subsistence-oriented economic ideas confronted with new technical and financial opportunities which they do not have the experience to utilize properly. There are, therefore, physical, economic and organizational problems arising from the changes happening within an established community.

Implementation of Public Land Distribution

From this point onward, Wadi Sarhan will be dropped from our discussion because PLDO here have had to apply an extremely modified programme to the existing farming area. Since there is also no more water potential in the new area, there is effectively no new Public Land to be distributed. In Al-Joaf, the situation is also special; cultivable lands are very small in size and extremely scattered; most of them are difficult to classify in potential. For these reasons it is best to discuss the PLD for Al-Joaf as a special case in Chapter Twelve. On the other hand, the remaining two case studies (Tabuk and Qasim) illustrate the central principles of PLD. In our examination of them some questions arise which will have to be borne in mind.

For Qasim: does one anticipate continued natural growth and hence establish properly organized new blocks of agricultural land on which this growth will take place? How, through extension and after-control, can existing farming be improved, so that old and new lands become approximately the same in productivity, etc?

For Tabuk: does setting up a new land settlement scheme necessarily involve the creation of a new project management structure? How far can a Land Distribution Programme be minimally involved in management and rely on separate agriculture extension support services?

From the earlier discussion, one can make a comparison between the situations in Tabuk and Qasim from a land distribution point of view, as follows:

Tabuk	*Qasim*
a) Land demand in areas traditionally under control and closed to unplanned colonization.	a) Slow but strong taking up of land by local people – local initiative.
b) Policy of establishing new agriculture.	b) Policy of improving existing resource uses as well as expansion.

Tabuk	*Qasim*
c) The change from nomadism to trade in foodstuffs and consumer goods.	c) The change from nomadism to a settled agricultural life.
d) A society not dominated by traditional values.	d) Dominant tribal relationships and the retention of much of the social features of nomadism.
e) Existing social and economic changes not linked in any integrated or planned concept.	e) Social change linked with economic change in the PLD programme.

In this study we are concerned with both practical and theoretical aspects of PLD. From an examination of the factors of planning, implementation and evaluation of the programme, we can estimate where the stress should be laid and where it should not and derive some general principles from observed practice.

Tabuk: On 9/2/89H (1969) the distribution of Public Lands was declared for a total area of 320,757 donums; these lands surround the town (Fig. 8–3). The first decisions were issued on 25/11/90H (1970), the number of allocable plots totalling 5,191. This figure is, however, open to change according to criteria such as the area needed for urban growth, the unsuitability of land when finally surveyed, etc. (see Table No. (8–3)). By 27/11/91H (1971), the number of applications submitted for agricultural utilization reached 2,766. Out of these, 2,245 applications were dealt with by the local committee and decisions issued for 2,027 applicants. Fifty-two applications remained with the local committee because the applicants did not give the requested data. Two hundred and twenty-eight land plots had been delivered to utilizers and 380 plots were still not taken up by allottees because they did not ask for them. The actual hand-over of land took place very slowly, since, for example, some allottees did not put the required boundary marks around their plots.

Up to the end of 1392H (1972), more lands were surveyed, such as those surrounding Bir Ibn Hirmas (Fig. 8–3). The number of plots declared for distribution here reached 4,782; out of these 3,125 plots (377 located in the wadi) were distributed to 2,972 utilizers.

In all, in the Tabuk area 449,047 donums were surveyed.

From this total 29,390 donums of land were surveyed but have not been capability classified because water is not available for their utilization. There are two water-producing formations: Tabuk formation which is shallower, and for which permits can be obtained for drilling, and Saq formation, at greater depth, but which is used only where the Tabuk formation is not productive. All consumers prefer to drill the Saq formation even though it costs more because it is freer flowing, with better water quality and quantity.

PUBLIC LANDS SURVEYED AT TABUK AREA

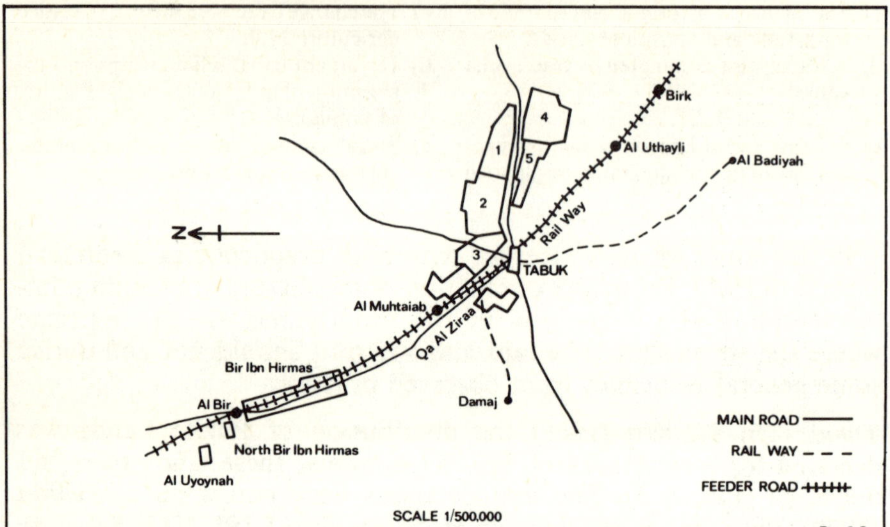

Fig 8·3

Some utilizers who had received their allotted land, rapidly carried out excellent agricultural works. Their total expenditures for land levelling, ploughing, well drilling, boundary fencing, and buildings vary considerably as the range of actual figures quoted for particular

Table No. (8–3) A summary of all the soil data and land classification in the Tabuk area.*

Location	*General Soil Condition*	*Area in Donums*	*Land Capacity Classification*
Surrounding	Sandy, sandy-clay,	227,230.9	3
Tabuk	EC: harmful salts,	43,951.5	4
	pH: 9, ESP: Fair,	10,000.0	5
	$CaCO_3$: 15%	39,575.0	6
Surrounding	Sandy-clay,	21,500.0	3
Bir Ibn Hirmas	EC: harmful salts,	7,740.0	5
	pH: 8.2, ESP: Low,		
	$CaCO_3$: 5%		

* Unpublished departmental memorandum.

plots indicates: 45,000 SR, 45,000 SR, 57,000 SR, 72,000 SR, 77,000 SR and 105,000 SR.

Some allottees have a desire to farm and utilize the land allotted for them, but one of the limiting time factors is the inadequate number of drilling rigs and crews available in the area. Approximately two months are needed to drill one well, and many land plots allotted to applicants and their families need from 1–4 wells according to their sizes and grouping arrangements.

Table No. (8–4) A summary of water conditions in the Tabuk area.*

Item	*Tabuk formation*	*Saq formation*
Depth (m)	150–270	400
Quality (ppm)	510–640	510
Quantity	Abundant	Abundant
Charge	Could be flowing	Mostly flowing
Utilization	Drinking – irrigation	Mostly drinking

* Unpublished departmental memorandum.

Qasim: PLMD surveyed areas both in Buraidah and Unaizah, the former alone considered here. The areas in Buraidah administration are shown in Fig. 8–4.

Table No. (8–5) Locations and the condition of Public Land in Buraidah.*

Location	*General Soil Condition*	*Area in Donums*	*Land Capability Classification*
Al-Melaidah	Sandy-sandy loam, EC 16 in 90% sample, pH: 10, ESP: 15 in 25% sample, $CaCO_3$: 20%	179,464	4
Al-Mostawy	Sandy loam – loamy sand, EC 16 in 25% samples, pH: 8.5, ESP: moderate, $CaCO_3$: 15%	11,400 105,881 27,490	2 3 6
Al-Botain and Qa'arah	Sandy – loamy sand, EC: 2.7, mostly pH: 7.5–8.5, ESP: Low, $CaCO_3$: 15%	521,800	3

*Unpublished departmental memorandum.

Table No. (8–6) The aquifer (Aqu) and depth in the Public Land area.

Location	*Saq Aqu*	*Tabuk Aqu*	*Manjor Aqu*	*Khoff Aqu*
Al-Melaidah	375 m	50–200 m	—	—
Al-Mostawy	—	—	available	250–300 m
Al-Botain and Qa'arah	—	available	—	250 m

Qasim possesses considerable agricultural potential. If this potential were to be rationally planned and managed there would be great beneficial returns to the agricultural economy of the region in particular and Saudi Arabia in general (see Fig. 8–2).

Undoubtedly, the abundance of water at the present time has eliminated the most rigid limiting factor which checked agricultural expansion and activities in the area for centuries. But at the same time the availability of water has created other problems. These problems and others, for example, allocated holding sizes, which follow from the

MAIN SETTLEMENTS IN QASIM

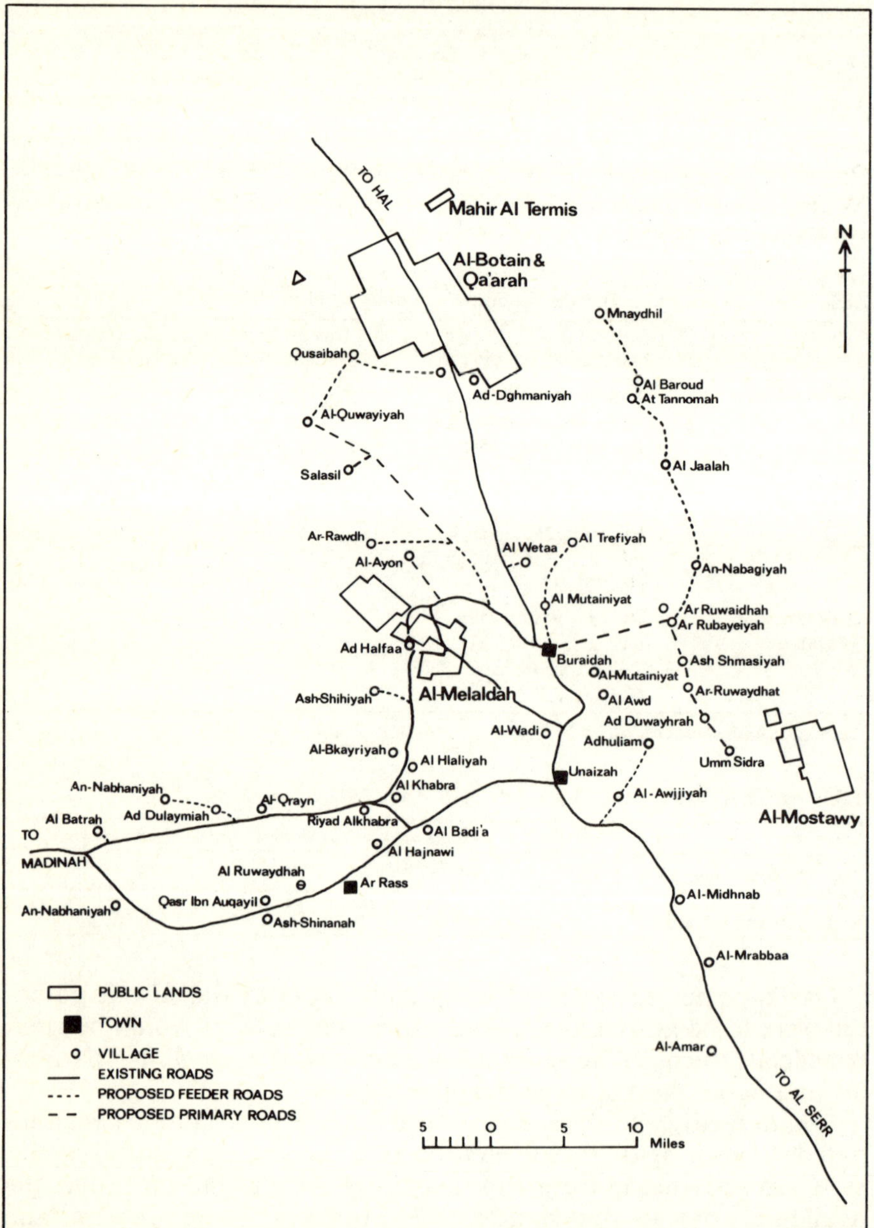

Fig 8·4

differences between Qasim and Tabuk will be discussed in Chapter Twelve.

To summarize: all the case study areas are dominated by Bedouins except for Qasim which is already a settled agricultural area. They all possess water potential with the exception of Wadi Sarhan. Al-Joaf is a typical agricultural oasis region with limited land for future agricultural expansion. The speed of change associated with the rapid growth of Tabuk town has in turn resulted from the political strategic evolution of Tabuk, the creation of physical and socio/economic infrastructures, partly in the private, partly in the public sectors. These case studies located in Area I show great variations even though they are all located in one region – the north of Saudi Arabia. Already a number of space-specific and locationally distinctive characteristics of each case study have been identified, each requiring that some special features be built into any PLD programme based on agricultural development. The difficulty, even impossibility, of applying one simple policy becomes marked. When one then also notes that neighbouring countries such as Iraq, Egypt and Syria have had to recognize the strength of regional circumstances (see Chapter Eleven), then it becomes vital to appreciate that Public Land Distribution for development is a highly complex process.

Chapter Nine

Public Land Distribution in the Context of Agricultural Development Requirements

The structure and procedures described earlier which currently exist have been created to conform with the general development approach outlined on pp. 74–75. Land distribution in Saudi Arabia today is therefore characterized by an emphasis on development which, in this context, practically means agricultural development. As the real problems for Land Distribution Programmes arise from this developmental emphasis and since it is not enough to distribute Public Land which has physical potential, a clear plan must be followed for development purposes.

Land Distribution is carried on solely for Saudi individuals, thus it means the mobilization of human resources to meet national and human needs. Since we are concerned with Land Distribution and not re-distribution this in turn means new farms and new farmers. Many of these new land utilizers have little or no experience of cultivation and so a management problem, both human and technical, arises.

The changes needed both to alter primitive agriculture to a modern state and to establish new modern farming are represented especially in the use of heavy machinery in farming and in the increase of expenditure on working manpower. Input costs rise when modern methods are adopted, hence, any lack of money will affect the desire of farmers to use modern farming methods. Therefore, the supply of capital becomes another critical factor. Trials have proved in many countries that agricultural credit systems can have effective results in bringing direct development benefits. By the application of higher inputs they can rise, because of this productivity to the point where the costs of production of each unit of production actually fall and the prices of agricultural commodities decline.

The Ministry of Agriculture and Water, through PLMD, has the right to supervise the allotted land from the technical point of view and to supervise the seriousness of its utilization by the party to whom it was assigned.[44] This in turn involves the MAW in all development sectors. In particular, it means that an intensive programme for each concern should be developed.

The machinery of Land Distribution has been established, the working principles are well known. What remains are the problems of proceeding from demand to reconnaissance survey to feasibility survey, and finally to what are essentially complex development projects involving all sectors of life in non-urban areas. This is the full requirement of agricultural development.

Saudi Arabia has initiated a development programme and the general strategy is clearly explained in the economic plan. What now matters is the devising of means of implementing this strategy through agricultural policy and practice. A water code is now being devised and is under consideration by higher authorities. When it is approved, it will need a new administration. Farm development subsidies mentioned in the economic plan are to be developed. Problems arising from this will have to be satisfied by regulations or by facilities that will have to be provided. PLMD has started to think of farm management, credits, plans, etc., as steps to build up and/or to speed up land development.

It is in this context of planning for development we now consider and evaluate the relationship between Land Distribution and economic development, first looking at case studies. It is the aim of this book to set out the basis of and fundamental requirements for the achievement of the programme of Public Land Distribution, so that we can suggest not a theoretical approach but rather a sound applied approach for the purpose of speeding up the programme.

Real land development requires the following:

Agricultural utilization plan and water utilization policy

An effective land policy requires *economic* and *social* infrastructures, which will enable economic efficiency of input use and progress in cultivating the land.

Agricultural utilization policy

As a result of the completion of studies carried out by the Ministry of Agriculture and Water through consultant firms, a comprehensive plan was laid down for: the purpose of decreasing the costs of agricultural production; raising production capacity in the agricultural sector; and the establishment of an economical balance of agricultural production to minimize the gap between domestic consumption and imports. Also recommended was the giving of financial priority to projects and programmes which increase the national and individual income and also to programmes in which increased yields could be economically produced.

Given that the new agricultural sector must be built on a sound scientific and technical basis, and within the constraints imposed by the environment, the main method followed in Saudi Arabia is a free investment system without restrictions or precise control; but one adapted through financial aid in a way that gains the optimum profit for the farmer producer, who in turn may make an ample and varied production available to the consumer.

This country has a good potential to achieve a high level of self-sufficiency as it has a variety of climates and soils. Depending on the quantities of water available and the practical experience of the cultivators, great crop variety is also possible.

These are the broad outlines of Saudi Arabian agricultural policy but a translation into its implementation is still required. Thus, for the preparation of programmes for Public Land, it has to be determined which crops are suitable for each area, such as seasonal summer and winter vegetables, fruit trees, field crops and fodder crops for livestock production. Specialized programmes required for each distribution area must start with a firm basis in physical feasibility but they are as yet difficult to determine due to inadequate research in the agricultural areas and information about specific crops, including crops recently introduced. Furthermore the farmers, with varied experience, still have the choice of utilizing recommended programmes, or not.

Water policy

Land distribution and agricultural development in the Kingdom is complicated by particular problems related to ground-water. The Kingdom depends substantially on ground-water resources to meet its requirements for drinking and domestic purposes, industrial requirements and irrigation.

Water is the main factor which limits the increase of agricultural lands in the irrigated areas of the Kingdom. This is, of course, due to the rarity of rainfall in this arid and semi-arid region (see p. 59).

In view of this, the only water resource that has to be controlled is ground-water and MAW has to design a water policy to develop the ground-water resources for meeting its water demand. Such a water policy requires minimizing the wastage of water, as for the most part the water is of fossil origin and is not being recharged as fast as current extraction rates; that water is used for development according to need. That surface water coming from rain must be conserved and stored and the search for further ground-water aquifers continued.

The Water Conservation Department has to prepare broad national policies and programmes concerning the development and conservation of water resources. Regulations for effective water control are required (see p. 143).

Farm management

Farm Management by definition is, "the practical aspect of the application of physical and biological sciences in ensuring the maximum economic return from correct resource allocation".[32] As most new utilizers are nomads or workers in non-agricultural sectors (see Table No. (7–1)) it is expected that they will have very little knowledge about agriculture. Guidance is needed in many things, for example, layout, soil resources, well location, water distribution and drainage canals and the location of building sites. A programme of operations should be accomplished at the right time, such as drilling a well, installing a pump, constructing canals, leaching saline soils, treatment with gypsum, addition of fertilizers and the sowing of crops.

Distributed land first requires reclamation. The operation of reclamation covers the following main phases.

Engineering Phase

This includes preparing a contour map on the basis of the minimum cost of land levelling operations and dividing the area into different plots according to the soil and topographical characteristics. In case of land topographical differences, partial levelling can be conducted by dividing the land into plots and then levelling each strip. It also includes determination of well sites so as to arrange for drilling in areas suitable for controlling irrigation operations. It also involves the determination of the layout of irrigation and drainage canals.

Agricultural Phase

Public Lands have desert soils with low fertility and sometimes harmful characteristics on which no cultivation has previously been carried out.

Soil Study

This step is necessary for the determination of the physical and chemical characteristics of the soil and for learning the best methods for their management.

Soil Improvement

At this stage, soil characteristics are improved mechanically and chemically through the flooding and leaching of saline soils, the addition of gypsum to alkaline land, the addition of organic matter or clay to sandy lands and finally the addition of sand to clay lands.

Planting Procedures

These include the selection of suitable crops, suitable methods of planting, service work, for example, ploughing, addition of fertilizers and other conditioners in the right quality and quantity, using the best methods at the right time. The quantity of irrigated water required as well as the method, time and number of irrigations is determined, and finally a suitable agricultural cycle (cropping system) is devised.

Under arid conditions, reclamation and land cultivation require large expenditure, much of which goes on digging wells and land preparation, while the remaining part is absorbed by equipment and seeds. It is therefore particularly important that the geographic, economic and social factors which affect the use of technology in farming are fully taken into consideration. The particular technologies of water distribution and utilization can strongly influence tillage technology. For example, some irrigation systems prevent or make more difficult the use of agricultural machinery. As a result, returns on costly investment can be unnecessarily low. For technical and economic success, the availability of suitable personnel for field operations in both phases is absolutely critical.

For the *engineering phase*, irrigation engineers are centralized in the General Directorate of Project Execution for projects in Riyadh. They collaborate with other workers for Public Land in preparation for utilization, for example, levelling operations, irrigation and drainage channels and land divisions.

Soil specialists – one fully qualified person in each area – can assist directly with the *agricultural phase*, by carrying out some field soil analyses and using the three mobile laboratories to determine the quality and availability of soils. Qualitatively, salinity, ESP/calcium carbonate ($CaCO_3$) ratio, etc., are all important in addition to the physical properties and other methods of reclamation for each land type. Once land has been reclaimed, the soil scientist will be required to monitor changes in the soil, also to calculate fertilizer requirements, and so on. The treatment of sandy soil, for example, differs from the treatment of clayey soil in preparation for irrigated farming as well as requiring specific precautions against deterioration.

The soil specialist usually provides the most important technical support to the new farmers in achieving maximum exploitation of land with minimum expenditure through the best methods for conservation and maintenance and in keeping the land in good productive status at all times.

When the *planting procedures* are reached, then the soil specialists should be mainly replaced by the irrigation agronomists. There are very few of these, centralized in the Research Department's three research stations located in Hafuf, Qatif and Qasim (Unaizah) and frequently their duties have to be performed by the nearest available technologists – the soil scientists. In co-operation with the extension officer and using soil survey data, the irrigation agronomist is required in calculating the quantities of water needed for irrigation, and so suiting this to the type of soil, as well as to the crop to be planted. Together, both can decide on likely crops and cropping patterns together with correct and suitable fertilizers and trace elements for plants and crops in the light of other studies – for example using phosphate fertilizers for lands where the rate of calcium is high. Chemical and other natural characteristics can differ so widely from place to place that it is necessary to determine specific methods and crops fitting for such characteristics. The expansion of cultivated areas has produced a need not only for regional surveys but also for regionally-specific recommendations on a very large scale – even after rapid preliminary survey. Agronomists, whenever possible, and extension officers are then responsible for the follow-up, step by step, of the development of the new land in co-operation with the new utilizers.

In addition to the above-mentioned direct and indirect relations between the soil specialist and land utilizers, the specialist can assist the local PLD committees by explaining the technical reports received by PLMD and evaluating the actual land investments made by the allottees during the probationary period of land holding. It is important therefore that soil specialists should be operational in each area where Public Land Distribution exists. It is intended that this should be done, but progress depends on the availability of Saudi and non-Saudi specialists.

Supporting Services

Success in any agricultural development depends ultimately on extension work, including financial, technical and even social aspects in a co-ordinated manner.

Agricultural Services and Extension

It is important to note that extension workers are not usually acquainted with land reclamation and settlement techniques as their work is generally connected with improving existing farm systems.

Accordingly the presence of irrigation engineers, irrigation agronomists and soil specialists, technically trained to assess and exploit unused land potential, is not only important but also necessary for PLD schemes. The lack of such trained personnel is, however, at the moment unavoidable and, for the time being in Saudi Arabia, the work of these specialists has to be carried out by extension workers. The bulk of the PLD work in the field executed by extension workers is in fact at the *planting procedures* stage involving crop adaptation, husbandry methods, and so on.

Field Organization

There are 63 Field Organizations situated in the agricultural areas in the country, divided into 11 Directorates, 21 Units and 31 Offices (Fig. 9–1). Most of these Field Organizations have a farm or nursery belonging to or rented by the Ministry of Agriculture and Water. There is always a Directorate situated in an important area. The administrative attachment of these Field Organizations is to the Extension Department of MAW but technical personnel (and their fields of work), operating within the Field Organizations are attached to their respective Departments of the Ministry.

The Field Organization is staffed with technical personnel, for example, the Extension Agriculturalist, Plant Protection Agriculturalist, Veterinary Doctor, and their Technical Assistants, but there are twice as many administrative staff as there are technical staff. It is a fact that all Field Organizations suffer from the same lack of technical personnel as do the technical departments within the Ministry. There is a great demand for qualified and experienced technicians and the shortage is only met by foreign assistance through private contract, private firms and bilateral agreements (see Table No. (11–3)).

The extension service is the backbone of the Ministry of Agriculture and Water, but, to become an effective service, severe reorganization is required. A strengthened extension service would facilitate the work of Public Land Distribution, the adoption of selected productive systems and improved farm practices.

Subsidies

In Chapter Seven (pp. 115–121) the farm development – small irrigation schemes – subsidy alone was discussed. These schemes, which are directed to Land Distribution Development are still being planned and money has not yet been allocated. Other subsidies which here require consideration are discussed below.

DISTRIBUTION OF FIELD ORGANIZATIONS

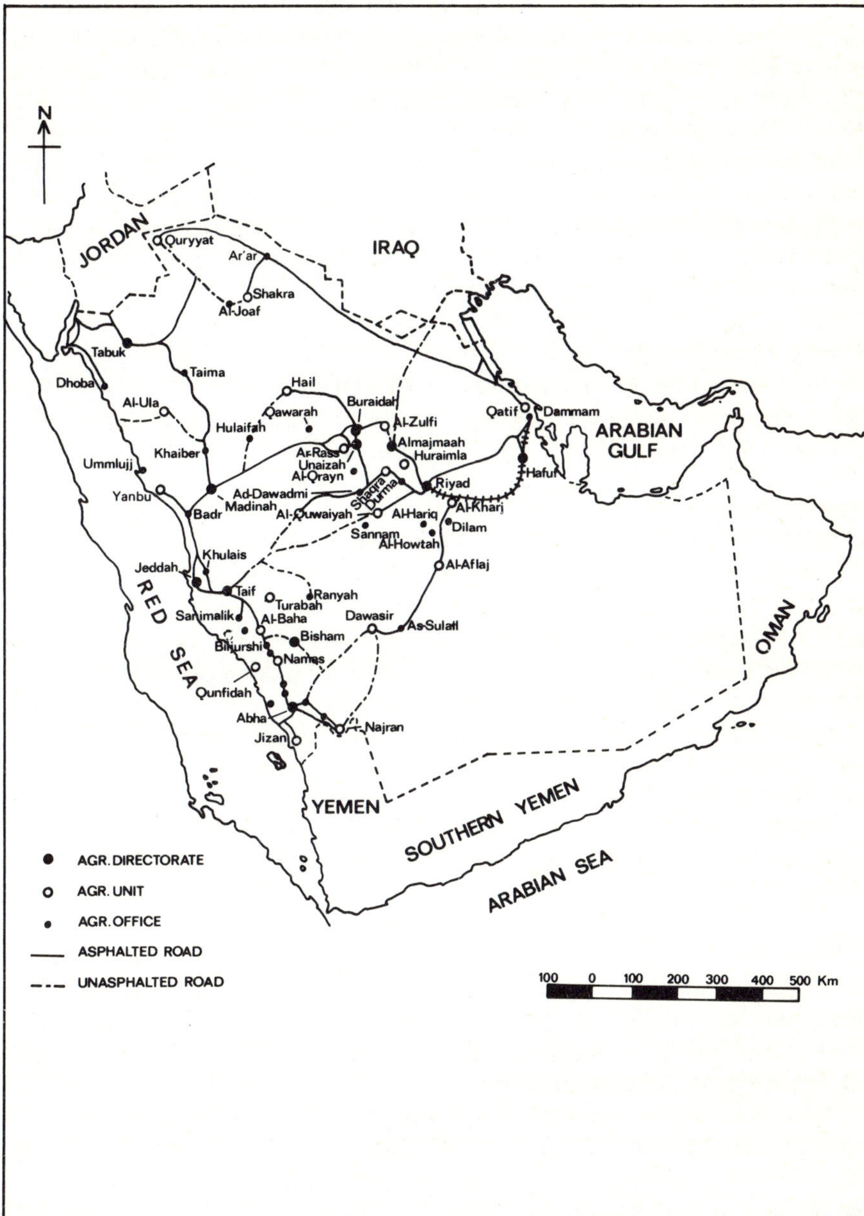

Fig 9·1

Agricultural machinery equipment

Until the 1391/92H (1971/72) budget, MAW owned a fairly large number of tractors and machines. Machine services at a low cost and furnished through Agricultural Field Organizations have included those of land levelling and preparation. These were sold with a reduction of 45 per cent and 25 per cent of their actual price, to co-operatives and farmers respectively. MAW allocated in the Budget for 1392/93H (1972/73) an amount to subsidize agricultural equipment for wheel and track-laying tractors and their attachments, land-levelling equipment and harvesters, mowers and threshing equipment. These subsidies are offered through the Saudi Agricultural Bank. Agricultural Bank branches and Field Organizations have only to supervise the use of equipment in agriculture.

Concentrated feed

On 10/6/93H (1973) the Council of Ministers approved a subsidy of 50 per cent for concentrated feed for poultry, cattle and sheep. This subsidy was originally in the Economic Plan.

Fertilizer

Cabinet Ministers also approved a subsidy of 50 per cent for the cost of fertilizer, both imported and produced locally. In MAW budget for 1392/93H (1972/73), money was allocated for this chemical fertilizer subsidy. A local fertilizer factory (SAFCO) exists in Saudi Arabia, for manufacturing nitrogen from oil gas to provide urea and ammonia fertilizers. Imported fertilizers are mainly compound NPK types. Fertilizer imports into Saudi Arabia increased from 1,477 tons in 1373H (1953) to 4,179 tons in 1385H (1965). At present it is estimated at about 5,000–6,000 tons yearly. Its consumption in Saudi Arabia is still low and only 2 to 5 per cent of farmers are applying fertilizer.[51]

Subsidies for wheat and rice: These are proposed but not yet framed.

Financing Credits

These are facilitated by the Saudi Arabian Agricultural Bank. This Bank was established by Royal Decree No. 58 dated 3/12/83H (1963) with a capital of 10 million SR, since increased to 53 million SR, increasable, in loan operations.

Its objectives are to give loans and financial facilities required in the agricultural development of the country and it provides a number of services including: firstly, finance for cultivation, stock raising, storage and marketing of crops, livestock, poultry, fisheries and forestry products; secondly, for land reclamation; and thirdly for financing the facilities required for the provision of water needed for the purposes mentioned above.

Loans started being made in 1384/85H (1964/65), and the Bank gives loans to persons, societies, companies and organizations in Saudi Arabia working principally in agriculture. These fall into three categories.

Short-term loans for the purpose of farming seasonal crops. Such loans should not exceed twelve months. The number of loans increased from 52 in 1384/85H (1964/65) to 1,730 in 1389/90H (1969/70).

Medium-term loans. These should not exceed five years. They are mainly for purposes such as the establishment of farms, wells and channels, the purchase of livestock, poultry and machinery and the reclamation of relatively small farms and other medium-term investments. The number of loans increased from 573 in 1384/85H (1964/65) to 2,563 in 1389/90H (1969/70).

Long-term loans. The date of recovery of loans for the reclamation of large-sized farms might reach twenty-five years.

The Bank has no right to give the above-mentioned loans except after verifying within reasonable limits the probability of loan settlement.

Most loans were mainly made for irrigation equipment at the beginning of this scheme and these represented over 70 per cent of all loans made. This percentage has decreased whilst the percentage of loans for other purposes has increased, such as animal and poultry, animal feed, fertilizer, constructions and seeds.

Table No. (9-1) The percentage of total loans in 1384-1389H (1964-69).[51]

Item	*1384/85H (1964/65)*	*1385/86H (1965/66)*	*1386/87H (1966/67)*	*1387/88H (1967/68)*	*1388/89H (1968/69)* %	
	%	%	%	%	*Short*	*Medium*
Engines	39	48	41	43	—	37
Pumps	36	28	17	15	—	16
Drilling and constructions	11	8	16	27	4	15
Fertilizer and seeds	5	7	3	3	5	5
Livestock, poultry and fodder	4	4	9	8	24	15
Wages	—	—	3	6	34	—
Ploughing and levelling	—	1	3	2	22	2
Miscellaneous	9	4	8	4	11	11

Since irrigation in Saudi Arabia relies on ground-water, irrigation engines and pumps have been the main types of equipment obtained with loans from the Bank. For the period 1385–1389H, the number of loans for engines and pumps given were 7,440 and 4,655 respectively.[51] The Bank also gives loans for fallow land. The broad meaning of "fallow land" in Arabic in this context is land left uncultivated seasonally or not cultivated but owned by registered certificate.

Fallow land plots of small area (up to 1.5 hectares) which depend on hand-dug wells are granted loans for several specific purposes. First, normal water-pumps not exceeding 8 hp engine with all accessories, second, a plough or operational hours of ploughing or levelling by tractor not exceeding 360 SR can be used on medium duration loans of five years against non-transferable guarantee. Third, short-term cash loans for transfer and installation of irrigation equipment, and fourth, *short-term* loans in kind, for example, oil, diesel and seeds can be made.

When a farmer has reclaimed the land and cultivated some of the area with fodder crops, he will be granted another *medium-term* loan for four years for animal husbandry purposes.

Fallow land plots of medium area (1.5–4 hectares) irrigated from surface wells are treated in the same way as those mentioned above, except for equipment which will be more expensive. Some *short-term* loans may also be given.

Fallow land plots of medium or large area, irrigated from artesian or deep wells are granted loans for suitable irrigation equipment for five years against non-transferable guarantee as well as having the facilities noted for plots of small area above.

Loans for Public Land Development

According to Saudi Agricultural Bank regulations, strictly speaking, none of the new utilizers of land under PLDO should obtain loans because all applicants should provide the Bank with the ownership deeds when they ask for loans. Such ownership deeds can only be issued after the probationary period of three or more years has passed. Therefore, in giving the developers financial facilities during the probationary period and to ensure the repaying of loans given to developers, the following special steps are taken.

The Agricultural Bank, according to the instructions given to it, does not finance well-drilling operations in Public Lands but instead it asks land utilizers first to drill the wells with their own resources and the Bank will afterwards supply loans for irrigation and other equipment.

Special conditions are laid down when an allottee applies to get a loan from the Bank, thus:

1. The allottee who forwards a real estate guarantee may be given a loan for a period of five years.

2. The allottee who cannot forward a real estate guarantee can submit a sponsorship guarantee and may be given a loan for a period of three years.

The allotment decision "deed" may be mortgaged in advance as a guarantee in accordance with PLDO and its Operational Procedures, but only after getting written permission from MAW (see Form No. 7, Appendix I).

Article Four of the Bank's Ordinance, however, states explicitly that long-term loans may be given for the purpose of relatively large sized lands reclamation. The meaning of "reclamation" is interpreted in two different ways:

(a) From the scientific point of view, it means the mechanical and chemical operations that change the land from non-arable land to productive land, such operations being the leaching of saline soil, removal of hard pan from the bottom of soil profile, the establishment of drainage channels in lands having high water-table, and large levelling operations in lands having an uneven topography and which require this levelling if they are intended to be exploited.

(b) The technical meaning of the term "land reclamation" on the other hand is the preparation of land for agricultural production such as supplying the principal production means, for example, simple levelling operations, ploughing and the establishment of irrigation channels.

Since Public Lands which are going to be distributed have already been proved to be economically feasible to develop, usually through cultivation, they do not need the operations specified in interpretation (a). Therefore, it can be held that for PLD purposes the relevant meaning of land reclamation in Article Four of the Bank's Ordinance is that stated in interpretation (b). In this way the allottees can get *long-term* loans and repay them in instalments according to the product of their lands.

Extension of *medium-term* loans to ten years is sometimes necessary in order to give the farmer an opportunity to invest in the most efficient way, especially in the case of the farmer who drills a well at his own expense. Preparation of land takes time before the farmer can repay the loan from his agricultural income. Insisting that the farmer repays within two or three years makes him short of money and unable to apply adequate programmes. The Ministry of Agriculture and Water has therefore supported the idea of extension of *medium-term* loans but extension of the date due on *long-term* loans is still under discussion in the Ministry of Finance and National Economy.

To provide successful opportunities for the financing of allottees and to help them utilize their lands for the best purposes, agricultural and extension programmes should be applied alongside the financing operations. The farmer's choice whether or not to follow these programmes (see pp. 144–150) is then controlled by monetary discipline.

The Bank now has a branch in Qasim, and the need for having a branch in Tabuk after land distribution began became clear. This branch, connected with the Madinah Branch, began its work in Tabuk on 1/1/1391H (1971). The Bank issued the eighth annual report about its activities in the fiscal year 1391/92H (1971/72), and this included a summary statement about Public Land Distribution with a special note on the Tabuk area as follows:

"The Public Land Distribution programme is developing and the Ministry of Agriculture and Water has declared that more than 3.5 million donums are subject to distribution. Moreover, other areas are to be distributed. Tabuk area was one of the first areas where distribution took place as water was available therein. The Bank offered the beneficiaries suitable loans for drilling the wells and flowing water was found in most wells in the Tabuk area."

This means that the costs of utilization will not be as great as if pumps were required and each well can irrigate up to 100 donums. In Wadi Sarhan a committee from the Bank visits the agricultural areas from time to time to satisfy any needs, but a branch has not been established due to staff limitations and higher priorities in other areas. It was asked for by MAW when the Bedouin Settlement Project was ended (see p. 132).

Supporting infrastructure

Co-operative Societies: The co-operative movement began in Saudi Arabia in 1340H (1921). Within a period of ten years there were 39 registered co-operatives up to 1390H (1970) serving more than 17,000 members and a capital of 3.5 million SR (Fig. 9–2).

The Ministry of Labour and Social Affairs supervises co-operative

Table No. (9–2) Location and types of co-operatives as of 1389/90H (1969/70).[20]

Type	*Central Region*	*Eastern Region*	*Western Region*	*Southern Region*	*Northern Region*	*Qasim Area*	*Total*
Agriculture	—	2	3	1	4	1	11
Consumer	9	3	2	2	1	1	18
Services and Electricity	2	—	3	1	2	—	8
Women's activities	—	—	1	—	—	—	1
Vocational	1	—	—	—	—	—	1
Total	12	5	9	4	7	2	39

CAPITAL SIZE DEVELOPMENT IN CO-OPERATIVES

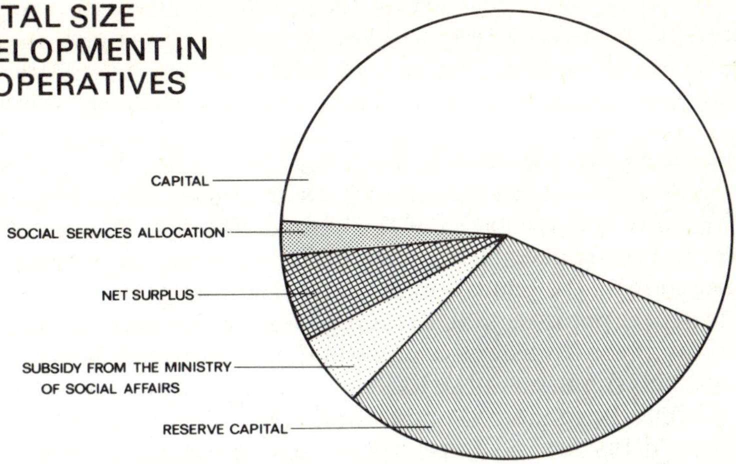

REFERENCE: Report of The Ministry of Labour and Social Affairs, 1349H page 345

Fig 9·2

administration, registers, and regulations. Co-operative activities include the procurement of agricultural requirements such as seeds and fertilizers, but in the area of agricultural co-operation joint responsibility is held with the Ministry of Agriculture and Water.

The slow growth of co-operatives (see Fig. 9–3) is due to the lack of co-operative officers and an absence of understanding of the real benefit that co-operatives bring to farmers.[51] For instance, a subsidy

CLASSIFICATION OF CO-OPERATIVES IN THE KINGDOM ACCORDING TO THEIR TYPES

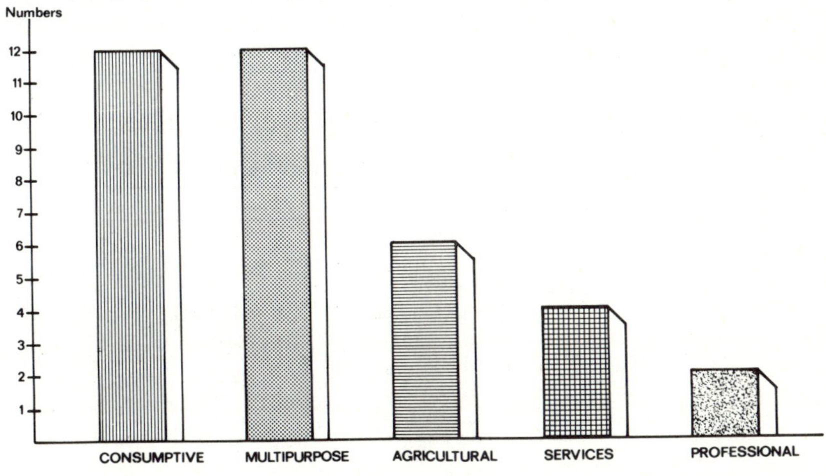

REFERENCE: Report of The Ministry of Labour and Social Affairs, 1349H, page 353

Fig 9·3

of 45 per cent for agricultural machinery is given to co-operatives while the subsidy given to individuals is ony 25 per cent (see p. 150). Agricultural co-operatives are an answer to the difficulties of many small new utilizers of Public Land to be found in this country.

Community Development (CD)

Saudi Arabia began a Community Development Programme in 1380H (1960) with the assistance of the United Nations. The first Articles of the CD Law stated the objectives of community development as: "in order to raise the educational, health, economic and social standards of the rural population in the Kingdom, on the basis of extending the services of the Ministries concerned to the rural area in a co-ordinated manner to supplement the local efforts, community development projects are to be organized in the rural area".[1]

The Ministries of Labour and Social Affairs, Agriculture and Water, Education and Health, are participating in this programme, each Ministry concerned providing the technical staff required. The Ministry of Labour and Social Affairs is to provide the project directors, the male and female social workers and clerical staff. All agricultural equipment and implements required for the implementation of the agricultural self-help projects, such as well-drillers, selected seeds and fertilizers are to be provided by the Ministry of Agriculture and Water. Agricultural services include pest control, distribution of seedlings, chemical fertilizers, demonstration plots and farms.

The local community is helped by a multi-sector approach method which deals with all aspects of life (economic, health, social and cultural) in the community. Since there have been no previous studies on the social and cultural background of the country, community development as a concept has had to begin from a zero point and to stand on its own.

Centres provide services to about 170,000 people in 58 small towns.

Table No. (9–3) The distribution of community development centres.

Zone	*Rural CDC*	*Urban CDC*
Northern	1 – Qurayyat	1 – Unaizah
	2 – Ha'il	
	3 – Hawailan	
Western	4 – Qob'a (Madinah)	2 – Madinah
	5 – Wadi Fatima	3 - Makkah
	6 – Turabah	
Middle	7 – Ad-Diraiyah	4 – Riyad
	8 – Laila (Al Aflaj)	
Southern	9 – Khamis Moshait	
	10 – Jizan	
	11 – Al-Hassa	5 – Qatif

These centres are facing the same difficulties as co-operatives. It was found that the UN concept of Community Development could not achieve success in Saudi Arabia, mainly due to the fact that the principle of reliance on the initiative of the people has not yet proved workable.[45] The need for local initiative to develop social and economic resources puts them under a strain far beyond their capabilities. At the same time there were State funds for assisting co-operative societies which were never spent in the CDCs, because they could not satisfy the UN concept criteria.

Community Development is a process of controlled social change. In its application, it acknowledges specific historic-political, socio-economic and cultural peculiarities and adapts for them. It respects the religious values and beliefs of the people. As a concept it remains an important humanizing influence since our age is the age of planning. Planning has become State policy and planning has become the means of the State control.

Marketing

The Saudi Arabian market is oriented to private entrepreneurship and a relatively free market where there are no restrictions on trade. The agricultural export is negligible compared with the import; the import of agricultural and water equipment and materials is essential for agricultural production. The import of food materials similar to the local products while superficially beneficial to the consumer may depress local effort unnecessarily.

Marketing problems are in fact one of the chief limitations on agricultural development because of existing deficiencies in the basic marketing facilities.

Communication and transportation studies point to the urgent need for rural roads on which the trucking rates per ton/kilometre are sometimes over three times the rates on hard-top roads. There is consequently geographic variation in prices and also unfair marketing practices based on volume and price variations in supply and demand. The trans-peninsula paved highway is a big step in the right direction though a comprehensive system of farm-to-market roads has not yet been achieved. Other roads and current feeder roads studies portend additional significant progress.

The development of product standards, through grading, standardizing and packing to minimize physical losses and reduce cost is essential. Packing and grading facilities may be provided as an activity of private entrepreneurship.

Storage and refrigeration needs for maintaining perishable vegetables and fruits are great. Storage facilities will have to be provided to reduce the seasonal variations in price. The Ministry of Commerce has an active and long-standing interest in these industrial areas of agricultural production and it already creates and implements standards for agriculture and food products, studies specific standardization problems for local produce and advises on measures for preventing the adulteration of foods.

To summarize: the opening up of new land presents the Kingdom with challenging opportunities of establishing model farming based on modern agricultural knowledge and practices.[34] The success of land development depends very largely upon the establishment firstly, of the right kind of organizational set-up; secondly, upon the financial assistance to and public investment in a new land development infrastructure; and, thirdly, upon the technical assistance available. Land distribution and development is a complicated and difficult task requiring great skill and the co-ordination of different agencies.

As usual, Ordinances in Saudi Arabia signed by H.M. the King have outlined the policies and left the details for the operational procedures to be developed out of working practice. This system makes modification to include more detail relatively easy as long as, through administrative feedback, such additions are accepted by higher authorities.

Chapter Ten

A Comparison with non-Saudi Muslim Land Distribution Policies

Here we have chosen a group of countries so that we can compare and discuss Public Land Distribution, management and related problems. Libya, Syria, Iraq and Egypt were chosen because they have great similarities in their background of land ownership, derived not only from the Islamic religion but the economies, soil and traditional ways of life. The areas in which we are interested are countries which are desert areas with a rainfall of less than 4 inches. Saudi Arabia and the other countries are similar in that they have very large arid lands but their efforts to develop land in the past and present, by one way or another, for the benefit of their citizens have not been uniform. For the sake of this comparison we will limit ourselves to discussing the development of ideas, regulations and categories of Public Land management. As a result of this examination we can note similarities and differences and lead on to the identification of important matters of principle.

Syria and Iraq may be considered as an extension of the Arabian Peninsula arid region. They have practised Land Distribution in the past but with different approaches and different conclusions. In Syria and Egypt, agriculture is the backbone of the economies. In Iraq this dependence is less striking and Libya has great similarities with Saudi Arabia from the point of oil revenue, physical characteristics, and the needs of infrastructure (Fig. 10–1).

When Islam spread from the Arabian Peninsula to the neighbouring countries such as Iraq, Syria, Egypt and also Libya during the Islamic conquests, Crown Lands and State Lands were established. These were called *Fai'* lands (community property) (see Chapter One, p. 9). The remaining lands were left undistributed, occupied by farmer cultivators for as long as they paid land tax (*Kharaj*) to the State. In this early period a great number of landholders were, and remained for some time, non-Muslim. The land itself as property became State domain held for the whole community. When non-Muslims embraced Islam they were given equal ownership rights according

COMPARATIVE LOCATION MAP

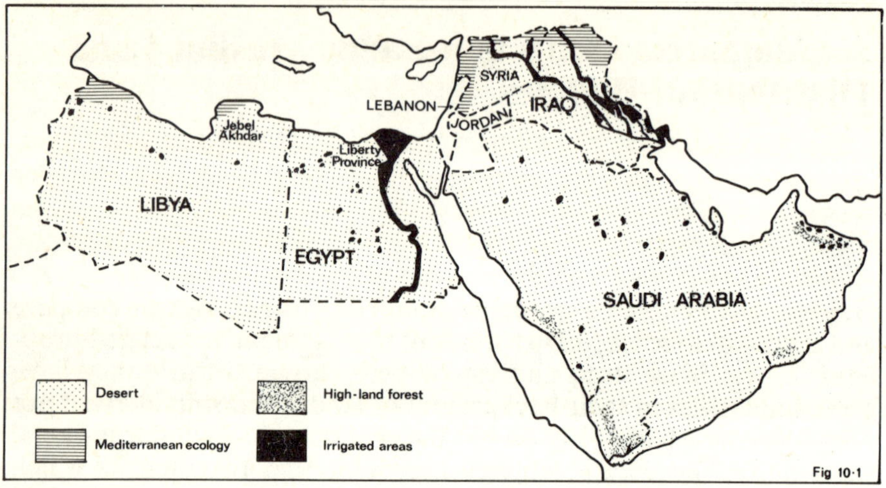

to Islamic law. Formerly non-cultivated lands (dead lands) were declared State Lands which could be distributed to Muslims by permission of the rulers.

Changes through time brought the land systems nearer to basic Islamic principles. The clerical work was usually left in the hands of the natives. Community property land which was cultivated by tenants was well recognized in these countries. As has been said before, the desert is a common inheritance shared in all four countries. The process of settlement was generally similar everywhere outside the riverine lands of the Nile and the lower Tigris-Euphrates lowlands. The original tribes were, of course, pastoral nomads following seasonal pastures with their herds of camels, sheep and goats.[22] When they found that cultivation was economically advantageous, they began to settle. These groups occupied and used dead lands as they desired and held them, where possible, against rivals. They exercised the effective control of these lands on a day-to-day basis.

The Ottoman Code introduced in 1278H (1858) for land and right registration systems (*Tapu* in Turkish or *Raqabah*, meaning "neck" in Arabic) was a bureaucratic innovation whose main purpose was to establish an imperial claim in order to tax every piece of land.[58] Land ownership needed registration and this led to taxation. It has also led to the establishment of a form of individual ownership different from the communal rights held by tribal sheikhs. The State, as owner of the land title (*Raqabah*), collected one-tenth of the crops produced, according to the Islamic system of *zakat*, and could give the right of utilization to somebody else when the land fell free. This transfer was subject to the payment of a certain registration fee or due to the holder of a grant from the Ruler (Sultan). These land grants came to be considered as *mulk* and developed as private estates, not taxable in their own right. Turkish land codes brought about this situation in many other areas of the Ottoman Empire.[41]

One particular characteristic was the way in which great land estates originally granted for bureaucratic purposes became transformed into private properties, in which the traditional Islamic safeguards for the community's and individual's right to use land became weakened and sometimes destroyed.

If we compare countries that were ruled by the Ottoman land code and land registration (*Tapu*), we find that these were supplemented, amended and amplified by subsequent Ottoman legislation or orders, always designed for purposes of administration and bureaucracy. Effectively they applied to all cultivated areas. Bedouin claims based on traditional usage were limited not to lands actually tilled for cultivation, but to the bordering desert and steppe. As they were sometimes pushed into the desert they still claimed lands they had abandoned. These are called customary prescriptive claims to land and were also in the past called *lazma*.

The Ottoman land code failed to settle land title, especially in Libya, Syria and Iraq. To be successful, any land system must be suited to local needs and conform to local ideas and conditions. In Saudi Arabia, the tribal system grew in value and the Bedouin concept of territory was only affected by outside forces during the Ottoman period and to a limited extent in Hijaz and in Al-Hassa. King Abdul Aziz built up Saudi Arabia out of conquest and land control rested on the power of the King as a real chief of tribes who commanded tribal allegiance (see Chapter Two, p. 17). As such, the whole land concept in Saudi Arabia has grown up from different roots to those affected by the Ottoman system.

Libya

In the past, one must regard Libya in part as Mediterranean and also in part as Arab. First, there was a pre-Islamic period when the major part of the coastal zone was dominated by the Greeks. This zone has been Mediterranean rather than Arab for many centuries; being close to European countries it has been strongly affected by them and their culture.

Second is the Islamic period of water and land systems during which tribal strength was based mainly on the Jabal Akhdar and the deserts of the interior, both relatively unaffected from outside (Fig. 10–1). During the Turkish period an amalgamation of elements of Ottoman Civil Code was applied. The Turks were concerned with collecting taxes through sheikhs of the tribes, as cash on each head of herds and a tenth of the harvest. The working relations between Bedouins and Turks seemed satisfactory, largely because of the absence of Turkish interference with tribal and pastoral groups.[41]

It seems that the land tenure system in Libya is a mixture of tradition and law. It was customary for the Ottomans to conduct a general survey of the land of subject territories and assess the revenue which could be exacted from the indigenous people. The Turks could not control the semi-nomadic tribes and their sphere of influence was limited to the coastal oases.[22] This is why Arab inhabitants were affected only to a minor degree by the Turkish regulations. Before the Italian occupation, nevertheless, the tendency in land ownership towards the end of the Turkish occupation was for communal *mulk* to be transferred to private *mulk* particularly in the coastal areas. State ownership of land was poorly developed in Libya during the Turkish occupation.

The more recent and short-lived Italian period had as its main policy colonization by Italians. The result was the destruction of all customs and laws that hindered Italian colonization. Tribal, Islamic and adopted Ottoman elements were all pushed into the mountains and the interior containing a mixture of strategic and less fertile areas. There was also Italian suppression of any tribal resistance and revival.

The third period is that of the Libyan Arab State. The new State was formed by a crystallization of tribal localities. It took over all the rights held by Italians, but the re-creation of a fatally weakened tribal system proved impossible and the new fluctuating situations brought confusion. Then came oil which freed the State of many of its economic limitations.

There are now two main elements in land control. Firstly, there remained some traditional customs and assertions of partial claims by the remnants of the weakened tribal system, with attitudes to territory rather than land, based on usufruct and ancient rights handed down from one generation to another. Secondly, there is the insistence of the newly emerged State on its central right to allocate land and to determine its use, the location of State Land, and also land disputes. It was indicated in a FAO study that "the rights of possession on tribal lands are vague and the ownership of much tribal land is disputed between the tribes and the State. However, it is widely recognized that the rights of the occupants are only the rights of usufruct while the State holds the property title known as *Raqabah*. Furthermore, tribal lands are not registered in either the name of the State or in the name of the resident tribe. Tribes, sub-tribes and individual tribesmen all claim rights of long-standing usufruct."[17]

Legally speaking, as almost all tribal lands in Libya are not registered, they are considered as State Domain. Nevertheless selling and buying of tribal lands is carried out according to tribal custom and usage and any regulation of individual action has to come from the sheikh of the tribe. The tribesmen have the right to veto any transfer of land and each segment of a tribe lays claim to the land it wishes to cultivate or graze at any time. This would seem to indicate that tribal tradition is stronger than religious rules and Government laws.

Libya has two main features which give it some similarity to Saudi Arabia: nomads which made up about 80 per cent of population before the discovery of oil, and oil revenue. Libya has now become the second largest oil producer in the Near East, ranking after Saudi Arabia. In its area of 1,750,000 square kilometres, in 1385H (1965), the population was estimated as two million of which 75 per cent were engaged in agriculture as settled cultivators or nomads.[17]

The background of Libyan agriculture was similar to that of Saudi Arabia in that livestock and livestock products were dominant and have been the most important items of export in the past.[23] The majority of the rural population were nomads and semi-nomads living under traditional conditions and subject to harsh climatic forces, sand, wind and rainfall hazards. There is a large total area of non-developed cultivable lands and thus there is also a future for agricultural development, and particularly for land settlement.

In 1374 (1954) the expressed agricultural aims were to establish settled farming in all areas suitable for individually owned-commercial farms, and the reclamation, development and distribution of State-owned lands. Observations and experience in Libya indicated that nomads and semi-nomads are willing to lead a settled farmer's life provided physical, economic and social factors permit them to do so.

Experts in land settlement planning, rural sociology, land registration and farm management were needed, especially to establish the recording of land titles and to advise on the establishment of the necessary Government services to develop the programme in the future.

Three main decrees regulating tribal lands were promulgated: one in 1341H (1922) covering registration of land property; the second, Law No. 9 of 1379H (1959) dealt with tribal conflicts over land; and the third, Law No. 12 of 1383H (1963) covered compensation for confiscated lands. The development of tribal lands and the resettlement planning of former Ente farms were both important for nomadic sedentarization.

Libya approached land distribution through a National Agricultural Settlement Authority, NASA, which was established in 1383H (1963) and attached to the Ministry of Agriculture as a Public Agriculture institution.

It has the authority to distribute State-owned dead lands, appropriated for agricultural settlement, by usufruct agreement or on a lease basis or contract for a specific period. It has also the authority to transfer to users waste lands that have potential for production. It also has other responsibilities such as the development of agriculture on all such lands, increasing agricultural production and the improvement of rural areas in general, through:

1. The development of farms, wherever they may be, which have reverted to the ownership of the State from a former development.
2. The encouragement of individuals to reclaim and develop their own virgin lands.
3. The dissemination of co-operative consciousness among the farmers and encouraging them to organize or join co-operative societies.

This vast power and responsibility is, however, very much beyond the present capacity of NASA and it also brings NASA into conflict with the Ministry of Agriculture and other authorities.

Legislation was promoted in 1388H (1968) to limit the functions of NASA to the settlement areas only and at the same time community development in these areas was to be co-ordinated by the specialist authorities. It is clear that NASA began as an autonomous authority for Land Distribution and settlement with other big associated responsibilities. Then its status was depressed and its functions limited to settlement areas only and for settlement purposes. In Saudi Arabia by contrast, the Public Land Management Department is a governmental body within a single Ministry, growing with less original authority and its responsibility limited to the period before the distributed lands are cultivated.

Land distribution in Libya carried out by NASA falls under two main categories. First, the Dead Land, dry farming land and newly reclaimed land for new settlement are mostly located in the Jabal Akhdar region. They depend on rainfall, ground-water or mixed water resources.[27] Because Dead Land reclamation requires special experience, technology and funds, NASA is reclaiming and developing the land before distribution takes place. Distribution is then carried out on either a private ownership or on a lease basis according to conditions. Second were the "Ente lands" including ex-Ente lands mostly located in Cyrenaica (Tobruk) and Tripolitania. These lands were inherited from the Italian government and classified as:[29]

Lands still under the direct control of the State Property Department, but mostly leased by individual farmers.

Holdings or lands legally belonging to the State, but in effect "owned" by individuals or tribesmen with no fees paid to the State Property Department. Moreover, State ownership is not recognized in these cases because the people claim that these lands belonged to them before the Italians confiscated them and these holdings have been reoccupied by the farmers.

Holdings in dispute between the Government and tribes. The Government pays annual fees to some of the previous owners and while this is not regarded by the Government as proof of title it gives strong support to the legal claims of the rest of the claimants.

Where the tribal farmers have occupied the Ente estates on the basis of previous claims they consider the Ente farms as their traditional home territories (*watan*) and in this case any payment to the State is held to represent only rent for buildings. The Ente farms have been valuable in demonstrating clearly that under good management and utilizing advanced techniques of exploitation, many areas could be made to produce valuable trees and field crops and could support a rural community at a relatively high standard of living. Their takeover also proved that such developed land was very sensitive to misuse which could damage fixed capital, produce land deterioration and a regression away from commercial farming.

It is clear from the evidence that Libya, with a mixed inheritance of land systems, land tenure and land appropriation, has experienced many difficulties. In Libya, land development precedes a contract or lease basis of distribution and so Land Distribution is more like a simple distribution of restricted titles. Thus the efforts of individual utilizers are limited in ways, whereas in Saudi Arabia, in order to ensure cultivation, land is distributed for utilization before the grant of private ownership is given.

Libya, like Saudi Arabia, in no way reflects the tendency in other parts of the Middle East for the rise of a dominant landowning class.[41] The inhibiting factors behind this fact are mainly negative. First, in both countries poverty in the nineteenth century discouraged investment in real estate and made it difficult for any individual to accumulate large amounts of fluid capital for land purchase. Second, the dominance of traditional tribal economic and social life gave no real opportunity for the development of a powerful landed interest. Third, the shortage of water for agriculture, the main physical obstacle to economic development made landlordship less attractive traditionally than, for instance, in Mesopotamia. This last can in time and with modern technology now be overcome by the application of more capital to the land.

Libya, like Saudi Arabia, increased the output of its agricultural sector between 1382–1387H (1962–1967) but as a proportion of the national income this has fallen to 11.5 per cent.[29] The discovery of oil and its impact on other sectors has in both cases accelerated the migration from rural to urban areas.

The first development planning in Libya, 1382–1389H (1962–1969), was devoted to physical infrastructure such as roads, harbours, airports and social sector (housing, schools, hospitals, education, etc).

The second development planning phase, 1389–1394H (1969–1974), was concentrated on social services sectors besides the development of non-oil sectors, of which agriculture is one. In general this is similar to the Saudi Arabian Development Plan. But still in Libya's Second Plan the greatest portion of allocation of capital to agriculture, about 40 per cent of the total, is to be allocated to marketing, credit and subsidies. These are absolutely vital if production is to be expanded. In the case of Saudi Arabia, subsidies were started a little later, in the 1392/3H (1972/73) budget for wheat production, fertilizer and farm machinery equipment, and marketing facilities await the completion of the infrastructure plan.

The similarities in general between Libya and Saudi Arabia exist on the basis of physical characteristics: of the tribal system, the potentialities and also the planning for future development. Dissimilarities grow out of basic differences in historical experience, many of which follow macro-locational differences. Affected directly by more external forces, Libya has inherited a complex series of laws concerning land control and, in its recent independent history, has less clear tribal characteristics. Libya tackled this situation by establishing one semi-governmental body dealing with all aspects of land control and distribution. Most important was the attempt to digest land once prepared for cultivation but then evacuated and much less important, the Dead Land not previously tilled.

Rights on tribal land are defined by one law as either complete individual ownership, right of usufruct or specific rights in relation to the State. Settlement areas are reclaimed first before distribution, and once the land is ready for distribution, already developed, it is to be utilized on a lease and contract basis.

In Saudi Arabia, cultivated land inherited by the State from previous régimes is mostly in Al-Hassa and in a few small-scale areas. These are utilized on a contract basis and managed by the Ministry of Finance and National Economy. Land claimed as tribal land and previous settlement areas such as *Hejar* are differentiated as either private ownership in case they are cultivated or Public Land in case they are not cultivated or utilized, this very much following *Shari'a*. The only semi-governmental body or corporation concerned with land was formed for the preparation of the Bedouin settlement area in Haradh.

Public Land in Saudi Arabia which has water and soil potential is the concern of a governmental body, the Public Land Management Department. As PLMD continues to grow it may reach a stage when it is strong enough to be established as a semi-governmental corporation with co-ordination authority. At such a stage it would be in a position to pursue Public Land development with more freedom from governmental structures and to co-ordinate its work more completely with other community authorities.

Finally, in Libya, marketing has had a remarkable backing. This may be due to the fact that Libya, in the past and present, has been more open to trade and exchange as a result of its Mediterranean location and position between sub-Saharan Africa and Europe.

Syria

Land laws and regulations in Syria are by origin a mixture of traditions and laws, the latter being imposed in the fifteenth century by the Ottomans. Enforced sedentarization of many of the tribal groups of the interior was accomplished through the growth of tenurial contracts between the *effandi* class who, like the Mogul zamindars had become acknowledged by imperial authority as landlords, and the Arabs who tilled the land, in many cases as hired labourers on a share-crop basis, and undertook to reclaim land on the basis of crop-sharing until the peasant finally acquired land for himself.

During the French mandatory régime Ottoman laws were amended.[47] One law passed in 1346H (1926) is of interest to us as confirming the existence of two categories of State Land. Firstly, there was Public Domain Land which was registered in the name of the State, and was at the disposal of the Directorate of State Domain. Secondly, there was the land over which the State claimed formal possession according to the Muslim concept. The Old Ottoman prescriptive right was given legal status by this law so that persons who brought non-cultivated land into cultivation could acquire ownership if they could prove a period of cultivation. For the occupation to be legal, a licence from the State was necessary.[58] The Muslim concept of State ownership only retained its validity for unregistered land, which could be land in the effective rather than the legal occupation of individuals or land non-cultivated and unoccupied.

The French also passed a decree in 1361H (1941) whereby desert Bedouins' territorial boundaries were laid down in favour of Bedouin chiefs.[47] These boundaries included vast sparsely populated areas which could be treated as State Domain. At that time a head of tribe or a head of a group (a "notable one") could register Common Land (*mushaa*) under the name of the head of a tribe or under a name of an individual instead of a group or a family.[58] This created private landowners with very large estates. Also registration took place for non-cultivated land or vast desert areas which were not able to be cultivated by a person or group in the past. Some registration of grazing right for a group or tribe took place, and in time such groups came to feel that this was a sort of private ownership. In all, the effect of these decrees was both to increase communal land and also to create absentee ownership by individuals who had been able to obtain registration title but who were not themselves cultivators. The decrees ruled out any central control by a Public Domains Administration.[47] By contrast, in Saudi Arabia, King Abdul Aziz completely abolished both traditional tribal rights for pasture and tribal collectively-owned districts in 1345H (1925) and, by implication, created a larger concept of State Land which later could be regarded as Public Domain.[17]

After independence, Syria was faced with Bedouin entities owning very large estates on an individual or collective basis, besides the absentee private ownerships, all created by the French. The Syrian constitution and early Government was not in a position to abolish these ownership conditions. As a result, the law of 1369H (1949) was passed to regularize the existing situation and administer the domains and desert land in a way almost similar to the Ottoman Code. A tendency to establish individual ownership continued, the idea behind this being further to break down the Communal Lands and secure individual titles to plots of land.

The law of 1372H (1952) which declared that all *mawat* lands (Dead Lands) were subject to the administration of State Domain, still validated private ownership titles but put an end to the strictly illegal occupation of what could be considered State Land by tribal groups. It declared that only title deeds to specified areas were to be recognized. The law stipulated that no new prescriptive titles could be acquired over *mawat* lands because they had not been recorded in the registers of Immovable Property or in those of State Domain.

Unregistered State Land in these circumstances could not be retained on the basis of customary law which was now not recognized, but neither was its occupation legal on the basis of the Civil Law. Title was still valid for *mawat* lands for any area not exceeding 200 hectares per person and a similar area for every member of the family of the recipient. This could allow a fairly large unit of 2,000–3,000 hectares for a family, by implication referring to range land with some dry farming.

Because the concept of State Land was still not positively defined, this law brought confusion to the legal status of occupants of unregistered State Land. In Jezera, which is extensively cultivated, 1,000 hectares is considered a small farm – the International Bank recommended 1,000 hectares as a single maximum for Syria – and in Syria there is no shortage of land. In these circumstances, a partial limitation on areas held seems strange. Large-scale cultivation needs heavy investment and also large-scale resettlement by the State requires working capital and public services, which the Government sometimes cannot afford. If private enterprise were to develop unused but usable land, limitations on effort would be counter-productive to new land development. It was therefore left to the Syrian merchant class to consider investing its capital in mechanized agricultural use of the largest possible holdings of available land. This produced not only a group of absentee landlords of relatively small holdings as in the neighbourhood of Aleppo and Damascus but also large commerical land exploiters.

In Syria, in Damascus, merchants and city notables began to be absentee owners and held agricultural lands in the distant countryside – similar to the notable men in Florence in the thirteenth century, where they and other *borghesi* held most of the countryside of the Tuscan region. Grain production was emphasized on the new land and almost doubled between 1363H (1943) and 1373H (1953). The national revenue of Syria relies mainly on agricultural production.

Under the 1373H (1953) law, action was taken for the distribution of tribally occupied land to its individual Bedouin occupants. "In this case the State has not distributed land to new owners but has confirmed the tribesmen's right to hold individual ownership of land formerly occupied collectively."[58] This gives the tribesmen the right to take an income from the merchant tractorists who cultivate the land. It gives the *Sheikh* of the tribe who has more capital than other tribesmen an advantage through tractor ownership to obtain direct income and more prestige, a similar position to that of the Iraqi *Sheikhs* with capital for pumps and irrigation equipment.

Also in 1373H (1953) a Government decree controlled the conditions for distribution of the State Land to individual purchasers at a price equivalent to 25 per cent of its real value and for plots up to 50 hectares. Warriner noted that there is no need for a general measure for redistribution of ownership because the land is sparsely populated and any further available land would not be cultivated by investing entrepreneurs, unlike in Egypt.

In Syria, during the 1370s (1950s) the country appeared to be developing and there was no need to think in terms of maximum and minimum holdings on the new large, mechanized, mainly wheat-growing estates. Here, holding grants not only ensured the farmer an adequate living standard, but should have enabled him to produce for a growing market and receive adequate returns on investment. It was the hope of the *medium-* and *large-scale* Syrian farmers to retain the lands already owned or received. On the other hand, the landlord–share-cropping peasant relationship in the longer occupied and used lands did produce social and economic unrest for frequently the merchant landlord was no more than a rent collector. The reaction to this latter situation was excessive and in 1378H (1958) drastic land reform (during the first UAR), was introduced, imposing *everywhere* a maximum 80–120 Ha. irrigated or 300–400 Ha. holding rain-fed land for an individual landowner and/or with a family respectively.[58] This blindly followed Egyptian Land Reform but was even more rigid in that it did not permit private sales of land to small farmers as the Egyptians did. This law was ultimately reversed because it was felt that it did not suit Syrian conditions or even satisfy many claimants. However, grain production was reduced (though cotton was increased) to almost half the level in 1378–1380H (1958–1960) compared with the average of 1370–1374H (1950–1954). In 1382H (1962), an amendment of this law was approved, raising the maximum holding from 80 to 200 Ha. for irrigated land and from 300 to 600 Ha. for rain-fed lands;[58] even this, in production terms was an unsatisfactory compromise.

Looking at land laws in Syria, we noted at the beginning that they are a mixture of traditions and laws. The laws first imposed by the Ottomans were modified out of recognition by the French. Independent Syria turned back to the Ottoman system then followed the codified Egyptian Land Reform approach and has now finally begun to consider real regional needs.

Saudi Arabia did not experience this confused history. It began with tradition, was affected only to a limited extent by the Ottomans and has mostly recognized the need for regional adaptations. In Saudi Arabia there have not been any radical and severe ideological changes such as those in Syria. Syria, which began with tribally-rooted attitudes to land, has not yet developed modern legislation capable of integrating traditional and modern social economic customs.

Syria, a country with an agricultural background, has a very large land and water potential available. Still sparsely populated by tribesmen, merchants have increased individual and private enterprise investment but have only tapped part of this potential; whereas in Saudi Arabia oil revenue is the main source of national income and there has been not as much incentive for private commercial agricultural development; tribesmen's and merchants' interests have not seriously conflicted. Syria has still to develop its agricultural resources and, through agricultural exports, obtain foreign currency for equipment and infrastructure.

Iraq

During the Ottoman period there was no general registration for the settlement of title. In the northern parts of Iraq grants for registered title were made around the towns. In Southern Iraq the code was not applied even in theory. People were afraid of military service and the taxation implications of registration.[58]

Up to the end of the Ottoman period, the basis of land ownership was the tribal *dirah*, a large area not limited to land actually tilled, but including also non-cultivated land or sub-marginal marsh land, over which the tribe exercised a customary right of occupation. The customary tenure of the land – as collective ownership – belonged to the whole tribe. Tribesmen cultivated land collectively. Grain products were divided between them and their *Sheikh* to provide and maintain Arab hospitality. The *Sheikh*, head of the tribe, spoke on behalf of the tribe and was responsible for communal welfare. In a sense, each tribe was a miniature State.

In the north, land tenure originated as in Syria where dry farming predominated. In the south the matter was more complex. Land and water are more than plentiful but with very ancient irrigation systems with complicated requirements, land control was also more complicated. Between the Tigris and Euphrates (see Fig. 10–1) requirement duties for irrigation, such as strengthening the river banks and canal clearing, needed tribal organization and a pseudo-managerial structure in which sub-*Sheikhs* and minor *Sheikhs* were appointed as managers on behalf of the Head *Sheikh*.

By the end of the twelfth century H (nineteenth century), grain trade and export possibilities increased throughout the Arabian Gulf.[57] The profits motivated tribal *Sheikhs* to strengthen their power to acquire land as personal property. Such profits came through pump irrigation which was introduced to some two-and-a-half million acres. The pumps were installed by *Sheikhs* and city notables who developed a landlord status in which the position of share-tenant in terms of security, income, etc, was much worse than in Syria. *Sheikhs* took up to 80 per cent of the crop, sub-*Sheikhs* worked as bailiffs, and rack-rented share-croppers led a bare existence.

After the Ottoman period an extraordinary feature in Iraq originated from the very large estates held by tribal *Sheikhs*. The *Sheikhs* became estate owners, and in the south they owned, together with merchants and other large owners, all of the land. Tribesmen became share-croppers with no rights or status, neither individual owners nor labourers. This occurred because during the mandate bureaucracy period tribal land associated with *Sheikhs'* names in the capacity of Ottoman tax collectors became owned by the *Sheikhs*. Registration of title was carried out under the Land Settlement Law of 1352H (1932), which gave the Government the right to settle the title of the land and established the procedure of registration, and, due to the strong pressure from tribal *Sheikhs* to introduce a system of land registration for their benefit, most *Sheikhs* succeeded in registering tribal land as their absolute property.[57] This conferred legal rights on a previous customary tenure. After the *Sheikhs* really became estate owners, they stopped taking traditional responsibilities for tribes or tribesmen. Land belonging to the villages was registered as a village headman's property. The great holdings thus are tribal in origin and have only recently become private property as a result of the appropriation of tribal land by the tribal *Sheikhs* in the twenty-six years (1352–1378H 1932–1958). During this period, production was in fact doubled as changes in land tenure were accompanied by expenditure on canals, pumps and drains in the south and by credit systems in the north. Nevertheless, compared with its real production potential, Iraq emerged with low agricultural productivity and a depressed peasantry.

Dawson recommended that the settlement of title should come after land surveys. The land cultivated by each tribe should be registered as leasehold tenancy from the State.[22] This was not done.

The Land Reform introduced in 1378H (1958) concentrated on land distribution and ignored specific conditions in Iraq: people, land, physical characteristics, oil revenue, vast arable areas, tribal society and low productivity.[59] This law closely followed the Egyptian Law of 1372H (1952) whereas the agricultural situation in Iraq was completely different. Agricultural production in Iraq fell even further after the law was passed. Grain production was 17 per cent, rice 20 per cent, cotton 16 per cent.

No land surveys were carried out before land redistribution which proceeded, very slowly, over some five years. The expropriation of privately owned holdings of more than 250 hectares irrigated land and 500 hectares dry-farmed land was ordered and the land distributed to occupying cultivators in plots ranging from 7.5–15 hectares irrigated land and 15–30 dry-farm lands. Co-operative societies were introduced for new owners, theoretically with modern and wider scope.[59] The Law of 1378H (1958) also included provisions covering the distribution of State Domain and of land held in unsettled title. State Domain which includes grazing or other uncultivated lands is still undefined, and while the scope for Land Distribution was much wider, it brought conflicts with tribes and heads of tribes. Iraq was faced with problems in the north (similar to those of Syria) with notable merchants.

Here Land Distribution was interpreted only as title settlement, carried out through land registration without any clear development policy by the governments, and without forecasting expected results.

In Saudi Arabia, national policy from the beginning sought to avoid large estate creation and *Shari'a* was applied to solve claims. No development of crop-sharing was allowed in tribal areas and registration was carried out mostly for existing cultivated areas already in private ownership. No great land-grabbing merchant class developed. In Iraq Land Reform Laws emphasized the concept of maximum limits for dry farming holdings, whereas in Saudi Arabia laws were regarded as pertaining to investment in uncultivated lands, a totally different concept. Since the investment in uncultivated land is not fully detailed in the Islamic Creed, local traditions were applied to them (see p. 22) but traditions differed from one province to another, reflecting different environments and adaptations of them. Thus local traditions were applied by judges. In northern Iraq, the Ottoman code of equal division was followed, which leads to the break-up of holdings, while in the south inheritance falls to the eldest son and holdings are kept undivided. In Saudi Arabia *Shari'a* law was generally applied in which all sons have equal shares and daughters have a half share. This of course leads to land fragmentation.

Egypt

The identification of holdings in Egypt was initiated by decree in 1299H (1878); an appreciable cadastral survey was carried out and completed in 1326H (1906). Turkish legislation had also recognized the necessity of a foundation of reliable cadastral surveys for land tenure. Three-and-one-third million individual holdings were recorded during this settlement,[22] comprising most of the cultivated irrigated land. However, in Egypt as elsewhere in the Middle East the place of the nomadic pastoralist must not be forgotten.

There was a continuous stream of nomadism entering Egypt in the past from the Western (Libyan) Desert and the great deserts to the east (see Fig. 10–1).

The process of assimilation of these groups can be divided into five different types.[14] Firstly, absolute nomadism by pure non-assimilated nomads has survived together with, secondly, the semi-nomads, travelling only short distances but not sedentarized. Thirdly, there was partial assimilation where Bedouins occupied the agricultural zone immediately adjoining the desert and served as guards, this zone appearing only around cultivated areas. In time they became numerous and claimed the pieces of land on which they had grazed their flocks. Such land claims were cumulative and were the chief method of acquiring land by one-time nomads. The possession of land led generally to fuller assimilation in sedentary society as a fourth step, as the value of owning land was realized. Later, intercourse with cultivators helped to bring nomads socially closer to sedentary communities and encouraged them to turn to agriculture. Often still living socially as nomads and retaining tribal structures, in time they were assimilated completely into peasant society. Now, almost all nomads in Egypt are assimilated in this way, producing the main differences between Egypt and Saudi Arabia.

Egypt is the gift of the River Nile, the source of irrigation for the main agricultural areas. It is one of the most populated countries in the world with high cropping rates, high yields and high inputs of water and fertilizer.

A great majority of land holdings are less than one acre in extent and until recently[59] most of them were components of very large estates, almost feudal in character, extending to several thousand acres in which farmers worked as both labourers and tenants with the capital provided by the owner.

The dominance of very small operational holdings is mainly a result of the highly concentrated demand on land which created a man–land ratio problem.

The dominance of large land ownership units, however, as a socioeconomic and political phenomenon is the result of particular responses to environmental forces. As in southern Iraq, the demands of irrigation agriculture are for a structured and ordered complex of social, economic and technical elements. In pre-Islamic times and surviving through later periods including that of the Ottomans, the Egyptian response has tended to be autocratic politically as well as technically. During the nineteenth century the financial rewards obtainable by concentrating on one major cash-crop, cotton, encouraged commercial landlordism but concentrated capital and revenue as well as land in the hands of a few great landowners and entrepreneurs.

By the 1370s (1950s) there appeared, from the point of view of Land Distribution no alternative to major reform and this was based on ideological change. The implications were a radical change in the distribution of land ownership as well as social change, controlled and co-ordinated in rural areas through co-operatives acting as financial mechanisms and to maintain the high yields already achieved.

This situation is completely different from that of Saudi Arabia where there is no such pressure of population or feudalism and where there is available capital and the possibility of practising agriculture in an extensive way.

The ideology in Egypt is to increase production even on formerly highly productive estates. Capital theoretically can be provided and services supplied through official co-operatives. Egypt had become too dependent on cotton exports and there has been a swing to vegetable and fruit export. Farm areas in Egypt can be extended only, and at great cost, by new irrigation schemes. Land Redistribution Reform can only solve local problems and be designed to maintain agriculture as the main source of income and wealth.

If we look at the laws concerned with Public Land, Agriculture Reform Law No. 178 dated 1372H (1952) stated that an individual has the right to own *any* Public Land, fallow land and desert land areas beside the maximum limit of existing cultivation of 200 Faddans (F) for an individual and 100 Faddans for a family.[36] (One Faddan equals 0.42 hectares.) That Law was replaced by Law No. 148 in 1377H (1957) where the maximum Public Land so owned was limited to 200 F. Beside this area, 100 F of cultivated land for an individual and 200 F for a family were fixed as maximum limits but the desert land was still left to unlimited claims.

Public Land as such started to be identified under these Laws until Law No. 119 dated 1379H (1959) further clarified the situation of Public Land to be reclaimed and prepared for distribution. In 1381H (1961) the modified Law No. 127 classified Public Land and Desert Land as in the cultivated land category. The maximum limited area (for any land type) was not to exceed 50 F for an individual and 100 F for a family. In 1383H (1963), Law No. 15 laid down that foreigners have no right to own any type of land (Cultivated, Public or Desert). In 1389H (1969), Law No. 50 limited the maximum ownership area (individual or family) of any kind of land (Cultivated, Public or Desert) as not to exceed 50 Faddans.

Public Land, unutilized, could be sold under tenure to individuals in favour of its reclamation, in units of not more than 50 Faddans each. It could be distributed for reclamation by an individual in units between 2–5 Faddans. Such individuals would have to guarantee reclamation within 7–10 years in "cultivated" and desert areas respectively. Its cost should be paid by a 20-year credit with an interest rate of 3 per cent but in case of cash 10 per cent reduction would be given. The owner has no right to disposal during the period of reclamation and, if several individuals are involved with contiguous plots, tenure would be determined by a committee. Desert Land could be rented in units of not more than 10 F for individuals.

Looking at the development laws of Desert Land in Egypt, one finds that there is no attention paid to desert (in the sense of non-irrigated land) at the beginning owing to the priority paid to cultivated land. When the need appeared, as population pressure continued to grow, laws limited the permissible area of allocable arid land until finally all land, not matter what its quality, was controlled in the same way. The aim is to avoid the creation of very big estates, in the knowledge that an individual's capability to develop true desert land could be ignored. The expansion of the new agricultural areas which are mostly located in the deserts depends upon irrigation potential and mainly on the expansion of Nile Water utilization. Land Distribution in practice is entirely limited to reclaimed land for new settlers who were farmers chosen from heavily populated and congested areas.

It is clear that there is a complete difference between Saudi Arabia and Egypt especially from the point of social and physical backgrounds. This is in part the effect of long periods of alien rule in the case of Egypt. Saudi Arabia has a tribal background and it is not affected so much by others. Its people reject radical change and have been able to maintain Islamic Land Concepts. Capital is available for building up infrastructural services and individuals are encouraged to develop the new land. Mostly these are Bedouin with little previous agricultural experience. The promotion of land utilization, relying on State subsidies, credit, services, and other facilities to back development by individuals is part of a new Land Development Policy of agricultural expansion, while in Egypt Land Distribution has had to concentrate on a social egalitarian approach to increasingly scarce resources.

General principles which can be considered from Saudi and other examples

First, all the conditions in Egypt were unique to that country. Almost all Bedouins were assimilated in the distant past. The Egyptian land title settlement, begun in 1299H (1879) and completed in 1326H (1906), referred completely to intensively irrigated cultivation. During this period a cadastral survey for land tenure was achieved.[22] All three-

and-one-third million individual agricultural holdings which existed were recorded. It appears that there was no need for a Public Land in the sense of Dead Land policy in the past because unutilized land was virtually unusable for tillage. As settled population has increased, however, laws and regulations have gradually developed and Government control has had to be extended universally because of the shortage of land resources.

The matter was different in Syria, Iraq and Libya, originally tribal areas in which change has been relatively recent. As in Saudi Arabia and Iraq, the discovery of oil has no doubt contributed to the sedentarization of many of the nomads and to the growth of the semi-nomadic segment of the population. Although the pure nomads of Iraq live in the interior of the desert around the borders of Saudi Arabia many of them have been able to work in the oil fields as labourers, drivers and guards and to build homes near these fields. They have sent their children to schools and become more and more associated with urban life.

Sedentarization is not an end in itself, but a means of bringing nomadic populations into the mainstream of economic growth and social change. Problems do not end when nomads are settled; on the contrary there emerges a new set of problems which cannot be solved easily. Important differences exist among individual countries with regard to the techniques which have been adopted in the effort to stimulate land development. In recent years, Egypt and Syria have undertaken a programme of socialization and Iraq has taken steps towards a more collectivist organization. But as yet it seems uncertain as to how far in this direction it may wish to go. On the other hand, Saudi Arabia has continued to foster and encourage private enterprise. Libya is in a transitional state and policies have not been clearly framed.

From this discussion it appears that each country has its own distinct setting for land distribution. The chief lessons learned from the countries discussed are as follows.

1. *No legislation can be simply and successfully transferred from one country to another*

If a particular régime is successful in one country, this may be because it was designed to satisfy certain specific conditions and regional needs, that is, there has been care and devotion in the design.

Saudi Arabia's capability to meet, through the framework of modern legislation, its needs[47] during its development was made possible mainly by a combination of tactfulness and firmness on the part of Saudi rulers. King Abdul Aziz during his rule over fifty years was a fine example. They were able to persuade the *Ulama* (religious learned people) to accept such modern innovations as the radio and the wireless, and also to control the speed with which others pursued change.

It is true to state that policies framed to fit a defined national situation are more likely to be effective than those which are not.[47]

2. *Laws and regulations should be flexible and designed in broad terms*
Countries are faced with many unforeseeable problems and difficulties during the implementation of land laws, some of which cannot even be taken account of in theory. If such laws are designed in broad terms to meet basic requirements, it is much easier to make modifications according to local needs and changing circumstances.

In the case of Saudi Arabia, whenever there was a need for a new regulation, it was issued by the King and was framed in elastic and in broad terms.[47] Concerning Public Land, the use of the land must be in accordance with legal justice. Legislation expresses the social policies of the country and must be adaptable to the physical characteristics of the land and human adaptations to these characteristics.

Details dealing with flexibilities can be left to administrative regulations and procedures. This means that it is desirable to have a simple and general written ordinance which expresses the social policy of the country and to have clearly established administrative procedures to carry out this ordinance.

3. *Avoiding the build-up of large estates prevents much land-control trouble*
In Syria and Iraq, land tenure problems originated in the building up of very large estates. King Abdul Aziz abolished traditional tribal rights during his effort to unify the country of Saudi Arabia and in so doing removed the basis at least for large-scale individual takeovers of tribal rights. PLDO was designed also not to build up very large holdings.

4. *There should be no confusion over land tenure, land titles and land appropriation*
Some of the countries discussed ran into a series of difficulties because land control had no clear conceptual base. In Saudi Arabia, the master key is still the *Shari'a*. King Abdul Aziz intervened in major tribal claims on the basis of *Shari'a*, while other minor claims could be simply referred to *Shari'a* courts. Ultimately in Saudi Arabia it is the concept of utilization and usufruct which underlies all.

If *Shari'a* is applied, land left unutilized for a period of three years has its ownership rights cancelled and the land can return to the State as custodian for the whole people. Equally if a utilizer can prove that during three years he has constructed a dwelling, planted trees and improved the land then his individual rights can be registered in his name free of any fee. But always there must be proof of productive and serious use, which, if proven, cannot be dismissed by ideologically based action.

5. *Avoiding radical change is vital*

In a community that is highly tribe-integrated and deep-rooted, it is dangerous to introduce strange legislation which does not derive from what is already accepted, especially if this does not satisfy cultural, ecological and economic requirements.

Land Reform in the full sense is faced with many difficulties. The standard package of recommendations on Land Reform is irrelevant to appropriate Land Distribution policies for Saudi Arabia where there is no population pressure on land. The wealth and prosperity of the Kingdom does not require a limiting of enterprise. There is also the simple practical point that the granting of land to a potential farmer is of no particular benefit to him unless water is available and this implies effort on his part given some technical and financial assistance.

6. *Tight managerial programmes are not applicable for land development everywhere*

In Egypt, policies for agricultural development were linked, either before or after, with general development planning and carried out in tightly controlled managerial operations with expanding provision of services to farmers.

Tight managerial operations of this sort are really impossible in countries with backward agriculture and administration which is still in the process of being developed and has severe personnel shortages.

7. *The avoidance of small-size holdings if there are other possibilities*

In Egypt, the underlying forces behind Reform Policy imply the acceptance of an average farm size of one Faddan. This makes mechanization almost impossible.

If a country has a peasant population already attached to the land, willing to work hard on small farms, it is wrong to crush this initiative, but if a country has abundant land relative to demand, it would be wrong to try to make small farms, for there is scope for enterprise and growth.

8. *Advantages of ownership*
The evidence is in favour of granting ownership to individual landholders or rights to individual land use to a group holding ownership. The advantages of ownership are that it provides what people generally want, and what agriculture needs. It does not automatically transform utilizers into efficient modern farmers but it generally provides a suitable foundation for improvement. Change for the better is the most that can realistically be expected.[47]

An effective Public Land Distribution Programme is therefore aimed at increasing ownership *per capita* and not at the redistribution of individual ownership as land reform does.

If we accept these general pragmatic principles, it can be claimed that all have positive morals for Saudi Arabia. These lessons will also allow us to proceed to discuss those elements which could be utilized to make the optimum use of land distribution.

Saudi Arabia differs from most countries in four major aspects which affect the planning of land development and agricultural production.

1. The development of agriculture as a result of the exploitation of newly-developed water resources will always be confined to well-determined and relatively limited areas.
2. The distances between centres of production and consumption are very great and the possibilities for economic development in the intervening regions are remote.
3. The commercial possibilities in these separated centres are such that communications which cross the negative intervening areas are vital to allow the increased volume of production and consumption.
4. Climatic conditions in spite of aridity are sufficiently favourable to permit agricultural production to increase substantially.

As we pointed out before on p. 158, Saudi Arabia is developing and flexibility exists for creation, strengthening, modification or change when need arises.

To sum up the discussion: vigorous development and settlement programmes entail sufficient resources for land preparation, establishment and perfection of a water system, adequate extension, provision of sufficient farmer training, educational facilities, an operational farm credit programme and the provision of marketing facilities. The result of these activities and the rest of a complete package of improved practices can result in rapid development if economic incentives are provided.

Chapter Eleven

Variables Which are Specific to the Saudi Situation

Middle Eastern peoples have come to realize that they live in one of the most vitally strategic regions in the world and that it has become essential for the survival of their countries that they should be fit for a rugged world in which only strong and prosperous nations can survive. Revolutionary techniques were adopted in order to bring about the desired changes in some parts of the area; elsewhere non-revolutionary developments have been regarded as appropriate. Saudi Arabia falls into the latter category.

Saudi Arabia as a major unit in the Middle East joined the race possessing two basic features. Firstly, it emerged in the twentieth century with a basically independent past and an almost unique Islamic cultural purity. The acknowledged existence of deeply-rooted traditions and social values was responsible for the survival of urban village and Bedouin communities with territories of their own, in the sense of accepted occupation. Secondly, it represents a rather conservative outlook in governmental attitudes towards innovation.

The communities composing the new State were characterized by almost complete isolation, certainly from major world movements and even largely from each other. The Government, in its forging of the State and aided by oil revenue, undertook expanding programmes of economic and social development, including education, communication networks, free health services and social security, and it has adopted a programme for economic development without making any demands on the people other than an acceptance of controlled and cautious change.[45] In so doing, it aims to retain these positive aspects of existing social habits and traditions consistent with the religio-cultural values of the whole community.

It can be observed that the people have become very concerned with the establishment of services in their community as a basic duty of the State. These services are necessary for development, notably the supply of expert advice and training, modern techniques and capital and sometimes equipment. In this concept, the State at the present time is regarded by its people as acting as the representative of the whole society, performing the functions of the Arab chief who had the full responsibility for the moral and social welfare of the members of his tribe.

Fifty years ago the rulers of Saudi Arabia, as part of these duties, adopted a general policy of land distribution. The basic concept of their right to do so is already accepted. The PLDO was issued six years ago and is now one of the basic tools to achieve the goals of national policy. The PLMD has been established for the implementation of the PLDO. It has fitted itself between different Governmental bodies, administratively placed within the Ministry of Agriculture and Water with co-ordination responsibilities as regards the Water Resources Development Department, Water Conservation Department, Agricultural Services and Extension Department and Agricultural Field Organization. Also, outside of the MAW, the PLMD has functions of collaboration especially with the Agriculture Bank, the Ministry of Interior (notably the town planning offices), the Ministry of Finance and National Economy (Public Domain) and the Ministry of Justice.

PLMD is therefore one of the established means of promoting the national interest. But what is the national interest as regards land and land use specifically in Saudi Arabia – excluding mineral and urban land and limited to Public Cultivable Land? In Public Arable Land use we are dealing with a set of complex economic, social, political and resource aspects and therefore other questions arise. What is the right place of Land Distribution in Saudi Arabia economic development? Is it to slow down the movement of Bedouins to urban areas by opening up areas suitable for their sedentary settlement? Is it for the increasing of production by encouraging exploitation of areas not utilized for agriculture before? Is it a matter of socio-economic stability? And, finally, is it mobilizing natural resources of arable land and water which are economically available?

The following discussion attempts to analyse the strategy of Public Land Distribution in terms of these questions.

In Saudi Arabia, the basic facts are as follows. In the first place, large nomadic populations exist which do not have specific titles to land but which demand socio-economic equality with their settled and urban compatriots. Libya has similar features. Secondly, relatively small and separated new areas of potential agriculture are being established for cultivation, this as a result of very recent resource surveys. Thirdly, there is a large rural population on small-holdings, rural under-employment, and a shortage of skilled manpower. Fourthly, the whole country, rural and urban, has a high exposure to imports, a high national capital availability and a general shortage of skilled manpower. Finally, Saudi Arabia, technically, economically and socially is in a transitional period. It is a country with a sparse population, comprising separated small-holdings that need lengthy intercommunications. It suffers from marketing difficulties and cost-distances which make provision of the services extremely costly.

These complex factors make Saudi Arabia a unique case and fundamentally affect all technical considerations.

Agriculture and population

The rural, basically agricultural population includes both settled and nomadic peoples. Within it, migration and labour mobility must be examined with reference to particular factors and processes.

Push-Pull factors: both the push factor from apparently unattractive rural areas to urban centres and the pull factor, the attraction of people to metropolitan areas are well-known in modern countries. In these, non-agricultural attractions of employment have produced no fall in agricultural production, since it is causatively associated with capital substitution for agricultural labour, due to mechanization and the application of new rural technologies.

In developed regions, for example Europe, the released rural labour always originated from a developed agricultural sector. As agriculture developed in technology and organization, the rural labour released was absorbed by the industrial sector and the latter sector, as more development was achieved, enabled more rural labour to be released. In Saudi Arabia this push-pull factor now exists in an embryo form.

In the Eastern Province the oil industry pulls labour from Al-Hassa and Qatif Oases where the agricultural population is decreasing. This is not due, however, to an increase in rural productivity, but to the growth of the oil and service sectors, the towns created along the Arabian Gulf and the consequent non-rural socio-economic "pulls". As a result of this, agriculture and animal production might fall. Now the already developed oil sector cannot possibly directly employ more labour because more capital-intensive investment methods are used.

In Al-Hassa and Qatif, there is a confusing situation. Date palm production, traditionally dominant, does not require much work, needing large labour inputs only for seasonal collection of produce. During other periods the date mostly needs a water supply but it is not very demanding. Even without irrigation, given the high water-table existing in the Oases it can survive and give some production. There are no statistical data available but there is observational evidence for a shortage of agricultural labour. Dates are left without trimming or wild grass clearing and so, while there is little or no contraction of the cultivated area, there is neglect and some decrease of under-palm cultivation - of alfalfa, for example.

Government employment opportunities for rural Bedouins, for example, in the National Guard, have greatly increased.

The urban areas attract labour to the general employment opportunities which come with oil affluence. A large number of taxi drivers in towns and lorry drivers in the long distance freight transport now growing were originally Bedouins. The towns also attract other people because of available high education and better residential accommodation. Despite this movement of labour from agriculture to towns which is necessary for urban functioning, the objective should be not to release such labour on a large scale but to slow down the rush to the towns in view of the present rapid population growth in the main urban centres, a growth which is already producing social and economic strains.

In the newly-settled lands labour shortages are now evident though these are regionally diverse. Generally the non-rural employment attraction even in these areas can result in immigration mainly into non-agricultural employment, as in Tabuk and other towns along the Tap line, where capital and cash-flow is greater than in the countryside. Therefore, the newly-settled agricultural lands which do in fact attract some labour have to compete with the greater attractions of the towns.

At the same time, there is concealed unemployment in the agricultural sector.

Estimation of non-utilized agricultural labour in Saudi Arabia, 1382/83H (1962/63).

1. Total cropped area, in acres, surveyed in 1382/83H (1962/63)	500,030
2. Total farm labour force	155,906
3. Cropped area per head of the labour force (1 ÷ 2)	3.2
4. Number of hours available per man-year (300 days at 8 hours)	2,400
5. Average number of hours required per cropped acre (assumed)	500
6. Number of hours of actual working per worker (3 × 5)	1,600
7. Actual work hours as percentage of required work hours (6 ÷ 4)	66.6%
8. Percentage of non-utilized hours per man-year (100 ÷ 66.6)	33.4%
9. Total available man-hours (2 × 4)	374,174,400
10. Total non-utilized man-hours (9 × 8)	113,468,385
11. Hypothetical surplus labourers (10 ÷ 4)	47,278

This estimate (the only one carried out) indicates that the available work time in the agricultural sector is much more than that hypothetically required. On this basis agricultural production could increase without any further growth in the labour input factors. The paradox that there is concealed unemployment in the agricultural sector, while at the same time wages for agricultural labourers are high and there is a labour shortage, is a result of both economic and social factors. Relatively, cash incomes are even higher in the urban areas where the demand for labour is continually growing. Socially, manual farm labour has never been well-regarded in status and the smaller agricultural areas are less attractive than the towns for social facilities. On a national scale, therefore, we find that the size of the agricultural labour force as estimated above is larger than the actual number of full-time agricultural workers. Some land holders who will describe themselves as farmers do not in fact till the land themselves – even in some newly-settled areas. In other cases, particularly in the older established Oases of the Eastern Province, the holders of land may now regard farming as a secondary occupation and, in fact, expend very little actual time on their holding. In the southern area, Jizan in particular, dry-farming, as in other countries, leads to highly variable seasonal demands for labour which when averaged on an annual basis will indicate statistical under-employment. One final result is that the hypothetical surplus labour, because it is voluntarily rather than forced to be under-employed, is not available to meet the demand implied by agricultural labour shortage and high wages.

In most developing countries, the low incomes obtainable in the agricultural sector, and sometimes land shortage, encourage the young working-age males to emigrate to work. The agricultural population which is left is then often supported financially by remittances from their relatives working in other sectors. This often means that human power – labour and motivation – shifts from the agricultural sector and production either decreases or stagnates.

In Saudi Arabia, the matter is completely different. Its characteristics, as noted in Chapter Seven display features both of developed and developing economies: oil-wealth, urbanism, cultivation and nomadic Bedouin. Great inter-regional diversity exists in the balance of emigration and immigration.

Unfortunately, there is a shortage of statistical information concerning these movements which have yet to be studied. On the one hand, there is the immigration of Yemeni labourers mainly, but not entirely, into agriculture. On the other, there is the abandonment of difficult highland arable land in Asir.

At a time when the growing oil revenues, through Government expenditure and investment, have enabled increasing demands for agricultural products of all kinds to be met by imports, domestic agriculture has not yet been able to compete in the growing market. In order to achieve this, Saudi Arabia has the physical capability of bringing new agricultural areas, free from many traditional operational constraints, into production.

Public Land Distribution among individuals, groups or tribes is one of the procedures taken in this context, but lands are distributed on condition that they shall be utilized and PLD can only be of benefit if utilization is effective.

Bedouins cannot simply adopt modern techniques for agriculture, they need demonstration, training and services providing them with the necessary good seed, fertilizer and other facilities. This is clearly essential in Tabuk, Al-Joaf and Wadi Sarhan. In Qasim the human ability to handle advanced techniques of exploitation is greatly superior and the area could be made to produce valuable products.

It is worth mentioning here that gradual settlement programmes differ from complete or full development projects, for example, Haradh, in the grade and rapidity of change implied in traditional type of living, and at the same time they do not need a revolutionary swing to modern technological methods. These programmes help in improving the production methods already used, as a first step towards larger future development: in other words, programmes of gradualism evolving a sequence of appropriate technologies.

The social factor is not an easy one to tackle. Tradition and religion strengthen the resistance to change by the existing social order, especially where radical changes are involved. These are the procedures followed in Bedouin Settlement in towns and villages of the Kingdom.

First, encouraging the Bedouins to settle in the villages and towns will create many social problems. If Bedouins are settled in towns without providing them with work opportunities that give them a reasonable income sufficient to cover urban living requirements in the town, an unemployed and highly discontented group will be produced. Moreover, the encouragement of villagers and Bedouins to move to towns might harmfully affect agricultural development policy. If settlement is to occur, the best way is to settle villagers and Bedouins in areas to which they belong, after conducting studies of physical land potential in these areas to ensure the availability of good water and soil. Royal Order No. 4169/3/M states the necessity of checking on water conditions in areas to be settled, since shortage of water for agriculture is the main physical obstacle.

The necessity of water availability in lands to be settled is absolutely critical, because, when water and agricultural capabilities exist settlement operations can attain the designed objectives. If, however, there is insufficient water for growth settlement operations will be useless. The Government becomes obliged to provide public facilities and it is forced to provide drinking water to settlers, transporting this water long distances. The Bedouins have frequently made very strong pleas for such support in locations totally unsuitable for viable permanent settlement.

The Ministry has carried out studies of water conditions in some areas in the Kingdom, identifying areas which could be distributed according to the Public Land Distribution Ordinance. Other lands should not be distributed unless studies of the water situation in them are carried out and unless the availability of agricultural water and soil has been proved. This is to ensure that settlement only occurs where job opportunities can be made available and that it will not be harmful to agricultural development in areas that have water and soil potential. In this sense, public facilities will be provided as investment, rather than open-ended support.

Second, when settlement takes place, it should be ensured that tribes are not settled very near each other in order to minimize contact between them; this is in order to prevent territorial conflict of the traditional kind. The desire of members of one particular tribe to utilize adjacent Public Land plots distributed to them in blocks should be encouraged even in areas of low water potential in order to enable them to combine their resources for well drilling and digging even if these wells produce a little amount of water. This is to discourage them from migrating to the towns even at the cost of temporarily encouraging high-risk agriculture.

Third, most tribes have some central gathering place at which Government facilities such as clinics, emergency water supplies and so on, can be concentrated. They should be discouraged from fragmenting into smaller groups, each with its own nuclear site, since this makes more difficult and more expensive the provision of such facilities and also obstructs the implementation of permanent settlement programmes.

When applications from tribal people for settlement in large villages in which a living could be earned in ways other than, as well as in, agriculture, then the preparation of a detailed scheme of such settlements in these villages should be jointly discussed by the PLMD, town planning offices and other agencies concerned with participating in PLD local committees.

Small and separate holdings

So far as the size of holdings is concerned, extreme smallness in size is certainly detrimental to efficient or increased production and under Middle Eastern conditions it can be shown that large-scale farms are more efficient than the small in that when land is divided into small units, its productivity return against inputs will be lower.

Table No. (11–1) Small farm holdings as a percentage of all holdings.*

Country	*Year*	*Less than 0.5 Ha*	*Less than 1 Ha*	*Less than 3 Ha*	*3 Ha*
Japan	1960	34	64	95	—
Egypt	1950	53	—	—	92
Greece	1929	37	—	—	86
India	1954	39	—	—	84
Saudi Arabia	1966	—	55.6	75.9	—

* Economic Research: US Department of Agriculture, "Changes in Agriculture in 26 developing nations, 1948–1963." Foreign agricultural economic report no. 27, Washington DC, 1965 pp. 37–43.

These five countries: Japan, Egypt, Greece, India and Saudi Arabia, are characterized by small size farm holdings. In Japan, farm holdings of size less than 1 hectare represent 64 per cent and in Saudi Arabia represent 55.6 per cent. Less than 3 hectares represent 95 per cent in Japan and 75.9 per cent in Saudi Arabia. The other countries lie between these two limits.

On the basis of various criteria it can be shown that the optimum local inhabitants and capable users of the land are also given priority in the allocation of land for farming. Secondly, the size of the distributed area per person, as an average, will be 5–10 hectares, thus avoiding the further creation of minute holdings.

The initial work of Land Distribution is of course applied first to new areas which have large water potential. In well-established agricultural areas in Qatif, Public Land Distribution becomes relevant when the limited Public Land available can be used for increasing the size of existing holdings and some official machinery is required, not only to organize the division of land between existing farmers but also to carry out water and soil investigation.

A complex of factors

Although in combination very rare, a complex of factors can be found in Saudi Arabia. These are a relatively large rural population. Referring to Chapter Seven, Table No. (7–2), we find that 66 per cent of the population are working in agriculture. Agriculture, as previously indicated is a traditional sector in which one can expect a low level of productivity, resulting from some particular factors.[4]

First, there are the traditional and inefficient techniques and practices, and these are used in farming at all stages from ploughing the soil to marketing the final products. Second, there is the under-utilization of available resources and factors of production. In the traditional period most of the factors of production were highly marginal so that when the producer found an alternative income he began to neglect the marginal elements. This trend of decline in the traditional production has continued and is still evident at the present time in many places. Traditional production has been severely undercut by a vigorous oil sector while the modern farming sector, although rising steadily, is far from satisfying domestic needs even at a subsistence level. A third factor may be added: the subsidizing of imported products in the past, such as rice, wheat, barley, sugar and meat; the attention paid to urban areas and consumer demands, the ample availability of foreign currency derived from oil resources and changes in consumer taste.

The rural population itself has been also heavily exposed to imported consumer and capital goods of all kinds – a rare situation for an undeveloped country. In the past few decades new exogenous factors have affected the traditional way of life, not only by disturbing its economic internal structure but also by exposing it and leaving it open to all the impacts of a dynamic and rapidly developing outside world. As a result, most of the traditional values and criteria of behaviour in all fields of activities have become increasingly irrelevant.

Since the majority of the population is in the agricultural sector, this sector has the greatest potential purchasing power for creating and expanding the domestic market for non-agricultural products.

Migration to the urban centres was associated with a growth of income which in turn increased the demand for food; however, local production could not keep up with this rising demand. To fill the gap between demand and supply, imports have vastly increased.

Table No. (11–2) The early effects of the oil boom on food imports to Saudi Arabia.[4]

Year	*Imports (Millions SR)*	*Index*
1367H (1947)	22	1
1383H (1963)	397	18
1385H (1965)	591	27

The rural population lives and works, when agricultural, on small or very small holdings in which there is under-employment. Ministry of Agriculture and Water statistics record the fact that the average working days per year are only about 170. It is true that young working men tend to rush to towns for job opportunities but many families still live on a small or very small holding, preferring to live in the area where they originated. Agriculture on the whole appears to maintain a static population, most rural out-migration appearing to do little more than absorb the natural increase.

In a country in which there is no shortage of capital and a high average but variable consumer demand, the normal diet has completely changed from dates, milk and wheat to vegetables, fruit, canned food, and various other foodstuffs. Towns and villages have been enlarged or created within a short time and construction work is seen everywhere. The inhabitants consume a large volume and variety of goods. Table No. (13–2) confirms the idea of high average incomes; most of the new utilizers, almost all non-farmers, in Tabuk had an income of 10,000–20,000 SR a year.

The shortage at the moment of skilled manpower and the relatively low technical expertise in agriculture has resulted in a slow technological response in agriculture to the new market opportunities.

Table No. (11–3) "Expatriate employees in the Ministry of Agriculture and Water".*

a. *By qualification*		
1. Without academic qualification		46
2. With academic qualification	a) Diploma or equivalent	211
	b) University Degrees (non-agricultural)	93
	c) University Degrees (agricultural)	162
	TOTAL	512

b. *By field specialization*	Bsc	Msc	PhD
General agriculture & agricultural engineering	61	4	2
Agriculture economics & marketing	2	—	—
Soils and analyses	7	3	1
Agronomy	2	3	3
Food technology	—	—	2
Animal production	3	—	3
Veterinarian	32	4	5
Entomology	3	2	3
Plant physiology	1	—	2
Horticulture	3	1	3
Plant pathology	3	—	—
Extension	2	2	—
TOTAL	119	19	24

*Unpublished departmental data in 1393H (1973).

There are plenty of field specializations still vacant. Money is available and posts are also available but the problem is to find the right types of sufficiently skilled personnel.

Expatriate employees are faced with problems of completely different conditions and environment from what they know or expect. Mostly their stays in Saudi Arabia are short and by the time they start to become accustomed to the country they leave. It is, therefore, most important that more Saudi Arabian personnel are trained and employed in agriculture.

Previous Tables of expatriate and Saudi employees show that Field Organizations employ almost 500–600 field technical staff with

Table No. (11–4) The number of specialists required by the Field Organizations.*

Field of Specialization	*No. Required*
Agriculture & assistant engineer (various fields)	160
Veterinarian & veterinary nurse	43
Geologist & surveyor	10
Farmer & skilled worker	36
Unskilled worker & farmworker	124
TOTAL	373

*Unpublished departmental data in 1392H (1972).

technical training. Of these about 80 per cent are contracted foreigners working in various fields. The need is obvious for highly skilled manpower to implement the big budgets of the Ministry Departments, Field Organizations and other ministerial responsibilities.

A situation of total transition – technical, economic and social – exists in the country.

Technical transition is clear in the agricultural population. Riyad University established a College of Agriculture from which the first small class graduated in 1390H (1970). Now an agricultural school has been set up in Qasim, starting from intermediate education level and proceeding to secondary education and graduate level. The Training Centre attached to the Training Department in Riyad now has a programme to train Ministry of Agriculture and Water staff as well as farmers and their sons.

Concerning the transitional economy in Saudi Arabian agriculture, although rented farms and absentee ownership generally lead to less than maximum production, there is at the moment no alternative to this owing to the lack of indigenous agricultural knowledge in general and the necessity for introducing alien "know-how" through hiring labour or sub-letting holdings to agriculturally-experienced tenants.

In addition, the development of farm holdings requires adequate capital both for investment and as guarantee in case of failure, capital which is only available at the moment outside agriculture, hence the non-farmer landholder who is often a merchant. In Chapter Ten, we have seen how this and preceding factors in Iraq, and to some extent Syria, lead to land tenure situations with many disadvantages. It is therefore most important that in Saudi Arabia agricultural expansion through PLD is controlled so as to prevent the appearance of such detrimental effects of non-farmer private land control.

In the USA, Public Land Management Laws require participation in Public Land management of local users of the land.[46] This has been obtained most frequently by setting up advisory boards including local people who do not have official responsibility for managing the programmes and who would feed into the board information concerning local productivity, soil conditions and topography; they can also act as guardians of the general interest. In Saudi Arabia the duties of the recently formed PLD local committees could grow to include these functions.

Concerning social transitions, though there is very little data, one can note that up to 1386H (1966), the local market in Saudi Arabia was mainly for fresh vegetables and animal products.[51] Figures for importing these materials were 368 and 170 millions SR respectively. There was then no heavy demand for canned food. Now almost 90 per cent of fresh vegetables are produced locally and fattening of cattle stock, mainly from the Sudan, has begun in Qasim. However, another factor has emerged recently, the demand for canned and processed vegetables. Here a further two questions arise. Is it possible to establish agricultural processing products? And, the second, to what extent will these satisfy the local market?

From our evaluation of the variables involved, it is obvious that Public Land Distribution in Saudi Arabia is designed to create new holdings and viable production units eventually for farm owners, these owners preferably to be owner occupiers (*Faire valoir directe*).

The plan and the implementation of Public Land Distribution aim to encourage enterprise and to get maximum output against minimum inputs.

The plan must also control the balance of land holding in the context of social stability, while at the same time encouraging non-farmers to participate in farming.

Variables evaluated from questionnaire

From observation of those factors which appeared specific to Saudi Arabia, numerous variables were identified in PLMD. In order to maintain consistency between policy and implementation of PLD schemes an enquiry was made into Field Organizations seeking for real information concerning outstanding areas of difficulty. The answers, as shown below, included references to specific points of detailed practice, particularly in administration, but they also included some points which are significant to the whole policy itself. The need is for a consistent and flexible general policy which fits the specific Saudi Arabian situation without disturbing the central national philosophy, yet which at the same time can be translated into specific practical measures.

In order to assist in designing, on a continuing basis, relevant PLD programmes, PLMD sent this questionnaire to the Field Organizations inviting comment on the following points:

1. Specific situations needing to be clarified.
2. Problems facing the executive work of land distribution.
3. Requests from field organizations and local committees to facilitate the work of land distribution.
4. Suggestions and recommendations which could help in solving problems arising out of the application of regulations of Public Land Distribution.
5. Any comments concerning the Arabian Shield area.

Answers were received from 58 Field Organizations out of 63. It was noted that 50 per cent of the answers were not complete or unintelligible. This may be due to the fact that in only 18 areas are Field Organizations dealing with Land Distribution, or it may also be due to lack of qualified personnel.

Answers could be grouped according to the question-headings thus:

1–1 Enquiries about the old boundaries of the property rights in Public Lands or mountain areas and the relevant decisions.

1–2 Enquiries about the boundaries of buildings or farm lands.

1–3 Enquiries about the proprietary rights in run-off channels or on lands exposed to run-offs.

1–4 Enquiries about decisions for pieces of land granted by a local *Amir* but which have not been developed in full or which only have a well drilled therein.

1–5 Many enquiries why a simpler process of affirmation of land proprietorship should not be made through the local courts.

2–1 A deficiency in the number of the technicians and specialists supposed to be available in particular areas and requests that the required number of these should be appointed.

2–2 The demarcation of the villages and towns is not clear in several areas. There is frequent difficulty in determining whether land lies within or outside the boundaries of the jurisdiction of the municipality. There is no definition for the specialization of the Ministry of Agriculture and Water in the general plan for the Kingdom.

3–1 Inadequacy of the period allowed by the courts for notices regarding the validity of claims to proprietorship.

3–2 The method of demarcation of Public Lands from lands developed already.

3–3 It is necessary for a surveyor to be present permanently in the areas where there is distribution of land. He would determine the exact location of the land on site when distribution is declared (the local committee should have this information) before granting a piece of land to anybody.

3–4 A request that the local committee should be authorized to participate in the action of dividing the Public Lands from the developed one.

3–5 A request to increase the maximum size limit of the plots allocated from Public Lands.

4–1 It is suggested that a certain sum of money be collected from applicants for proprietary rights to land and a sum of 1,000 SR from any applicant requesting information about the development of a new land. Such deposits would be returned to the applicants when it is confirmed that they are genuinely willing to develop the land.

4–2 There is an increasing number of requests for areas of land to be allocated to several persons from one tribe who wish to be neighbours. To solve this problem, it is suggested that non-cultivable lands be distributable for utilization as lands for residence in addition to blocks of plots suitable for cultivation.

4–3 Lands should not be surveyed and declared for distribution and then the distribution decision withdrawn.

4–4 Authorization to be granted to the local committees concerned with Public Land Distribution to change the serial numbers of the lands where decisions are sanctioned for the distribution thereof.

5–1 Construction of dams in the areas of the Arabian Shield for controlling rain-water to be utilized in the Public Lands as existing regulations allow.

5–2 There are certain areas in the Arabian Shield where the land is prolific and water abundant: therefore these areas should again be considered for allocation.

5–3 Several requests have been received asking for lands to be granted in the Arabian Sheild Area. A need exists for ascertaining whether bonds of proprietary rights exist in these cases.

To reclassify some of these answers, judging from the responses to the questionnaire one can identify six groups of relevant points:
Group I – cadastral survey 2–1, 3–2 and 3–3.
Group II – regional connotations and variations 1–3, 5–1 and 5–3.
These questions had different answers depending on the regions' characteristics.
Group III - Dead Land and provisions for existing asserted rights 1-1, 1–4, 3–2 and 5–3.
Group IV – administrative procedure dealt with by local committees and various relevant requests 3–1, 3–4, 4–1, 4–3 and 4–4.

Group V – relationships between land rights and water rights 1–3, 1–5, 5–1 and 5–2.
Group VI – relates to the whole PLD problem, the nature of land rights and social policy, 1–5, 3–5, 4–1, 4–2 and 5–3.

When we look at the different groups of questions and answers we find exposed both the holistic nature of Land Development through PLD and the practical requirements of the situation in a particular regional context. For example, Group I dealt with administrative procedure but the answers to the questions raised will have to meet the specific requirements of the Saudi situation. For example, since part of the central policy relies on individual enterprise rather than State management, every proposal has to simultaneously satisfy private interest and public interest. Thus, Saudi Arabia is working towards a Public Land Development which avoids the build-up of very large estates. Therefore, a critical need appears for the careful definition of rights given under distribution and for control to ensure that Land Distribution results in real utilization. This is to ensure that the public interest in a water supply and in town planning is not adversely affected by the allocation of private rights.

The field organization questionnaire also illustrates that the field of responsibility of PLMD is either too small or too large. It vitally affects areas of responsibility in all the other departments in the Ministry and also in several other Ministries but at the same time the organization is itself no more than a single department in one Ministry. This arises because the PLMD is mainly responsible for assisting development in the Public Land sector. As a result, the PLMD makes itself responsible not only for the allocation of land but for a suitable development process (in terms of evaluation).

PLMD has developed both as a Land Distribution Agency and a Public Land Development Agency. This is too much for a single Public Land agency unless its structure evolves, but anything less will be too limited if Public Lands are to realize their full potential.

So, if it is not to fail in either or both duties, the PLMD has either to be given an autonomous position and obligations or the machinery for collaboration with other agencies has to be further developed at central and regional levels. This is not merely the result of universal administrative requirements, but owing to the nature of the specific Saudi variables discussed – sedentarization, great regional variations both in potential and socio-economic structure, and so on. The socio-political variations – for example, the Eastern Province is different from the Northern Province – are not themselves "historical accidents" but arise from major geographical differences in location, environments, etc.

Saudi Arabia is building its development on a systematic basis. The expenditure of oil revenue has led over the past twenty-five years to a broad expansion in some sectors of the economy, particularly in commerce, finance and construction. Investment by the Government generally is made in projects that private enterprise is not prepared to undertake. It also promotes and encourages the development of private enterprise such as industry, power and agriculture.

The development of new lands and the enlargement of existing farms by private entrepreneurs will be facilitated by the recent Public Land Distribution Ordinance and will be further encouraged by Government technical assistance and grants. The latter will be of great importance if Saudi Arabia is to avoid the trap: "In all the under-developed countries, Governments are anxious to get a move on with opening lands up for settlement, and it is an almost universal practice to settle the lands first and find out what they will grow economically afterwards."[39]

Land distribution calls for the mobilization of those land and water resources available and implies that we are to utilize the existing potential area to the optimum as best as we can. This, however, is not as simple as it sounds: "Unexpectedly difficult to get settlers for the land; or if settlers are found, to prevent them from abandoning their settlements within two or three years; if they stay, to prevent them from ruining the fertility of the soil."[39] This draws attention to the fact that the idea can best be achieved broadly speaking within the existing manpower in Government bodies and especially in the Ministry of Agriculture and Water, only by recognizing the implications of PLD for grass-root activities and high level national policy-making. Knowing the structure of Saudi Arabia, the situation of Saudi Arabia, and the situation of the comparative countries discussed previously, some universal requirements for a successful programme can be borne in mind. Firstly, it must be acceptable and attractive to farmers; secondly, it must provide adequate facilities for farmers; thirdly, these must include co-operatives, seed supplies and marketing facilities; and fourthly, it needs suitable trained personnel in large numbers.

For Saudi Arabia as for any other single country, these universal requirements have then to be translated into particular actions. These in turn can only be satisfactory if some fundamental questions are faced and answered. Does Saudi Arabia look for increased production? And, if so, production increases to what level? Is the country to subsidize "satisfactory" farmers only or to write off central capital inputs in the name of production? To assist more farmers, to settle more farmers, or open-endedly to increase production? For example, in Saudi Arabia, although wheat production has a negative value to the producers compared to fruit and vegetables (see Chapter Seven, Table No. (7–7)), a new programme is intended to subsidize its production. This is similar to the wheat production programme in Egypt which compels the cultivation of 33 per cent of land under wheat by law annually, although we know that the Egyptian situation is fundamentally different from that of Saudi Arabia.

Ultimately it is impossible to achieve an ideal technical compatibility between these and other questions because Public Land Distribution must always be based on some principles of optimum balance. This matter of balance is always in the hands of policy makers and the final decision is definitely political rather than technical.

To summarize the principles we can extract from the situation in Saudi Arabia: not only is each country unique but also within a given country regional and local differences may be so great as to vitiate the usefulness of even a national model unless this is very carefully framed. The policy will be moulded by specific interpretations of circumstances. Sound investments in agriculture at this time can contribute a great deal towards improving the economic and social conditions of the majority of people of Saudi Arabia. This is also in accordance with the main objective for the agricultural sector to increase agricultural production and to develop it in such a way that the soil and water resources can be utilized and safeguarded. This is such a complex multivariable matter that on the one hand there is a need for continuing flexibility, while on the other there must be consistency in major policy decisions.

Chapter Twelve

Public Land Distribution in Practice in the Case Study Region

In the Operational Procedure statement in the PLDO the following passage appears: "Primarily the final acreage to be allotted depends upon the total land area available for distribution and the number of applicants asking for it. The quality of land and the ability for its utilization are of secondary importance."

As a general policy statement this is understandable but during PLD implementation the three specific elements mentioned, that is, size of holding, land quality and the existence of utilization ability appear as very closely inter-related. In the short studies which follow the PLD experience in specific regions, the implications of this inter-relationship and the critical importance of the elements concerned are examined and assessed, together with other lessons learnt from practical experience.

Tabuk

As a frontier zone, Tabuk has all land centrally controlled and no land is available under traditional occupation rights. Land for distribution is available but there is also a high demand. There are five major allocable areas: three located to the north of the Tabuk – Madinah road and two to the south (see Fig. 8–3). These areas were divided into 5 hectare plots except for plots at the edges of main blocks. These are usually between 5–10 hectares. Fig. 12–1, (2), (3), (4), (5). The number of distributed plots reached 3,125 out of 4,782 laid out (see p. 137). Areas which are not distributed, are left, firstly, for public facilities and utilities needed in the future, secondly, for the expansion of established farms and, thirdly, as safeguards against adverse hydrological consequences and to give the required minimum distance between flowing wells (see p. 208).

According to PLDO the granting of one plot to each applicant is considered the minimum limit and two plots as maximum limit. Family blocks consisting of individual plots allocated to individual

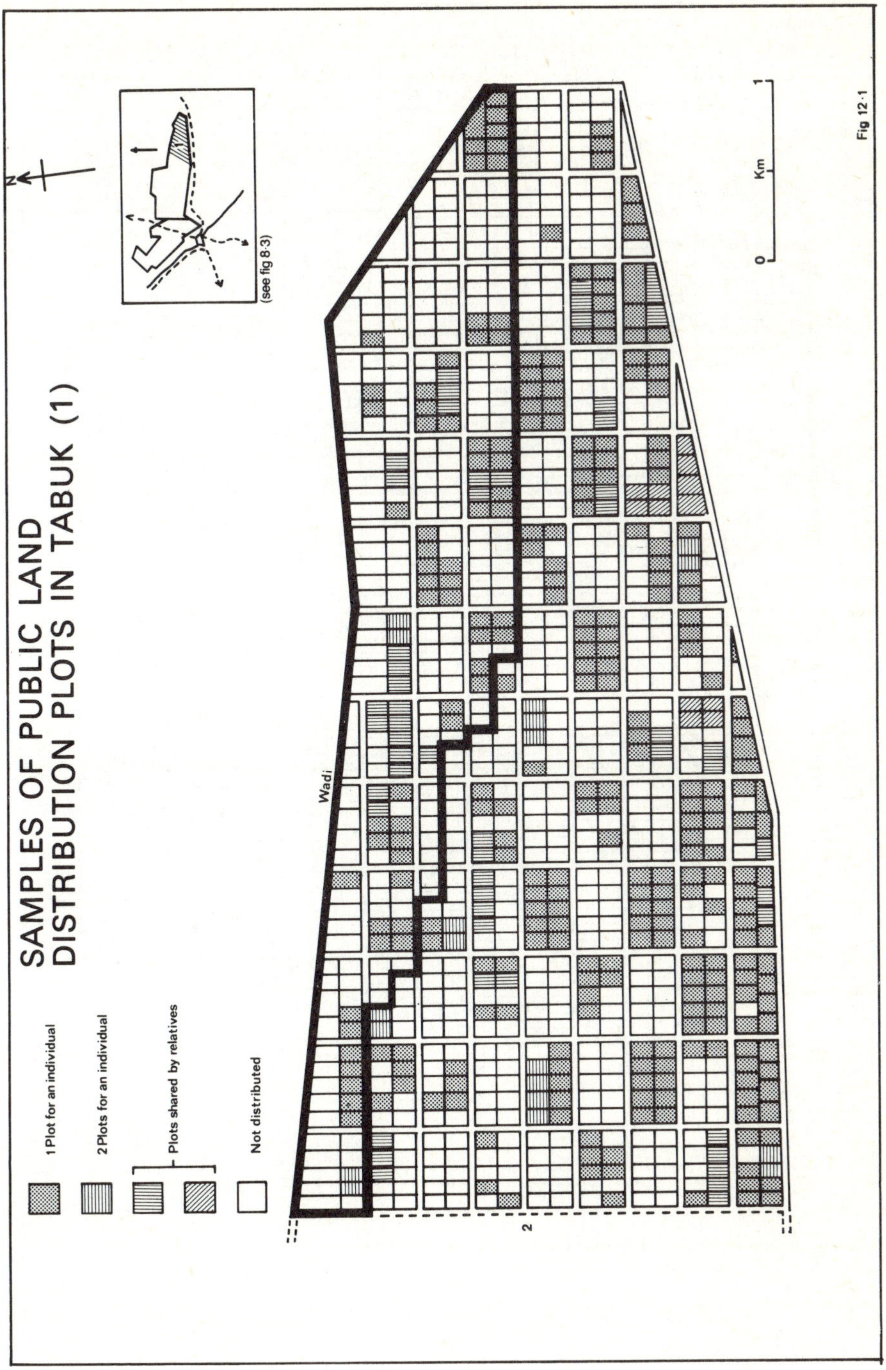
SAMPLES OF PUBLIC LAND DISTRIBUTION PLOTS IN TABUK (1)
1 Plot for an individual
2 Plots for an individual
Plots shared by relatives
Not distributed
N
(see fig 8·3)
Wadi
0
Km
1
2

Fig 12·1

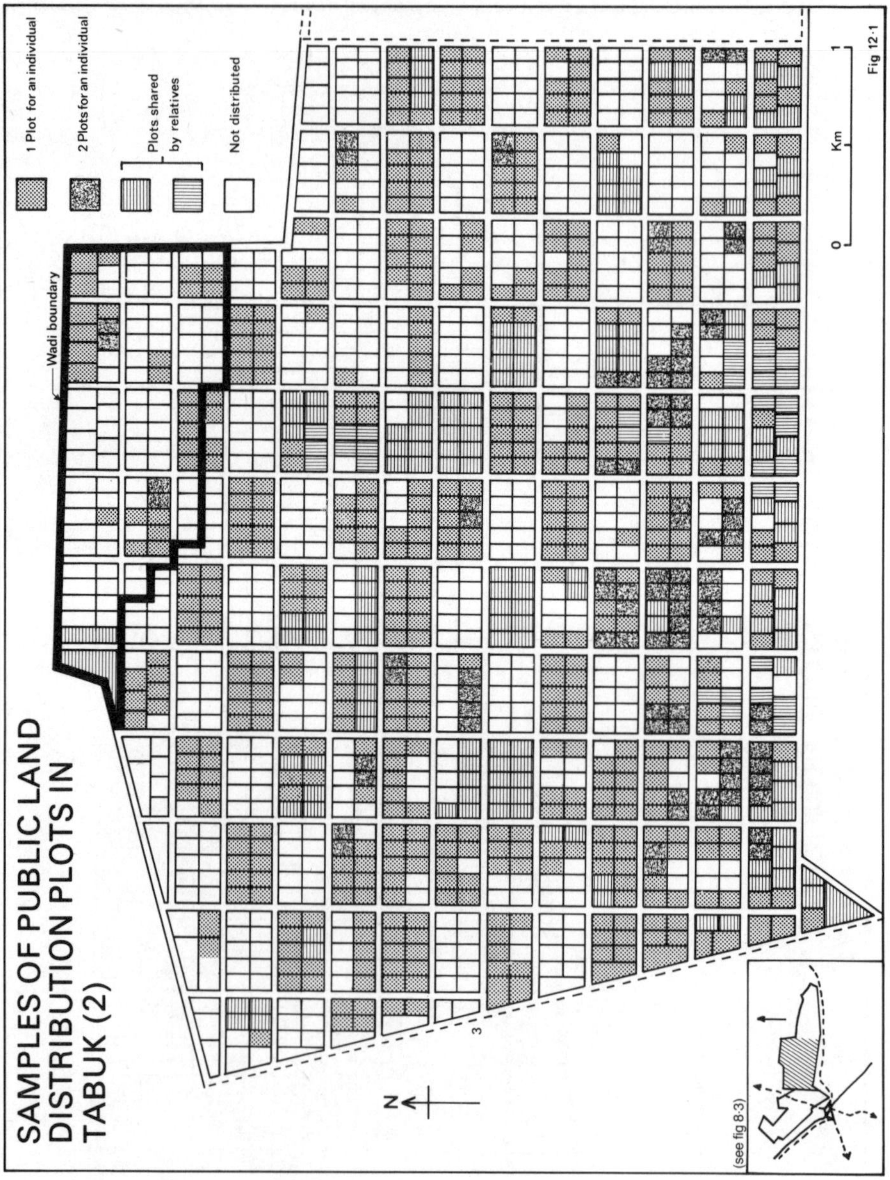
SAMPLES OF PUBLIC LAND DISTRIBUTION PLOTS IN TABUK (2)
1 Plot for an individual
2 Plots for an individual
Plots shared by relatives
Not distributed
Wadi boundary
N
3
Km
0
1
(see fig 8·3)
Fig 12·1

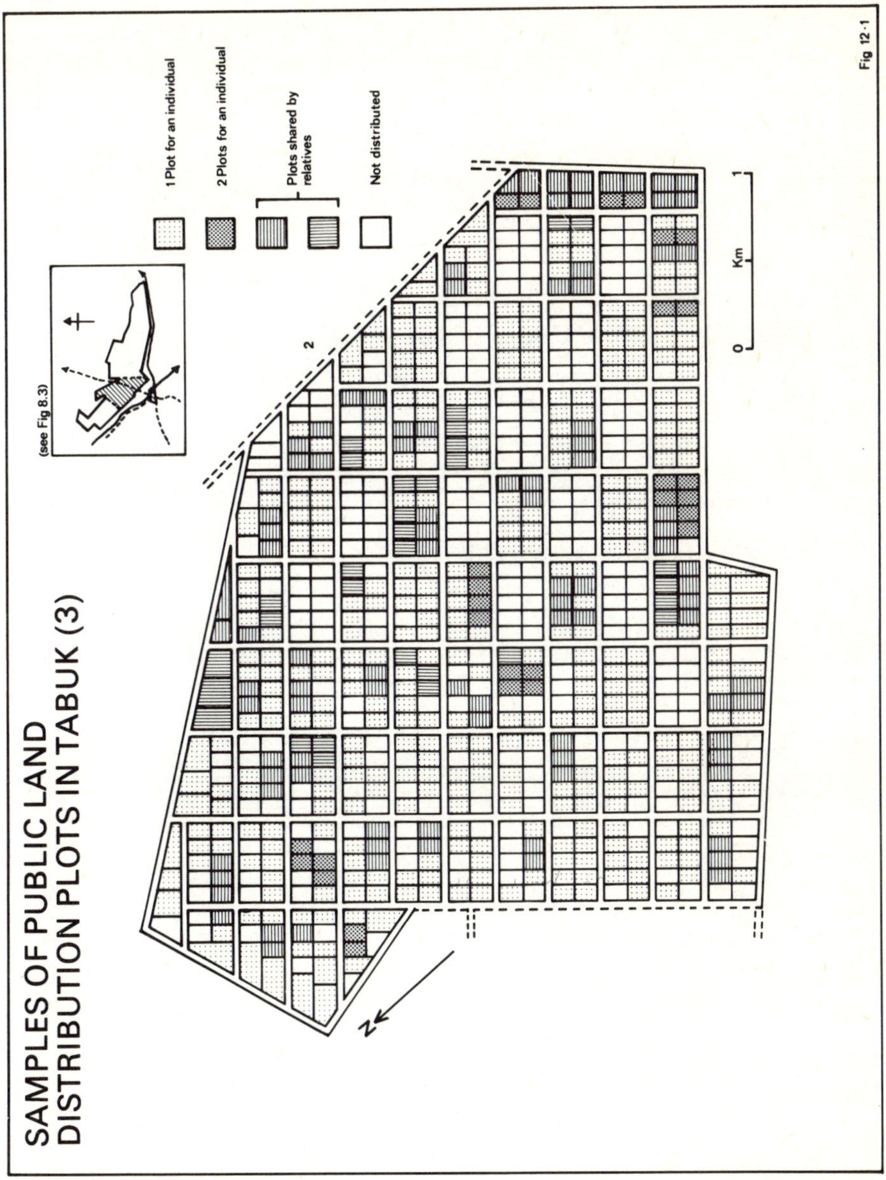
SAMPLES OF PUBLIC LAND DISTRIBUTION PLOTS IN TABUK (3)
(see Fig 8.3)
1 Plot for an individual
2 Plots for an individual
Plots shared by relatives
Not distributed
0
Km
1
2
N
Fig 12·1

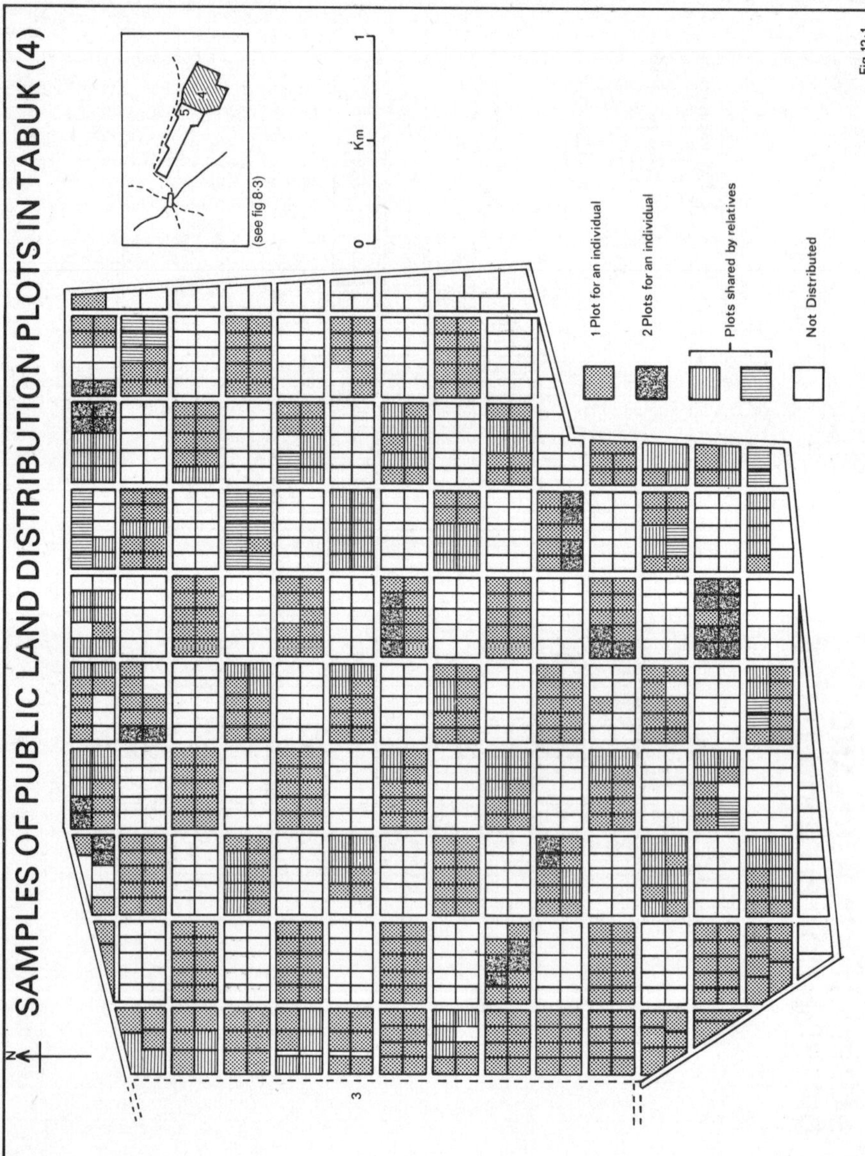
SAMPLES OF PUBLIC LAND DISTRIBUTION PLOTS IN TABUK (4)
N
5
4
(see fig 8·3)
0
Km
1
1 Plot for an individual
2 Plots for an individual
Plots shared by relatives
Not Distributed
3
Fig 12·1

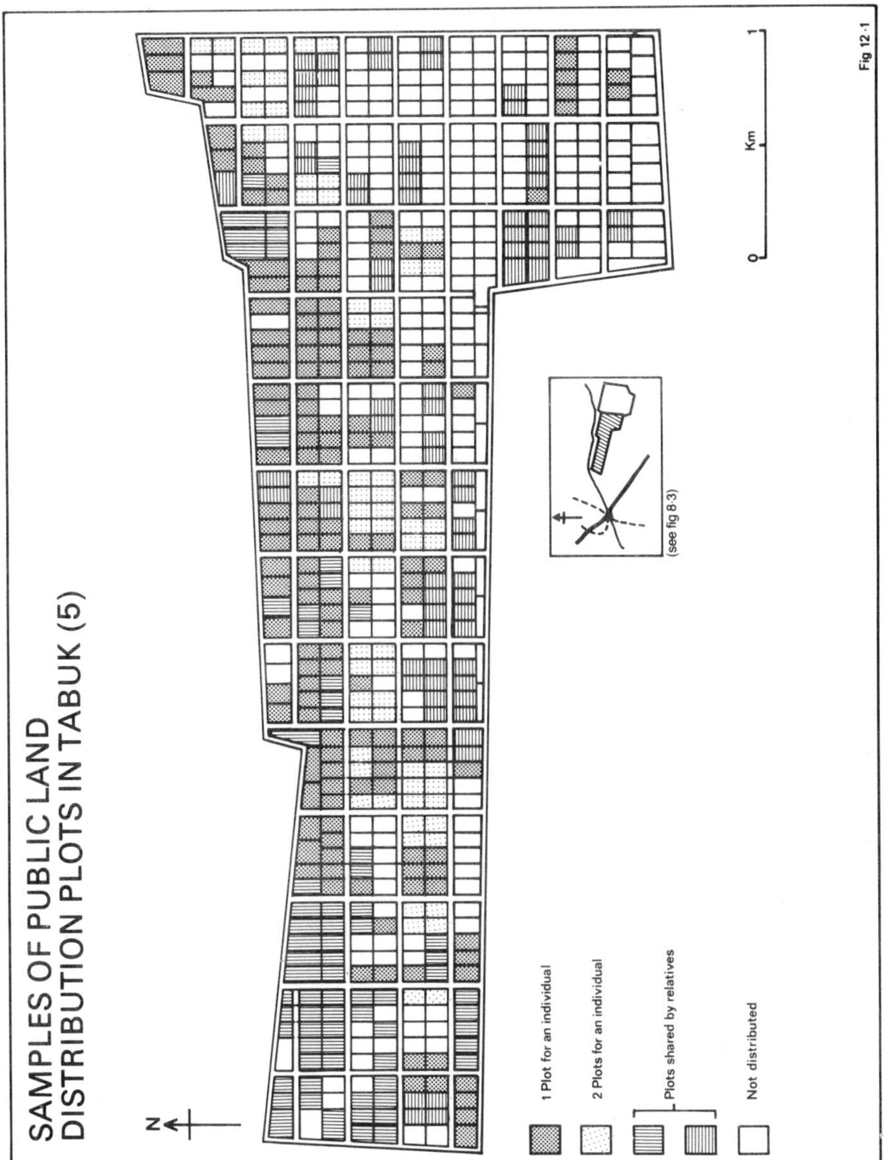
SAMPLES OF PUBLIC LAND DISTRIBUTION PLOTS IN TABUK (5)
N
1 Plot for an individual
2 Plots for an individual
Plots shared by relatives
Not distributed
(see fig 8·3)
0
Km
1
Fig 12·1

members of families are associated usually with ownership rather than cultivation, since even 5 and 10 hectare plots are viable for vegetables, fodder and tree crops, for example, citrus and grapes, and there is no necessity for larger production units. Nevertheless, the grouping of plots in this way can decrease the initial costs of water and physical development and their group utilization can confer a variety of benefits. The number of families among utilizers reached 193.

Table No. (12-1) The grouping index of Public Land plots in Tabuk.

Grouping Index	*No. of Plots*	*No. of Sharing Utilizers*	*Total Area (Donums)*
2	35	70	3,724.50
3	17	51	2,821.15
4	6	24	1,515.25
5	4	20	1,066.60
6	4	24	1,358.50
7	2	14	706.50
9	1	9	456.00
10	3	30	1,809.60
12	1	12	631.00
TOTAL	73	254	14,089.10

The distribution of lands has caused basic changes in the economic conditions of the town. In the past, the town used to depend upon trading, masonry and other enterprises, whereas the cultivation side was not of any significance and thus there were no shops where one could obtain seeds, engines, fertilizers or drilling machines. Since the distribution of Public Lands many subsidiary activities have appeared. For example, a branch of the Agricultural Bank has been established and three stores and shops have been opened for the sale of agricultural instruments, seeds and fertilizer. Such stores and trading shops sell vegetable seeds and light agricultural instruments such as sprayers, chemical fertilizers and feed for chickens (see p. 211 for public and private institutions).

The products of the newly-cultivated area, however, have not been sold on the commercial market except for one farm on 1/11/91H (1971) with a small sale of vegetables. This was partly due to cold winds which affected the growth of plants in the first season. Capital expenditure can be illustrated by agreements between the allottees and the drillers, privately negotiated, showing:

1. The cost of each metre (between 1–100 metres depth), 65 SR per metre.

2. The cost of each metre between 101–300 (which is the maximum depth), 70 SR/metre.

These are drilling costs only; and other costs such as the pipes, cement, and so on, are not included in this agreement. Capital outlay is obviously large.

Now there exists in the area six drilling machines which enabled the drilling of 23 drilled wells by the end of 1392H (1972). Most of these wells produced flowing water, each well being capable of irrigating 100 donums. More wells have been drilled since this date, about ten during the first four months of 1393H (1973). For the first time large areas cultivated commercially have appeared. The cultivated area had been expanded by 1,000 donums by 29/6/92H (1972). A further area of 1,000 donums is under cultivation and establishment.

The drilling of wells was followed by the building of irrigation canals and cisterns and the building of houses. Wind shields and fences were erected around the newly established fields in which cultivation began with the traditional date palms and wheat and the crops of forage such as alfalfa more recently added to field crops such as vegetables and various fruit trees such as citrus and grapes. House building and animal shelters are further additions to the landscape. Cultivation and the changes observable on the new lands now form important topics of conversation in Tabuk town, for the first time in history.

As we noted earlier, the population of Tabuk mainly consists of newcomers to the region, first attracted by non-agricultural opportunities. The applicants for Public Land are therefore mainly drawn from non-agricultural wage employment, Bedouins and merchants. While, as noted on p. 184, there exists statistical under-employment and under-utilized labour in the agricultural sector, in Tabuk many of the land allottees – the provisional owners – do not wish themselves to engage in field labour and there is in other respects a labour shortage.

As a result, the new farmers have to turn to immigrant labourers and/or enter into working agreements with hired labour in ways which were not originally envisaged.

Thus some new utilizers have given pseudo-tenancies to the field workers – often Yemenis – so that these workers operate the plots and give a share of their produce to the holder of the allotment certificate. There is also a financial incentive here, in that if the allottee-utilizer is to obtain a rapid return on his reclamation and planting expenditure he is forced to maximize production at the earliest possible stage; this puts an additional premium on cultivator labour. Thus the landholder may install a well and rent a 5 Ha plot to a Yemeni cultivator who would pay the landholder about 2,000 SR yearly. In addition, tree crops planted under a separate arrangement would be irrigated by the cultivator as part of the agreement. After 7–10 years utilizers will have got back their money expended on initial investment, for example, the cost of the well, and the trees also will have reached a productive stage. This process has already taken place and is illegal according to the PLDO. Its illegality is of course concealed by the utilizers who wish to proceed to obtain final property documents, issued on the basis of proven use of reclaimed public areas, to enable them to procure more money through a mortgage or a loan to cover the requirements and needs of further agricultural activities. In this way, the particular characteristics of the Tabuk region have distorted some elements in the original PLD policy although new production has in fact been established.

In the delimited areas there are plots not reclaimed so far. One major reason is the non-availability of drillers in the area but one must also note that many distribution decisions had not been taken even two years after the time of announcement. The Central Committee at its meeting of 29/10/1392H (1972) in fact recommended that no further plots should be distributed at this time in order that the whole position, in terms of utilization, pseudo-tenancies and water availability could be reviewed.

During the implementation of land distribution, the Tabuk Agricultural Directorate asked for more administrative employees, soil surveyors, soil specialists and others. Technical considerations appeared as more important than was envisaged in the PLDO and in Tabuk. The following problems were noted by the Agricultural Directorate as needing consideration and urgent solution. Some of these are particularly related to the Public Land itself, others are related to administration but there are also some which are significant to agricultural policy.

1. Lack of well-drillers in the area.
2. Scarcity of and high wages demanded by agricultural labourers and their lack of agricultural experience.
3. Unavailability of ploughing and levelling machines.
4. Lack of administrative and technical staff.
5. Since the allocated area for each plot of land was not less than 50 donums and not more than 100 donums, and the minimum allowable distance between wells not less than 500 metres, this created a problem because the distance of 500 metres cannot be maintained in holdings of this size if each holding has its own well.
6. The Saudi Agricultural Bank had no establishment in the Tabuk

area even though the arable land applicants were depending on agricultural credits to pay for the costs of land reclamation. Reclamation costs were too high for most of the applicants, who would not be able to reclaim the land or make any use of it without the assistance of the Agricultural Bank.

7. Agriculturists noted the formation of salts on the soil surface after ploughing and irrigation and the presence of high levels of sodium carbonate was suspected. This had implications for rates of water application as well as land management.
8. The non-availability of nurseries to supply forest trees and fruit trees.
9. The lack of an efficient pest and disease control system in the Agricultural Directorate.
10. The inadequacy of the motor sprayers.
11. Insecticides and fungicides sent to the Directorate by the Ministry (MAW) were insufficient to cover the needs of the area especially after the first summer when the new farms would be under cultivation.
12. There was a need to set up a pilot plot in the new farm blocks for monitoring and demonstration. This would necessitate the provision of extension staff (labourers and farmers) and seeds.
13. Some plots ready for distribution were in need of extra levelling since they had subsidence depressions caused by the building of asphalted roads and other work.
14. The unavailability of stores selling seeds, agricultural tools and equipment, insecticides, sprayers and dusters.

If we consider these problems identified by the Tabuk Agricultural Directorate in Tabuk and also the recommended solutions we can then analyse the nature of requirements for successful PLD development.

The responses from PLMD and the Ministry (MAW) to the specific points were as follows:

1. Advertise for drillers to provide a sufficient number to cover the needs of farmers wishing to drill wells on their lands.
2. Due to the lack of trained hands in cultivation the possibility of recruiting farm labourers with their families from neighbouring countries (such as Jordan, Syria and Lebanon) into the area, is worthy of consideration between Tabuk Governor, the Passport Office, the Labour Office and this Ministry (MAW). The farm owners' interest lies in the availability of trained hands especially in the early phase and, if this need could be met, a good start could be made. A reconciliation between regulations in force and farmers' practical needs would also have to be made.
3. Increase the supply of ploughs and levelling tractors.

4. It was recognized as most important to strengthen the Tabuk Agricultural Directorate with additional staff according to the typical establishment for similar directorates.
5. Reconsider the policy of increasing the area of Public Land distributed to each applicant. The present normal plot area is evidently not sufficient for profitability and all utilizers complained of this. The only solutions would be to reduce the distance between wells to 200 metres or to increase the allotted area to 100 donums minimum and 200 donums maximum. A farm with an area of 50 donums is not sufficient to meet present regulations. This problem was settled by adopting a distance of 200 metres as a minimum between two wells, but this may have adverse hydrological consequences. As a result, the PLMD in Circular No. 7635/18 dated 25/10/1390H (1970) recommended that various unallocated plots must be left without utilization to ensure that the quality of water shall not be affected in wells.
6. Urge the Agricultural Bank to set up a branch in Tabuk area and provide credit facilities to enable the farmers to dig wells, construct irrigation facilities and perform other works leading to the reclamation of land.
7. It is most important to consider installing an adequate drainage system to cover the whole of the cultivable area which will be distributed. This could ensure successful leaching of salts and prevent water-table induced alkalinity and carbonate problems.
8. Set up nurseries for forest trees and wind-breaks and fruit trees, on new land to be selected from the Public Land area.
9. A special plant protection team should be set up and fully equipped with sprayers and chemicals to work in the area.

10 & 11. Strengthen the plant protection team working in Tabuk by the provision of additional labourers, sprayers and chemicals.

12. Support the selected pilot plot's fields with supplies of seeds, fertilizers and labourers.

Besides these specific responses (which did not meet points 13 & 14) the Directorate mentioned other views and ideas which might be considered more concerned with extension resources than with normal development of new land. These were:

(a) The need to enforce following a triple crop-rotation which would limit soil exhaustion and the likelihood of production being reduced.

(b) Directing farmers to plant productive tree-crops on 25 per cent of their lands.

(c) Setting up of wind-breaks on the northern and western boundaries of each farm.

(d) Planting of wind-break trees along lines parallel to the asphalted road on both sides.

(e) The necessity of considering all the plots granted to members of a family (especially the wives of a male utilizer) as one unit, and that ownership of all such plots should be confirmed when 25 per cent of the total area of this unit is reclaimed – this when such a unit is formed by a written witnessed contract. This is recommended because there are many families commencing to till collectively their groups of separately owned plots.

(f) A co-operative agricultural society should be set up in Tabuk, such a co-operative to be encouraged by the provision of the services of the Agricultural Directorate's machinery (tractors and ploughs), services which should be granted either free of charge or at cost.

If we now group the questions and responses, the interlocking nature of the several sectors concerned in PLD development appears clearly:

Group I. Refers to technical problems, such as No. 5, No. 7 and (e). No. 5, which is concerned with the minimum distance between two wells, was settled by adopting a minimum distance of 200 metres. The possibility of increasing the maximum area distributed to individuals to 20 hectares instead of 10 hectares was also finally accepted as we note below. Plot sizes, of course, also are very important in relation to the idea of the establishment of drainage canals for the whole area; this also affects the internal communication system designed to surround each plot by a road 20 metres wide on two sides and another of 10 metres on the other sides. General Construction Directory technicians in the Ministry (MAW) are now well aware of drainage needs for the future but, since the final size of the area which will be cultivated is not yet known, this matter has to be kept under consideration. PLDO operational procedures in the field encourage utilizers to share and co-operate in water use and cultivation, but the Ministry still deals with individual allottees. This matter is still under the consideration of the PLMD Central Committee, its advisers, HE the Minister, and finally, in case of any recommended change, would have to be approved by HM The King.

Group II. Problems related to the absence of private sector supply facilities as in No. 1, and No. 14. The Ministry of Agriculture and Water cannot interfere in or with the private sector since this can only viably respond to demand. In fact such a response did appear and now three stores are available in Tabuk town where agricultural equipment, seeds and fertilizers are sold. Such stores also now sell minor agricultural equipment such as back sprayers, vegetable seeds, chemical fertilizers and animal fodder, and so on.

As far as well drillers are concerned, the number of wells drilled totalled 23 up to the end of 1392H (1972).

Group III. Relates to insufficient equipment and supplies noted in Nos. 3, 10 and 11. A decision was taken by the Ministry of Agriculture and Water in 1392H (1972) to discontinue the farm machinery service to farmers, all related equipment to be sold to farmers and co-operatives at less than purchase price. It was regarded as preferable to use farm management subsidies to encourage co-operatives and individuals to invest in necessary equipment. Farm machinery equipment is more in demand by Saudi farmers than any other equipment. Other types of equipment such as plant protection were still to be run by the Ministry since these require skilled handling. Shortages of supplies and technicians remained critical.

Group IV. Relates to administrative problems and technical staff as in Nos. 2, 4, 9, 10, 11 and 12. It is recognized that more emphasis is needed on the provision to the new farming units of informative and technical advice on irrigation methods and water use. Shortage of trained personnel remains a critical factor.

Group V. Refers to additional services as in Nos. 11, 12 and 13. In recent years, the Ministry has preferred to strengthen existing facilities as much as possible instead of creating new services. In the areas of PLD operation, however, the need is great and existing facilities are very limited. According to the evaluation, development programmes along with procedures for carrying out the work should be planned on an agricultural enterprise basis.

Group VI. Relates to agricultural enforcement measures such as: (a), (b), (c) and (d) (pp. 208–209). It is known that the Tabuk area is exposed to heavy wind storms and that it is imperative that windbreaks be established, especially in some localities of strong prevailing winds. However, the enforcement of agricultural practices and cultivation is not applicable even in theory in the country of Saudi Arabia and action can only be taken through strengthened extension and advisory services and financial inducements.

Group VII. Relates to new thoughts and ideas of mobilizing the services of other governmental bodies in Nos. 2, 6, 14 and (f).

A branch of the Saudi Arabian Agricultural Bank was established and loans are now provided for Public Land utilizers (see p. 154). Other items mentioned, even though they are relevant, are beyond the scope of the Ministry's work.

Most of the Ministries and other private and public institutions are now represented in Tabuk as shown below:

1. *Schools in the Tabuk area*

School type	*No.*	*No. of students*
Boys' preliminary schools	5	2,450
Boys' intermediate schools	1	312
Secondary schools	1	141
Girls' preliminary schools	4	2,471
Female teachers & secondary institute	1	104
Religious institute	1	136
Girls' intermediate schools	1	155
Army boys' school	1	610
Preliminary evening school	5	600
Intermediate evening school	1	120
Secondary evening school	1	100
Private schools (preliminary, intermediate and typing)	2	570
Children's nursery	1	120
	25	7,889

2. *Banks.* Branches of: Saudi Agricultural Bank, National Commercial Bank and Riyad Bank.
3. *Various Ministry Branches.* Ministry of Agriculture and Water, Ministry of Information, Ministry of Labour and Social Affairs, Zakat and Income, Ministry of Justice, Saudi Monetary Agency, Ministry of Defence, Ministry of Commerce, Ministry of Finance, Ministry of Communication (Roads, Post, Telegraph and Telephone), Ministry of Education, Presidency of Girls' Education, Ministry of Interior (Amirates, etc.).
4. *Various Crafts.* Trade, Carpentry, Blacksmith, Plumbing, Masonry and Agriculture.
5. *Trading Establishments.* Two trading agencies and seven brokers' offices.

This brief survey of experience in one PLD region illustrates very clearly, first, the complexity of such an operation and the need for co-ordination of many activities and, second, the very great demands made on one of the scarcest of resources, that is, trained manpower with a variety of skills.

Even so, the Tabuk region, because of the positive evaluation now being made of its location, is rapidly changing. Its passage by pilgrims entering the Kingdom may increase because roads are now paved and any pilgrim or individual can drive his own car to and from the Kingdom to countries to the north-west and to Europe. Freight is also growing and goods such as clothing, furniture, foodstuffs, concentrated fodder, engines, pumps, pipes, vehicles, meat, and so on, are being brought in through the Tabuk border centre to the region and the country. The effects of all this on new PLD agriculture have yet to be seen.

Qasim

In Qasim where, unlike in Tabuk, there was existing agriculture the lands surveyed for distribution were not adjacent to the existing farms so as to avoid problems and claims. These major allocable areas were divided into 5 hectare plots as in Tabuk (Fig. 12–2). Small areas adjacent to existing cultivation were left for the time being until adjacent farmers asked for land. As long as farmers have more water than they currently need they will irrigate adjacent land without permission. Qasim is an open area with few traditional prescriptive claims to land and its inhabitants are rather individualistic. A possibility exists of land still being taken up by individuals under the *Shari'a* system, strictly illegal and conferring no right of ownership.

The executive work of Land Distribution is not as easy as in Tabuk. Although a land survey was begun and the local committee in Qasim was formed earlier than in Tabuk, Land Distribution still goes slowly. Utilization decisions in Qasim have not exceeded 358, since most of the utilizers refused to take up their determined plots. The slowness of allocation is based on a variety of reasons:

A. *Specified area dispute*. Many an applicant requests land by specifically defining its area and boundaries, while the Ordinance states that applications can refer only to the land already surveyed and declared for distribution and that the distribution of officially delimited land is carried out according to a numbered plot design. A dispute can arise during the handing-over of the determined plots when the applicant refuses to take the piece allocated to him, justifying his refusal by saying that he applied for another piece of land. According to information available, many of the applicants refuse the pieces of land allocated to them because they prefer plots outside the surveyed land areas.

B. *After the discovery of water availability in Qasim, large areas of arable land suitable for agriculture were sold by the municipality. mostly surrounding the town of Buraidah*. This happened between 1370–1380H (1950–1960) to raise revenue for improving urban conditions. Some of this area was developed, but much still lies undeveloped and with this land available in addition to PLD land there is no pressure for PLD applications.

C. *Previous land grants in Qasim were made mostly between 1370–1380H (1950-1960)*. Some of the areas were given to well-known citizens in Qasim and the others to people outside. According to the PLDO, all undeveloped granted areas revert to Public Land status (see Chapter Five). Explanations of this lack of development lie in sociology, ecology and technology: for example, available equipment is not capable of reaching aquifers; shortage of finance; difficulty of obtaining modern equipment; a lack of technicians; the time-lag in

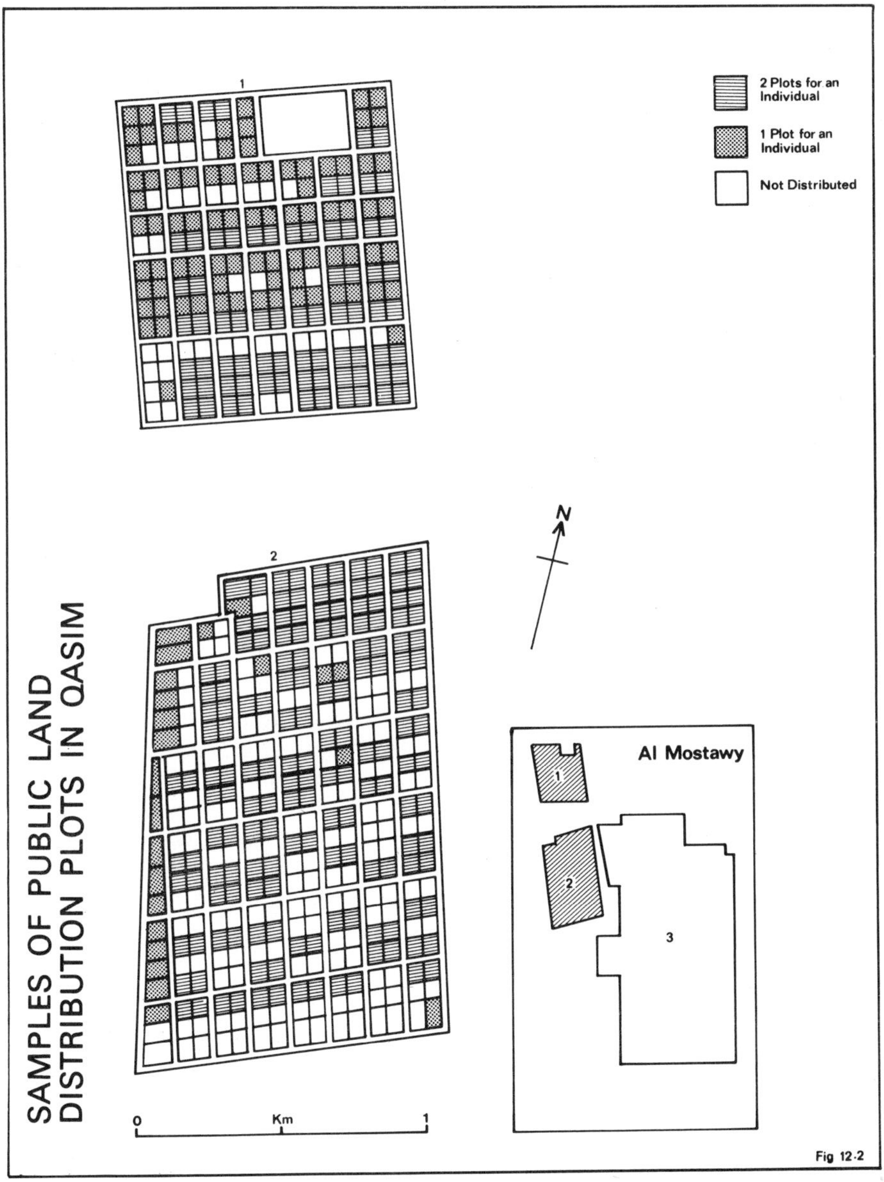
SAMPLES OF PUBLIC LAND DISTRIBUTION PLOTS IN QASIM
2 Plots for an Individual
1 Plot for an Individual
Not Distributed
1
2
N
Al Mostawy
1
2
3
0
Km
1

Fig 12·2

the development of granted areas, and so on. State policy is not in fact in favour of taking back previously granted areas since this is not regarded as beneficial. Higher authorities have approved several requests by the Ministry of Agriculture and Water for the giving of three years' extension period (see p. 80). This extra probationary period for previously granted areas is sometimes undefined.

D. *An individualist approach by cultivators.* Although Bedouins are still found in the Qasim area, their assimilation has already taken place to the extent that most of them are now farmers. The local committee noted in Qasim, when examining application forms, that:

> "it is a difficult job as the six members are required to find all these data about every applicant. They asked the *Amirs* of the villages to give information about people from their villages and found that it was not possible for them to supply such data, as the inhabitants had not yet even registered their names in the Civil Register (Passport Office). Therefore, if the committee is compelled to write down this information, it will be obliged to take the information from the application form on trust. If the committee is left to take the responsibility for this information it will state whatever it knows and accordingly will become responsible for any opinion given concerning the applicant, and this can produce problems, that is, requesting the committee to mention the income of the applicant which is impossible, as even a father may not know the income of his son."

If we examine Fig. (12–2), a sample of Public Land Distribution plots in Qasim, it is clear that all utilizers are individuals and no relatives or groups are mentioned. All information has to be accepted as based on an insistence on individual status – one characteristic of the nomadic past.

E. *The demand for individual farmsteads large enough to give adequate returns.* Size of land distribution is now a matter of real large-scale demand. Farmers and landowners in Qasim think not of subsistence farming but of commercially viable farming with provision for both self-perpetuating capital investment and capital formation. They are thinking in terms of square kilometres not donums and are backed by commercial capital.

The maximum limit for individual utilizers is only one-tenth of a square kilometre which is not considered worth the cost of the initial investment. To extend the maximum limit of Land Distribution, the local committee in Qasim was already informed of the approach adopted by the local committee in Tabuk, that is, that of giving groups of related utilizers priorities to enable them to have neighbouring plots, which can then be jointly farmed on a large scale. The Qasim Committee was also informed of the PLDO policy to strengthen the co-operative approach of giving organized utilizers contiguous plots to use as a co-operative farm. On the other hand, the authorities wish to avoid the build-up of large estates. In Article II of PLDO the maximum limit can be waived by the Council of Ministers in order to increase intensification of land use. Practical PLD experience suggests that the best way is to formulate plans and then to make changes in the light of the study of the problems encountered during execution. This can be done, given the time needed and the flexibility of PLD policy. Expanding the maximum distributed area to reach 20 ha has been agreed in some parts of the country where the legal maximum limit of 5 ha for an individual does not form an economic unit in terms of the comparison of effort needed for development with the actual returns from such an area. Royal Decree No. 22605/3F dated 14/11/1392H (1972) approved that the maximum area could be extended to 20 ha and a new paragraph has been added to the PLDO executive procedure comprising the following:

"It is allowed to exceed the maximum area mentioned in Item No. 2 of PLDO for the lands not yet distributed so that the maximum distributed area reaches 20 ha, on the following conditions:

(a) In areas where a large amount of arable land is available and where water is economically available.

(b) In areas where costs of the artesian wells are high or where flowing wells with high productivity are available for use on large plots.

(c) In areas where other primary costs for land reclamation are high so that the area to be reclaimed could give a good ratio of return to investment."

The above-mentioned excess is applicable at present in areas such as Qasim–Tabuk, where large areas of land as well as ground-water are available. The water production at some places in Qasim is 300–400 gpm and in Tabuk 200–350 gpm, as well as that from free-flowing artesian wells. The primary costs for reclamation, establishing a farm with an irrigation and drainage canals are high, for example, the cost of drilling casing and having a pump for a well in Qasim, has reached 45,000 SR and in Tabuk, up to 100,000 SR.

Problems of agricultural development in Qasim

The discovery of artesian water in the 1370s (1950s) paved the way for an early, sudden and considerable expansion in farming without prior planning of the application of irrigation water, adequate farming facilities and the improvement of farming methods and techniques. Problems arose because of:

Severe shortage of labourers and the high rate of wages

Both have increased as more attention has been paid by the wealthier Qasimis to non-agricultural activities and more holdings are worked by labourers and tenants. This situation encourages the replacement of such labour shortage by power machinery. The number of labourers engaged in agriculture in Qasim is estimated to be 11,401 - 16.6 per cent of the sedentary population.

Table No. (12–2) Facilities and utilities in main villages in Qasim.[59]

Village	*Population*	*Water supply* *Quantity*	*Quality*	*Public utilities* *Schools*	*Others*	*Distance to main roads (Kms)*
Al-Broud	100–500	—	—	—		58
Al-Botain	100–500	Enough	Good	1. Pri boys'	Clinic	9
Al-Tannomah	100–500	"	Medium	2. Pri boys'	Clinic	55
Al-Jaa'lah	500–2,000	"	"	2. Pri boys'		35
Hnaydhil	500–2,000	"	"	2. Pri boys'	Post	70
Al-Trefiyah	500–2,000	Enough	Medium	—		38
An-Nabgyah	500–2,000	Small	Bad	2. Pri boys'		23
Al-Awsjiyah	500–2,000	"	—	2. Pri boys'	Clinic	34
Al-Ghaf	100–500	Enough	Medium	1. Pri boys'	Clinic	25
Adulaymiyah	200–2,000	"	"	1. Pri boys'	Clinic, Court, Post	0
Ad-Dghmaniyah	100–500	"	Good	—		8
Ain Ibn Fhud	500–2,000	Small	Bad	1. Pri boys' & 1. Sec	Clinic, Court Post	45
Al-Wata'a	500–2,000	Enough	Good	1. Pri boys'		10
Al-Mutainiyat	100	Small	Bad	—		10
Al-Qusaibah	100–500	Small	Bad	—		20
Al-Midnab	2,000–10,000	"	"	1. Pri & Sec boys' 1. Pri girls'	Post Court	0
Al-Mrabbaa'	100–500	"	Medium	1. Pri boys'		0
Al-Amar	500–2,000	"	Below Medium	1. Pri boys'	Clinic, Post	6
Al-Robayah	2,000–10,000	Enough	Below Medium	2. Pri boys'	Clinic	0
Ar-Ruwaydhat	100	Enough	Medium	—		0
Salasil	100	Small	Bad	—		50
Ar-Rawdh	500–2,000	Enough	Below Medium	2. Pri boys'		25
Al-Ayon	500–2,000	"	Medium	—		0
Al-Bkayriyah	2,000–10,000	Enough	Good	2. Pri & Sec boys' 1. Pri girls'	Clinic Post Passport	0
Al-Qrayn	2,000–10,000	Little	Bad	2. Pri & 1 Sec boys'	Clinic Post, Vet	0
An-Nabgyah	500–2,000	"	"	2. Pri boys'	Clinic Court, Post	12
An-Nabhaniyah	2,000–10,000	Enough	Medium	1. Pri & Sec boys' 1. Pri girls'	Vet, Clinic	0
Ash-Shinanah	100–500	"	Good	—		0
Al-Hjnawi	100	Little	"	—		0
Al-Wadi	100–500	Sufficient	"	—		0
Riyad						
Al-Khabra	2,000–10,000	Little	Bad	1. Pri & Sec boys' 1. Pri & Sec girls'	Clinic Post	0

Pri = Primary School
Sec = Secondary School
Post = Post Office
Vet = Veterinary

Heavy machinery used includes tractors, ploughs and threshing machines. The lack of the right management and a shortage of mechanics and technicians reduces the capability of correct water use and conservation of water which is the real wealth of Qasim. Greater consideration of light machinery for the new and considerably large areas and also hand tools for small areas is important.

The misuse of water
The two most promising aquifers in Qasim are Tabuk and Saq formations. Both classified as (S_3-SI) medium to high salinity with low sodium. Traditionally, people of the desert love water because it was scarce in the past. They still think that the more that is applied to plants the more production will be achieved. Therefore, the problem of not needed high capacity pump installations arises. These cause over-exploitation of ground-water and, hand in hand with the absence of an artificial drainage system, hydrological and soil deterioration; as a result of the hot climate, salts become concentrated in soils and appear on the surface. Here appear some of the key factors of high cost production, waste of water and soil, and decreased production.

Insufficient control of disease
In subtropical irrigation conditions many diseases exist and they become widespread. Farmers now rely completely on the agricultural Field Centres for disease control because this service is free of charge. It is fair to say that for an area such as Qasim with 9,071 agricultural properties and relatively plentiful capital, disease control by the public sector is now being questioned as not conducive to enterprising development.

Al-Joaf
The famous ancient town of Al-Joaf lies in the central part of the northern section of Area I, and is connected by an asphalted road to Ar'ar town and also Tabuk (through Taima). There is also a road network leading to Wadi Sarhan. Al-Joaf consists mainly of the towns of Al-Joaf and Skaka surrounded by several villages. The number of agricultural holdings is 1,262 and the total cultivated area covers 15,800 donums. Ground-water is available for agricultural purposes, and can be tapped (see p. 133).

In Al-Joaf there is low land availability and high demand (see Chapter Eight, p. 130). Away from Skaka and Al-Joaf towns, the remainder of this area is hilly and rocky in which there are small cultivable patches widely dispersed, very small in size and mostly located in low-lying depressions surrounded by hills or rocks (see Fig. 12–3). These areas are mostly green after rainfall and traditionally used for dry farming or as pasture. There is thus little potential for agricultural development because there is so little suitable land to develop. There are no Public Lands left for distribution except those localities already used for the common interest and these areas could well be distributed since they could be utilized better for continuous

PUBLIC LAND AREA IN AL-JOAF

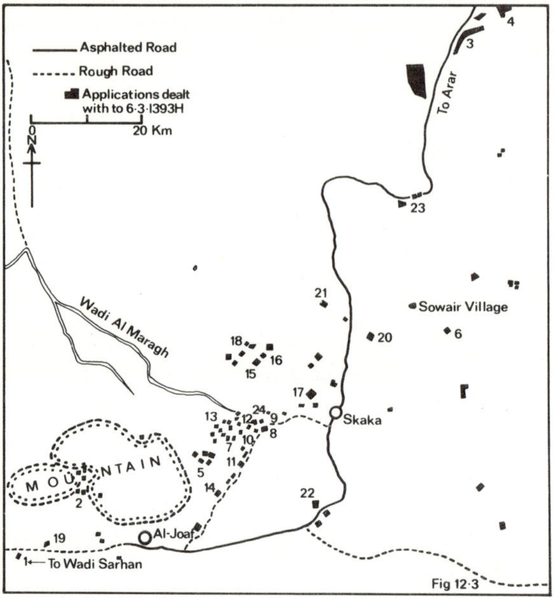

farming. The Ministry of Agriculture and Water decided to survey seventy-two such locations of Public Lands and prepare them for distribution. Their total area is almost 50,000 donums.

It was found that ground-water needed for Public Lands located north of Al-Joaf on the way to Ar'ar lay deeper than at other locations and potential utilizers here refused to receive their plots (see Table No. (12–3)). Most of the Public Lands are classified as Class 3, but drainage problems are expected. So far 260 decisions have been made for plots of sizes as little as 30 donums (3 has).

Such distribution of Public Land plots of less than 5 hectares *per capita* has required consideration. The Minister of Agriculture and Water has approved the distribution of less than the minimum plot area laid down in Article No. (2) of Public Land Distribution Ordinance on condition that there is no objection by, or hardship to anybody, and that such land should be utilized for agricultural purposes, given the following conditions:

(a) whenever it is in the interest of public welfare to distribute land among a larger number of investors without being restricted to

Table No. (12–3) Locations of distributable plots and decisions issued for utilizers in Al-Joaf area up to 4/7/1393H (1973).

Map key	*Location*	*Area in Donums*	*No. of Decisions Issued*	*No. of Utilizers Receiving Decisions*	*No. of Utilizers Refusing Decisions*	*Reasons for Refusal*
1.	Umm Tarfah	275	4	7		
2.	Fiadh Zallum	737	8		8	Deep Water & costly
3.	Al-Mo'atadel	5,151	77	15	62	,,
4.	Ba'agah	3,723	26		32	,,
5.	Riyad Hanen	110	4	4		,,
6.	Between Zallum & Sowair	256	5	5		
7.	Remth	42	1	1		
8.	Qonaitrah	1,173	21	31	6	Rocky & poorly drained
9.	Kasum	1,075	19	27	6	
10.	Sahal	507	9	20		
11.	Al-Hemah	877	11	9	6	Poorly drained
12.	Umm Faras	277	0	10		
13.	Wadi Nesy	185	3	2	1	Erosion run-off
14.	Mohegah	172	3	3		
15.	Qiyal	578	10	24		
16.	Qiyalat	455	8	10		
17.	Far'a	675	12	26		
18.	Qasum	182	1		1	Not specified
19.	Umm Kahf	164	2	3		
20.	Al-Hailah	776	6	1	10	Not specified
21.	Radat Al-Shamal	475	6	9		
22.	Radat Al-Kaay	136	2	3		
23.	Rai'a Al-Samen	717	9	14		
24.	Wadi Al-Maragh	501	8	13		
TOTAL		19,219	255	237	132	

the minimum area mentioned in Article No. (2) of Public Land Distribution Ordinance; and

(b) if it is deemed in the interest of public welfare to grant land of area less than 5 hectares to a neighbouring owner who already has developed and utilized land.

There still exists some Public Cultivable Land, and it is possible to distribute and farm these areas as small-holdings or give them to landless people in accordance with certain rules conforming with the local habits and administrative regulations. This is due to the fact that vast areas exist with a sparse population.

Al-Joaf is mostly inhabited by nomads who are now insistently requesting Public Lands, as a good number of them have abandoned their cattle and sheep and plan to settle and live by cultivation.

Al-Joaf area does not satisfy local demand for fresh vegetables and it was necessary that three truck-loads a week of vegetables be imported from Syria and Lebanon.

The distributed lands, once exploited, will satisfy the need for vegetables. Some of the towns located along the Tapline, such as Ar'ar, would consume the products of the land distribution at Al-Joaf.

Some co-operative approach has been recorded. A locality which has been distributed to members of a clan will be irrigated by a shared artesian well. Co-operative societies exist with a capital investment reaching 130,000 SR for poultry and dairy production. Concentrated fodder is imported from Lebanon and egg products are sold in Ar'ar town.

To summarize: Area I is considered the most promising agricultural area in the Kingdom. In Tabuk and Al-Joaf, the absence of agriculture on any substantial scale in these two areas has permitted a plan for development and settlement of the area on a model basis in accordance with modern techniques of irrigation but there is a shortage of land at Al-Joaf. Qasim was already an agricultural region in which the standard of farming is fairly high, fruit and vegetables are important products at present and commercial enterprise is vigorous.

Chapter Thirteen

An Assessment of Progress in Public Land Distribution and Conclusions

Methods of assessment

The PLD programme is relatively young and it has been implemented by a Department established only some six years ago. An evaluation of progress using quantitative criteria for measuring the degree of success of particular schemes is not yet possible, because no PLMD scheme has yet reached maturity. Nevertheless, some assessment has to be made because of the scale of the present operation. The area allocable for distribution is of the order of 3 million donums (compared with 4 million donums now cultivated) of which 20 per cent will probably be utilized. Production from Public Land which has been distributed is only now beginning to appear. In these circumstances all one can do is:

(a) (i) Examine the way in which the machinery – the organization of and administration for PLD – has evolved in the light of experience.
   (ii) Refer and make comparison to universal elements to be found in a PLD system anywhere.
   (iii) Examine progress so far made in the three types of programmes involving PLD.

(b) Examine the way in which the progress made in (a) matches the specific Saudi situation. What has been the Saudi experience as influenced by the particular set of resources, geographical social and economic characteristics of Saudi Arabia and how have PLD programmes been developed to suit this particular dynamic situation?

(c) Examine the way in which PLD fits national policies regarding development, social, economic and resource use factors.

It is only by an approach of this kind that one can assess the present situation and future possibilities.

First, an examination of the stage to which the organizational machinery for PLD has developed.

In Chapters Three and Six a survey of the evolution of PLD systems

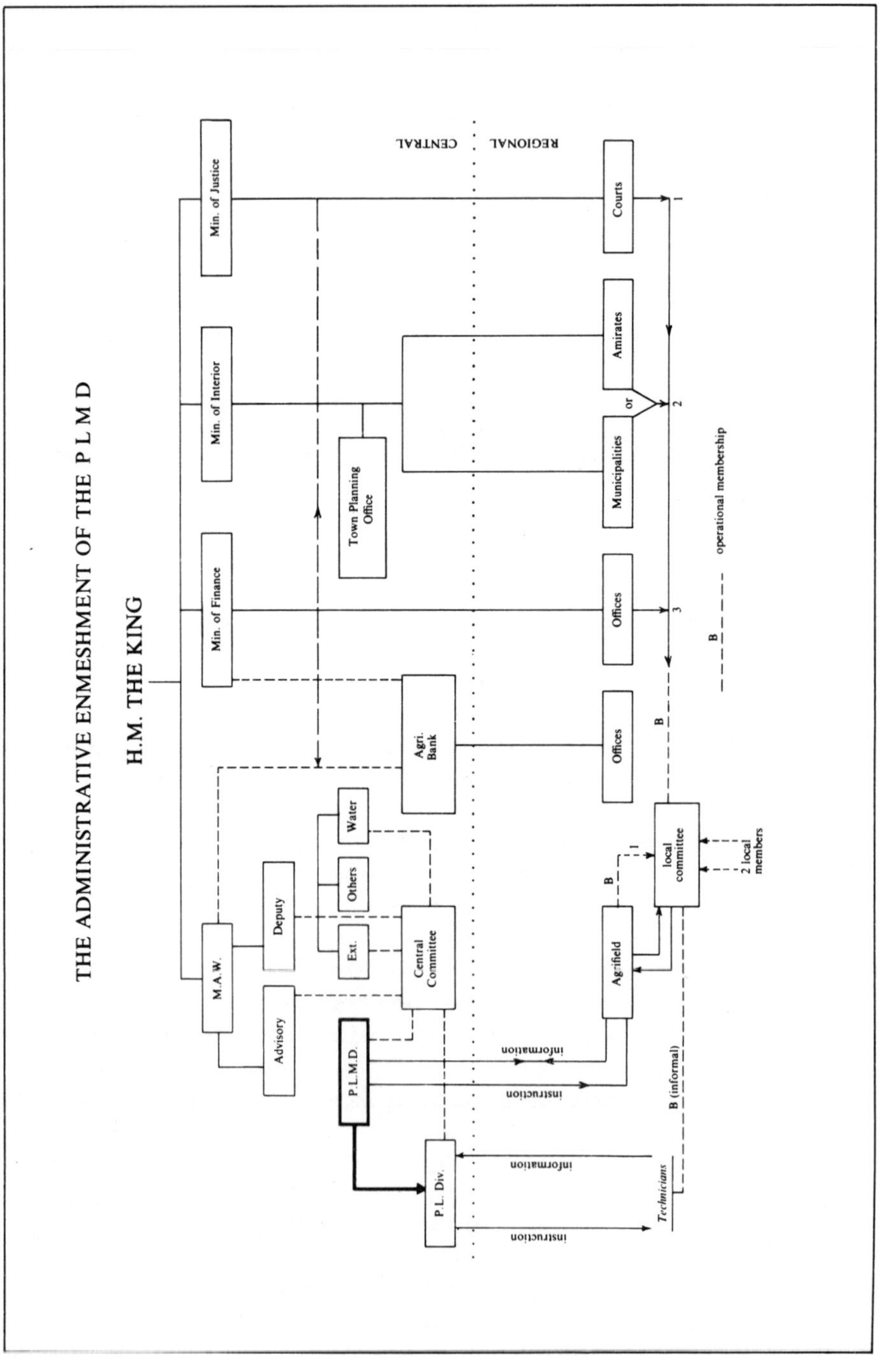
THE ADMINISTRATIVE ENMESHMENT OF THE P L M D
H.M. THE KING
M.A.W.
Min. of Finance
Min. of Interior
Min. of Justice
Advisory
Deputy
Ext.
Others
Water
Central Committee
Agri. Bank
Town Planning Office
P.L.M.D.
P.L. Div.
CENTRAL
REGIONAL
Courts
Amirates
or
Municipalities
Offices
Offices
Agrifield
local committee
2 local members
information
instruction
information
instruction
B (informal)
Technicians
B
B
B
1
2
3
1
operational membership

Fig. 13.1

was made. From that consideration it became clear that the present organizational system has some special characteristics. Fig. (13–1) shows the administrative network of the Public Land Management Department. Some of this results from the fact that any PLD programme involves sectors and interests of a very wide-ranging kind – legal, social, financial, educational and technical – and *any* PLD action requires collaboration with other specialist agencies.

This is also of course true of any agency concerned with land and water, the basic universal resource inputs. It was for this reason that it was recommended by the Regional Commission on Land and Water Use in the Near East, first session held in Lebanon, 1387H (1967), that governments should be advised to create National Committees for land and water use.

The main objectives of these Committees were to be:

1. From the findings of applied research programmes, to assist in establishing standard technical criteria for the identification of field problems, methodologies for field surveys and investigations and technical field development operations.
2. To assist in reviewing and developing technical work programmes for the applied research centres.
3. To assist in establishing a system for co-operation and co-ordination between the applied research centres.
4. To assist in introducing a system for co-operation and co-ordination between the applied research workers and technicians who are attached to interrelated sectoral Government services, namely applied Research, Education, Extension and Pilot Experimental and Development Projects.

A National Committee was suggested that should consist of representatives from all Ministries and institutions which deal with land and water use in a direct or an indirect way.

In Saudi Arabia, owing to the emergence of a PLD policy, some steps in this direction had already been taken. The response of the Ministry of Agriculture and Water was that the Central Committee, which was earlier formed in the Ministry of Agriculture and Water and whose function is to review land allocation recommendations and check the work done by the local field committees, could serve as a National Committee for the time being because it performs more or less similar functions to the suggested National Committee. The structure of the Central Committee has already been outlined in Chapter Five (p. 73).

The requirements for collaborative consultation at Central Committee level have become fairly clear. The Central Committee has the final decision-making responsibility for the PLD programme, with the

Minister of Agriculture and Water retaining rights of final approval, on the basis of proposals which come to it from the Public Land Management Department. Budgeting responsibility for the Department remains with the Ministry of Agriculture and Water, the Central Committee concerning itself essentially with allocations and general implementation.

Given the ability of the Department, in consultation with the Minister, to call on specialist consultant expertise, the formal structure established for the Central Committee would appear to be sufficiently strong. As, however, National Planning and Development policy further evolves and consequent changes in Ministerial fields of responsibility appear, it will be essential for the elements composing the Central Committee at least to represent the range of interests now included and to become fully involved in Public Land Distribution with all that this implies. As noted on p. 73, with reference to National Policy, the place of the Central Committee and indeed of the Ministry of Agriculture and Water in PLD depends greatly on how far national governmental agencies are organized on a problem-orientated basis, for example, Land and Water Use, Rural Affairs; or on a sector-orientated basis, for example, Agriculture, Water Resources, Transport, and so on. The Central Committee concerned with PLD is necessarily dealing with a multi-sectoral problem.

At the level of action and implementation, we have the Department of Public Land Management. As seen earlier, this Department has a very large spread of duties in connection with PLD as well as with range management and forestry. First, it must be satisfied of the existence in specific areas of suitable land and water resources. Second, the availability for distribution of such land (which concerns legal and religious agencies as well as the Court) has to be established. Third, there follows the need for survey identification of allocable lands. These first three responsibilities can be grouped under a general heading of "land supply".

Fourth, there is "demand". The application for Public Land to be distributed has to be organized, the applications themselves have to be examined and a variety of associated problems have to be dealt with.

Lastly, there is a group of factors which is associated with the transformation of potential resources into agriculturally-used resources. These are essentially technical, covering mainly soil, water, extension and management, agricultural subsidies, farm machinery and equipment.

In order to carry out these duties, the Department not only relies on its own central resources but also has to call on and expect the collaboration of other departments and Ministries. For implementation reliance on the local committees mentioned on p. 72 is also necessary.

As already noted, the PLMD, is under great strain because of personnel shortage. In the light of the general administrative and technical situation some decisions have been taken and some particular requirements appear.

The three groups of functions concerned with land supply, demand and technical transformation are strongly inter-related. For example, survey of land potential for the identification of land suitable for distribution is linked with surveys on the basis of which particular land use and management can be recommended, with all that this implies. The PLMD therefore has either to be established with the capability for carrying out all these functions, or else to be designed as a small, specialized agency with limited technical capability and operating as the focus of multi-agency collaboration. The range of requirements to make PLMD capable itself of dealing with all the sectoral factors, implies its elevation into what would be a Ministry within a Ministry. The alternative, in which PLMD remains the central focusing instrument but calls on other agencies, requires the establishment of a clear and effective network of collaboration and clearly defined responsibility for all parties concerned. So far, it is this latter mode of operation which has been adopted and which, with increasing refinement, will be maintained in the future. Any assessment of progress must take into account this fact and of the way in which PLMD as an instrument has been and continues to be developed as an effective means of PLD implementation.

What we expect in future years is that PLMD will be strengthened and gain more experience.

A high level of administrative staff will be appointed to organize official registration for lands utilized and others under utilization but covering only land distributed by PLMD. A national land register remains in the future and in any case would require an agency separate from PLMD.

In the interest of more effective rationalization of land and water survey and planning of use and PLD development, a standard soil survey and mapping will have to replace the present land classification as a basis for land and water improvement and management.

At the moment and as described earlier, PLMD has no regional technical offices but relies on the Agricultural Field Organization staff. Additional PLMD specialists would only be appointed to deal with special problems arising from PLMD work in specific regions. Also in each area where land distribution is carried on, a soil specialist or a farm management specialist could be appointed.

A high level of technical staff is also necessary for public and specialist divisions such as Bedouin settlements, soil classification, farm management, and so on, since they are necessary for Public Land development. Public Land utilization supervision could be coordinated by the technical staffs of PLMD and agricultural field organizations. National and regional systems of controlling such coordinated collaborative work then become necessary and are considered on p. 237.

ILO understood the importance of adapting technologies and developing local ones by saying, "If we want to develop our agriculture quickly at the beginning we could adopt technologies from other countries according to variations in local conditions while developing our own technologies."[35]

As noted before, the demand for trained suitable personnel is and will for some time continue to be greater than that which can be supplied internally in Saudi Arabia. Even the adoption of technology for an interim period will no doubt increase the need for calling on non-Saudi agencies and consultants. For the future, the indigenous development of technology and the provision of suitable personnel will require among other things a firm and continuing basis of relevant research. If PLD is to be effective, the results of relevant research are required to serve as guidelines for action; but also the personnel involved in PLD should, where relevant, have themselves a background in applied research or should know how to call on research expertise.

At the moment there is a Research and Development Department within the Ministry of Agriculture and Water but departmental terms of reference effectively mean that the Research Department confines its activities to agricultural affairs other than the land itself – crops, livestock, pest control, etc. Similarly with water; the Water Resource Development agency is almost entirely concerned with matters of hydro-geology, while the associated Projects Department is responsible for dealing with specific projects as they appear. The PLMD is left with the central responsibility of dealing with what might be called land quality and also with agricultural water utilization. If this responsibility was to be properly carried out solely by PLMD then a complete PLMD research unit, concentrating on applied research on land and water use, would be required.

Once again Saudi Arabia cannot, from the point of view of personnel, afford a proliferation of research establishments in the foreseeable future. It appears necessary from experience so far gained, that if PLD is to be effective, the PLMD should be allowed to concentrate on problem identification where problems appear in land and water use and be able to call on one or two research departments whose duties would be extended to cover these particular fields. The requirements again for the immediate future are fairly clear.

For Saudi Arabia, the development of agriculture has to depend mainly on the availability of ground-water resources due to scarcity of rainfall and its torrential nature. The widespread problems of soils are: reclamation, management practice of calcareous and sandy soils; poor fertility and difficult physical properties, mainly those related to water movement and retention. The most significant research needs lie in these two main fields of land and water use.

In the second session of the Regional Commission on land and water use in the Near East held in Cairo, 1389H (October 1969), a recommendation was made to establish and initiate the implementation of the regional applied research programme giving first priority to the study of the following problems, which the Commission had identified as being of most immediate concern to the region:

1. *Reclamation, improvement and management of sandy soils*, including
(a) Reclamation measures: fertility build-up, increasing water holding capacity, erosion control and stabilization of surface soil.
(b) Management and conservation: irrigation practices and methods, seepage losses, fertilizers and application techniques and suitable crops.

2. *Reclamation, improvement and management of calcareous soils*, including
(a) Reclamation measures: land preparation, measures against soil crusting and fertility build-up.
(b) Management and conservation measures: selection of suitable crops, fertilizer requirements and methods of application, tillage and cultivation practices.

3. *Reclamation, improvement and management of salt-affected soil*, including where applicable, the control of water-logging.

4. *Effective use of irrigation water*, including: determination of the most economic use of irrigation water, taking into account consumption, application efficiency, crops and cropping patterns.

There are, of course, other areas in which investigation is required, for example, farm husbandry, farm organization and management, marketing and so on, and some aspects of these are touched on below. Again the basic requirement is for co-ordinated collaboration at particular implementation levels in order to ensure that land distributed under the PLD programme is properly utilized. This also now involves the place of PLD and PLMD in regional, ministerial and national policies.

At the grass-root level much of this becomes evident in the local implementation of PLD. This includes local committees and agricultural field organizations.

Members of local committees are paid by the Government. The Ministry of Agriculture and Water makes payment to one half of the members while the other half is paid by other Ministries whose representatives participate in the local committees. In these committees, local experts are best chosen by the Ministry of Agriculture and Water with the help of the Amirate in the area. In those regions where there is no branch of the Ministry of Finance and National Economy, its members on the local committee are chosen from other Government institutions existing in the area. At the beginning, some of them were being allocated Land Distribution plots and, since they exercise allocation judgement as members of the committees, this matter is under consideration.

Almost all the administrative work concerned with completion, receiving, handling and filing of the application forms is dealt with by the agricultural field staff. Some of them ask for a secretary to join the committee.

Local implementation, however, also requires technical servicing at field level. It was not the intention of PLMD to have a permanent field staff within the department to deal with Public Land Distribution, since Agricultural Field Organizations could provide administrative and technical work to satisfy the needs of Land Distribution (see pp. 221–226). To ensure the best subsequent utilization of distributed lands, it was proposed, rather than to create permanent PLMD regional organizations, to send an inter-Departmental technical team to each area of Land Distribution. This would consist of four technicians, one each from Research, PLMD and the Extension Departments, the fourth from the Agricultural Bank. They were to have a close contact with utilizers and assist in land development. The idea was accepted by the Ministry of Agriculture and Water but the problem is that the Research and Public Land Management Departments do not have permanent technicians in all areas where Land Distribution is carried out. The correct procedure would appear to be the technical strengthening of the Agricultural Field Organizations – other than PLMD – on a regional basis (see pp. 225–226). The growing recognition of the importance of extension activities for agricultural development has underlined the necessity for increasing the generally limited numbers of skilled staff in extension services.

FAO has worked out the minimum requirement for the intensification of extension work needed as one field worker to 500 farms.

Requirements for trained manpower exist both at the professional and technical levels of the various types of farming in order to create more qualified staff for extension and determine the need for specialized supervision.

Still at the local level, the Ministry of Agriculture and Water is always in touch with other ministries participating in the local committees to persuade their members to be more active in decision-making concerning applications for Public Land. Effective steps towards a reorientation of agricultural extensions and services have been taken. Great difficulties in implementing these changes can be expected but a more efficient and more effective programme of service to agriculture has now claimed priority.

The relative slowness of progress can be explained in part by the novelty of the concept at the local level, for example, local administrators do not have a background of familiarity based on experience.

So far in this chapter we have examined the most important aspects of the machinery for PLD and the general lessons learnt up to this time. Let us now examine the situation in the context of the general concept of PLD and also in the light of the specific Saudi situation.

Universally, the distribution of land in any country must be regarded as a combination of practical measures. The motivation for, and the method of, such distribution is affected by some standard variables, so that all Land Distribution schemes have some points in common such as, the need for classifying Public Land, the evaluation of the potential of such land, the development of some acceptable tenurial systems, and so on.

In practice, however, each national system must be unique because it reflects a unique sets of variables. These are:

- Socio-Political.
- Physical resource availability.
- Economic demand and supply.

One can see in Saudi Arabia the appearance of a pragmatic system reflecting,

(a) the specific environmental and resource characteristics of Saudi Arabia;
(b) human characteristics ranging from factors of social structure to demography;
(c) the specific constraints, limitations and opportunities devised;
(d) as evidenced by response to (a) and (b), the Saudi Arabian Government's cultural and political philosophy.

The universal framework might be described as confirming certain general requirements, creating suitable institutions for agricultural development, building an honest bureaucracy and stable political system centrally and locally. It might be described as a change from a traditional custom-oriented society to the evolution of a system of values dynamically based on modern knowledge and techniques.

So far we have made a presentation of the facts and evolution of Public Land Distribution up to the present time. Land distribution has been considered as a useful tool to satisfy the national interest such as mobilizing national resources, adjusting holding size and achieving Bedouin assimilation. It also appears from our study that PLMD programmes and the procedure of Land Distribution adopted by the Government are flexible and designed as being particularly suitable for Saudi Arabia.

We saw also that the procedure is developing and modernizing to face the problems of Land Distribution and utilization. Now we must examine the possibility of abstracting some general principles to provide some guidance for Land Distribution and utilization in the future.

The shortage of data and the shortness of the period during which Land Distribution has been carried out cannot enable us to make more than an interim assessment of the policies to mobilize the potential possibilities available to speed up Public Land Distribution and utilization in a practical way for the hope of agricultural development. We have to make such an assessment remembering the inter-relationship of the many elements involved in Land Distribution and utilization. This is a lesson to be learnt not only nationally but internationally.

The basic need is to establish identification of objectives. The general objectives come from general planning policy. One element in this national policy is the objective of combining economic growth with national stability. The second is to build regional socio-economic stability. The third is to exploit natural resources which could be used for the benefit of the society.

Assessment and conclusions

In any assessment of how these demands have been satisfied we must turn again to lessons learnt from previous Saudi Arabian experience, primarily, the lessons learnt from the first and second trials of Land Distribution.

The situations which faced the first and second trials for settlement in Saudi Arabia have to be always borne in mind. The first trial (see Chapter Three, pp. 36–41) was directed towards tribal settlement stability. Its terms of reference were general – technical and financial expertise was extremely limited at that time; nevertheless this trial succeeded in satisfying to a great extent its purpose mainly of improving tribal political stability. In other words, it satisfied the first objective which we mentioned before. The second trial (see Chapter Three, pp. 41–49) had more technical and financial backing. This was directed at tackling the socio-economic problems arising from harsh environmental risks with which the Bedouins in the north were faced. This project succeeded in establishing agricultural communities, socially and economically reasonably well satisfied. Both trials had no advance planning because agricultural resources were not yet explored nor was physical infrastructure well established nationally. The third trial (see Chapter Three, pp. 50–52) was applied to specified areas mostly already having agricultural traditions and to be cultivated in the same manner. In this programme, the third objective began to be clear and at the same time other objectives were taken into consideration.

Secondly, the reactions and attitudes of the people concerned can be shown to be important. What has become clear is that the subjective appreciation of what is proposed or implemented has to be taken into consideration. For example, some people knowing Article 9 of the Ordinance, which implies that all granted areas in the past which are not cultivated, or those parts of plots which are non-cultivated should be liable to the application of the PLDO, feel that this is a type of expropriation. Others looking at Land Distribution maps (which are numerically divided as equal plots of 50 donums) see what appears to be an egalitarian plan to give people land holdings of equal size.

Thirdly, we can now compare the Saudi Arabian PLD programme with the experience gained by other countries which have applied Land Distribution programmes. From this other lessons can be learnt. For example, the key variables for land laws in Syria, Iraq and Egypt are basically social and economic, whereas in Saudi Arabia there is no social injustice in land holdings and at the moment there is great national wealth. In taking into account also the physical characteristics of these countries, it seems there exist some factors which produce similarities to the Saudi Arabian case study regions, for example:

Qasim. Similar to Syria from the point of having commercial agriculture, farming relatively large units, and the presence of individuals with capital obtained outside agriculture.

Al-Joaf. Similar to Egypt from the point of heavy pressure on land resource, low incomes, small-scale operation, capital shortage; here co-operative societies could add a new dimension.

Tabuk. Similar to Iraq in that potential developers have capital, physical potentialities exist but the land for political location reasons in a frontier position is controlled in availability by the State for non-economic reasons. If land is made available then private enterprise farming could rapidly expand.

Wadi Sarhan. As noted, a settlement scheme analogous to Libyan projects from the point of Bedouin sedentarization, carefully oriented technical assistance is essential in specific project terms rather than general PLD implementation (see Chapter Eight, pp. 131–133).

Given the fact that we can observe in the different PLD projects some regional variations in situations and in implementation practice it is clear that Saudi Arabia has already adopted a pragmatic approach to PLD. The universal factors affecting PLD still apply but the Government is responding to the unique set of national variables which appear to favour the adoption of a particular range of possible measures.

From these three programmes of Land Distribution and from experience gained so far in PLD one can identify three significant characteristics:

1. Saudi Arabia has worked out its general development policy and begun with general regulations and outlines for PLD within this policy.
2. General regional application is important so that no region of the Saudi community can feel that it is left without government care. This could produce benefits by slowing down the rush from rural areas to towns and avoid consequent social disturbance.
3. PLD is not a rigid policy for a fixed period and this allows modification and improvement.

The first lesson learnt is that distribution alone is not sufficient; follow-up assistance may often be required, adequate to put utilizers in a position to help themselves. The steps already taken are through extension, subsidies and agricultural bank loans. Also the need for an integrated relationship is realized, focusing the whole facilities of the Ministry of Agriculture and Water to develop the Cultivable and Distributable Land and mobilize the whole resources such as water and soil of different types and qualities in each producing area.

Second is that particular sets of factors govern the nature of the programme in any particular country. This includes characteristics, in the physical sense, of the country, the legal basis such as *Shari'a*, the possibilities of financing and technical shortage of personnel.

Third, Government activities necessary to prepare land for distribution may include non-agricultural elements such as building roads and schools. The new utilizers may be in need of large amounts of additional capital in order to set up economically sound farms; such capital allocation cannot be isolated from other sectors. Infrastructural provision as well as agricultural capital input involves not only PLD but general development policy.

For the country of Saudi Arabia it is feasible to ignore for the present the *short-term* returns on investment in PLD. It may be regarded as similar to an infant industry which needs generous investment to encourage early growth and at the same time to be supported in different ways to direct its youthful efforts.

For successful implementation in the Saudi situation some particular requirements must be met. The requirements can be identified at the input level, for example, nature and distribution of resources, nature of social organization, population mobility, and so on. The responses are partly technical and administrative.

The technical assistance and supervision sectors came up in connection with a Land Distribution Programme through their importance for the success of the programme and because of their contribution to the development of the country.

Technical assistance from different institutions could be channelled in an integrated way to give the best help to the utilizers and various types of land settlements.

For the achievement of success by governmental institutions working in rural areas it is required to consider:

1. Social and economic studies of services currently provided by these institutions and services which could be provided to achieve agricultural development in areas subject to distribution.
2. A common plan for the development of each distribution area. This plan should include agricultural services, agricultural production and animal production.

Many other aspects of Public Land Distribution programmes require the integration of the many aspects of development. This can only be technically achieved through effective administrative collaboration between the Governmental institutions which are related to agricultural development, in the Ministry of Agriculture and Water, and in the Department of Bedouin Affairs in the Ministry of Interior. Each of the above-mentioned institutions could help through its effective programme in the distribution areas and the services provided by them could be oriented. From what has been said about Ministries concerned with rural areas, it is evident that each Ministry is now responsible for all work related to its field. It is also obvious that more co-operation and co-ordination between services and projects conducted in rural areas will speed up the development.

As noted in Chapter Four, pp. 57–58, PLMD is only one arm of the Ministry of Agriculture and Water, working in collaboration with others in order best to achieve the desired results from its specific actions. Several Departments participate in the executively responsible Central Committee for Land Distribution as well as the economic adviser. Other advisers (law adviser and *Shari'a* adviser) not participating in the Central Committee, act in certain matters related to their specialist capacity. A senior geologist from the Water Resources Development is participating in the Central Committee. The Water Conservation Department at the moment issues permission for well drilling. When the Water Code (Ordinance) now under consideration is issued it will be responsible for the avoidance of water and land waste. A new departmental structure concerned with water use is under consideration and a new Department called "Water Rights" may be created to be responsible for administering the new code; a National Water Committee may also be created. In three other fields of great importance to the success of PLD changes and new developments are being considered within the Ministry (MAW), this in turn requires that some formal relationship with the PLMD be established.

Firstly, at present a working group (consultant company) is examining the feasibility of improving agricultural services and extension in the Agricultural Field Organizations. Utilizers benefiting from land distribution will be in need of an extension programme designed to help them to make the best use of their resources.

Secondly, the provision of plant protection services has placed a heavy burden on the personnel of Field Organizations. The Ministry (MAW) is trying to cease providing this free input service and other materials where possible and consider systems of subsidy that will more effectively encourage individuals to do things themselves, with possibly greater assistance through extension teaching and the strengthening of supporting infrastructures, for example, roads and supplies.

Thirdly, a programme was approved by HM The King in 1393H (1973) to train farmers and their sons in a Training Centre in Riyad. They are provided with financial support during the training period. Training or demonstration could be arranged in the same way for new farmers in a distribution area. The aim is to encourage utilizers to learn in order to know farming methods and products adaptable for the area. Particular emphasis should also be placed on the training of staff at different levels in all relevant activities of the project including practical use of the research work.

Fig. (13-1) illustrates the main elements involved in the relationships between agencies within the Ministry (MAW) and between Ministries.

The Ministry of Labour and Social Affairs does not come into the picture in the implementation of Land Distribution but it is responsible for the Community Development Centres which operate only in areas of sedentary farming population exceeding 20,000 and its co-operation is expected.

The Ministry of Justice has to appoint a religious judge in the Ministry of Agriculture and Water. Once this has happened, it is believed that courts will have a better chance of solving problems, especially those of a religious nature.

In this complex situation in Saudi Arabia, the main agencies concerned with agricultural development then are: the Ministry of Agriculture and Water, Agricultural Bank, Co-operative Department, Community Development and Agricultural Education. The Ministry of Agriculture and Water remains the backbone of agricultural development.

Within the general structure, the PLMD holds the responsibility for Land Distribution and supervision during the period of utilization. Utilization covers cultivation and farming as well. Utilizers have began to acquire technical assistance from the Ministry of Agriculture and Water, since it is responsible mainly for agricultural development. According to its terms of reference, the PLMD has found itself dealing with and involved in all matters related to Public Land Development besides the Public Land Distribution.

In examining the mechanism for land distribution and the contribution of different institutions to land distribution, one can now see that there still exist places for strengthening or modification. In Fig. 13–1 the administrative network which has been established to deal with the complex needs of PLD is illustrated.

Early in the programme of work and also becoming apparent in the functioning of Government machinery the regional question arose. Fig. 13–2 illustrates some aspects of the relationship between Central Government and those field operations which have regional connotations. The implementation of Land Distribution should combine both in the field and in the specific areas to supply the needs of the various interrelated services that utilizers require. Land Development at present carried out in a few areas has given rise to a nucleus of work groups and their results have been fairly satisfactory. But, as Land Development expands to cover other distributed areas, then the regional level appears to be the most effective for integrated programmes. When a large proportion of farmers are participating in development of newly distributed land, these programmes need designing at regional levels in order to organize direct and indirect assistance to them. Any such development would affect so many sectors and interests that this highly complex matter cannot be considered at this time but in the near future it will be one of the vital aspects of development.

Once the feasibility and need for increasing the effectiveness of the PLD programme, by ensuring that the requirements noted earlier

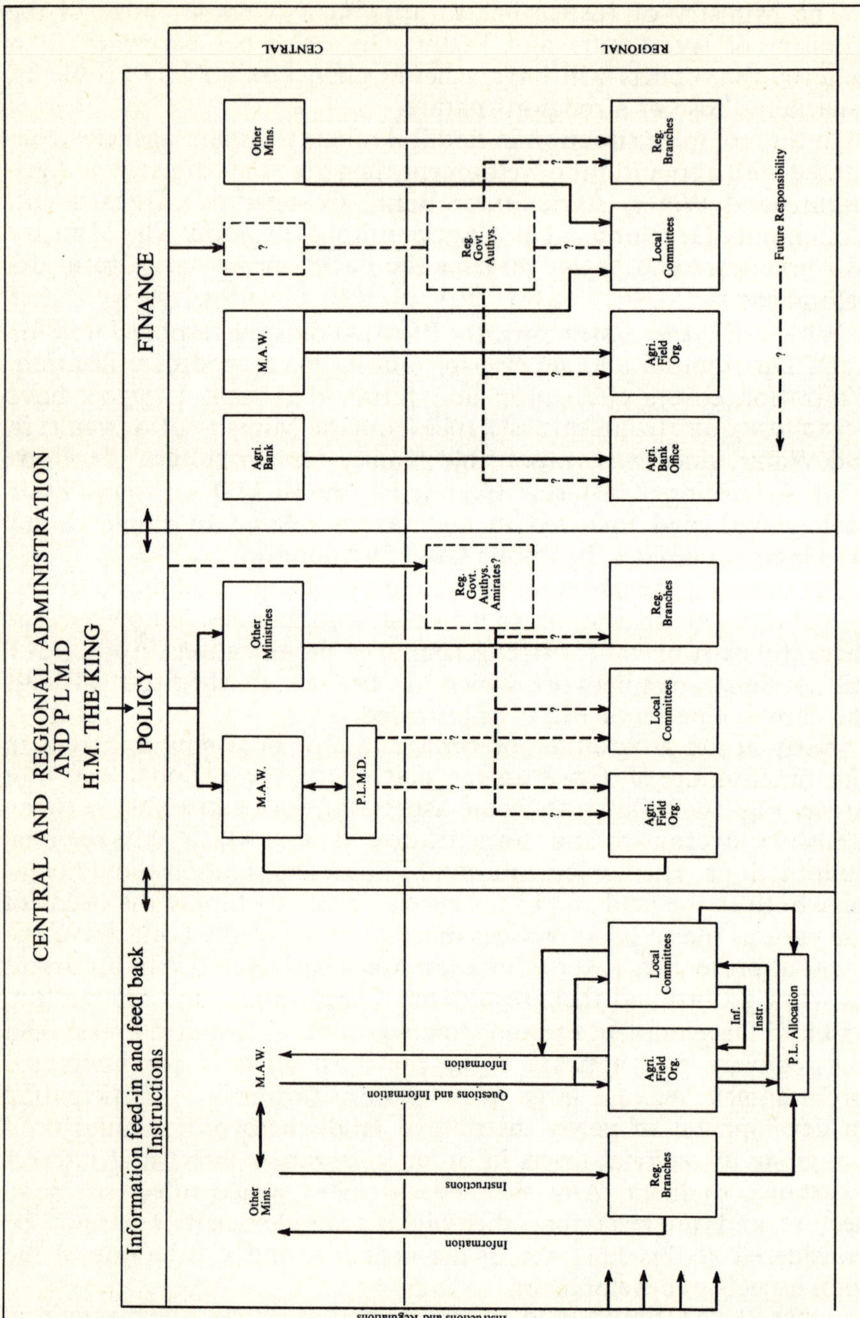
CENTRAL AND REGIONAL ADMINISTRATION
AND P L M D
H.M. THE KING
POLICY
FINANCE
Information feed-in and feed back
Instructions
CENTRAL
REGIONAL
Other Mins.
Reg. Branches
Reg. Govt. Authys.
Local Committees
M.A.W.
Agri. Field Org.
Agri. Bank
Agri. Bank Office
Future Responsibility
Other Ministries
Reg. Govt. Authys. Amirates?
P.L.M.D.
Inf.
Instr.
P.L. Allocation
Information
Questions and Information
Instructions
Instructions and Regulations

Fig. 13.2

are met through some kind of regional approach, is accepted, then this raises the whole question of regional planning and regional administration.

Here, however, we cannot explore the whole field of regional planning but must confine ourselves to noting what developments there have been in the matter of Governmental regional administrative structure and to assessing how the consequences affect the work of the PLMD.

The principle of creating a regional administrative organization was established in the Royal Decree No. 12 of 1383H (1963). This divides the country into several administrative provinces,[13] each one subdivided into "districts" and each "district" into centres (see p. 55). The new feature of this organization is that the provincial Governor would become an administrative officer co-operating with a provincial council and the representatives of the various Ministries.

In accordance with this organization and relevant to PLD is the proposal that every Ministry has to consider the opinion of the Provincial Councils, as regards the planning of State-owned unused lands (Public Lands) near towns or villages for sale or utilization and where no municipalities exist and any offer for sale of State-owned utilizable agricultural lands within the province boundary.

Other features are clearly going to be of importance but since the country was not yet ready at that time for the implementation of such organization, the decree was not then applied. Now a further modification of this organization is being carried out. Creating a new regional administrative organization with the general structure of regional Government to deal with rural development could be expected as a logical measure. If such an organization were brought into existence whereby the whole Government service sector could co-operate and co-ordinate within a Provincial Council, then it could deal with all matters related to Public Land utilization. For example, a Western Region master plan has been prepared for the Ministry of Interior by consultants, and this presumes not only the growth of a regional planning approach but also of a regional administration. Further regional studies of rural development programmes immediately lead one to assume that PLD projects will have to be tied in with regional development and regional administration.

It is true that in developing countries all over the world, and especially in the Middle East, projects for development and modernization are always begun in urban areas before rural areas. The ideology behind this is to build up the service sector. However, as noted above, rural projects distinct from PLD are now proposed in Saudi Arabia, linking agriculture with other sectors.

This means a combination of offering direct and indirect assistance to new land utilizers on a national level while at the same time including implementation on a regional level. That would combine, both in the field and in a specific area, the various intertwined and interrelated services which the utilizer needs.

The opening of new lands like Tabuk and Wadi Sarhan involves the creation of new communications, roads and schools (see Table No. (3–3)). There would be less uncertainty in previously settled areas like Qasim because the resources and markets of such areas are known, but everywhere non-agricultural services and facilities are essential for the success of PLD-based agriculture.

For example, as we have already noted, the Agricultural Bank has branches in districts and technicians in the field and their offices are usually located in Agricultural Field Organizations.

If regional planning is to be given high priority, then, along with the work of other agencies, the PLMD requirements for effective implementation of established PLD policies (see pp. 242–244), must clearly be phased in. Similarly, the administrative and technical mechanism for PLD must be phased into the embryo regional administrative structure.

This will not be easy because, while considerable reformist changes in the style of Government have taken place in Saudi Arabia over the last twenty years, policies remain highly centralized and power remains in the hand of His Majesty the King. Formal bureaucracy has grown up on this basis and channels of executive policies are equally in accordance with the existing power system. Not only, therefore, is the phasing in of PLMD and other agencies, with new structures necessary for organizational reasons, going to take some time, but also the phasing in of PLD, with all that this implies concerning development and rural change. This can only proceed at the same rate as the evolution in the style of Government. The emphasis so far has been on stability and change, and this desirable combination will dictate the speed of the evolution in the style and philosophy of Government.

The third method of assessing the progress of and position reached by PLD, which we noted on p. 221, is the way in which PLD has fitted into national policies.

Saudi Arabia is already at a point of utilizing a great range of resources and Government income where specific goals are competitive. The overall picture in policy-making is reflected in the amounts and timing of Government investments in different programmes and the intensity of particular administrative mechanisms organized to their implementation. The broad generalized goals relevant in the Five-

Year Plan can be outlined as, firstly, to improve efficiency and increase output of agriculture;[19] secondly, to achieve an equitable distribution of resources and welfare for this and future generations, and thirdly, a relevant rural contribution to, and participation in, overall development.

Initial policy implementations were of widespread income increases and social and welfare improvements among the large number of population engaged in sedentary, nomadic and semi-nomadic agriculture.[32] The physical infrastructure, both in national productive sectors, for example, electricity, transport, communication, and so on, and in urban areas has been given great emphasis in recent years. There is a consistency between development requirements and trends in the economy as a whole and the general manpower supply available for development. The present specific shortages in manpower – technicians, semi-technicians, or manual labourers – point to the need to release the large numbers in rural populations, who are working below capacity, for work in other economic activities.

Saudi Arabians are moving towards urban and industrial employment whereas agriculture has a decreasing pull. The move towards developing and breaking away from traditional agriculture is appreciated even more in the light of extreme shortage of manpower for administration, planning and management. Saudi Arabia has yet to start the development and transformation of the several agricultural sub-sectors and the linkage of the overall sector to other sub-sectors of the economy. The agricultural sector has to grow, agricultural production units and farms have to be enlarged. MAW and other Governmental bodies have initiated a far-reaching set of policies which relate to settlement, development, production and prices. Agricultural policy is represented by many inputs, mechanisms, institutions and actions initiated by the Government.

The six conditions which are directly necessary at the farm level to promote agricultural development are: favourable commodity prices,[32] favourable input prices, capital and credit, available technologies and relevant material equipment, knowledge and communication, and finally, appropriate tenure conditions given the existence of potential land resources which can be exploited.

Favourable tenure environment is accepted in Saudi Arabia as implying owner-operation under which the individual making the investment realizes the full return on it. Ownership is a necessary condition of tenure to assure incentive in development through the favourable conditions which are mentioned above. The move towards ownership is somewhat complicated in Saudi Arabia, since utilizers must frequently make considerable investment in land preparation and water systems. It is further complicated in certain locations of settled agriculture where functions of ownership, management and labour are all provided by separate persons with different knowledge, capital, skills and economic incentives (see also Chapter One).

Table No. (6–1) shows the proportion of cultivated land held under three main types of tenure. The PLD programme, however, has added a new factor. Allocated land carries with it from the beginning a Utilization Certificate which legally entitles the allottee to utilize the land for agricultural and animal production. The allottee automatically benefits from the full range of MAW services and also from the Agricultural Bank; he may also benefit from any schemes which are specifically devised to assist PLD allottees. Under *Shari'a* Law (see Chapter One) the allottee becomes the owner of the land once he has utilized it. The legal PLMD requirement is that utilization must be practised during the first two or three years after allotment in which case a deed to the land grants the new owner full rights under *Shari'a* Law. As noted in Chapter Five the Third Phase PLD programme administered by the PLMD has had to proceed in this tenurial matter with pragmatism and flexibility. No revolutionary concepts of tenure have been introduced and in this sector the programme has remained in step with the national situation.

Land distribution after the general survey of agricultural potential, for example, soil and water, followed the economic aspect and was limited to potential areas in general, where, before the Ordinance, land granting happened in the whole country. Land Distribution is considered as a transitional stage to develop large agricultural units. Land Distribution development was facilitated by Government impact so that the general trends for subsidies were now established.

Clearly, the financial needs of PLD have to be seen as part of the total development needs, which in turn form the basis for national development investment policies. Briefly, the financial needs of the PLD programme can be outlined as follows.

All the other farm-level requirements stem from national agricultural policy, the basis of which has been the encouragement of general and specific increases in agricultural production; variations in the programmes affecting particular commodities have occurred and will continue to do so.

The possibilities for the expansion of the agricultural area in Saudi Arabia are of course limited by the physical environment. The general distribution of potential land for agricultural land expansion as evaluated in the six areas surveyed are shown in Fig. 13–3.

SAUDI ARABIA CULTIVATED AND CULTIVABLE LAND

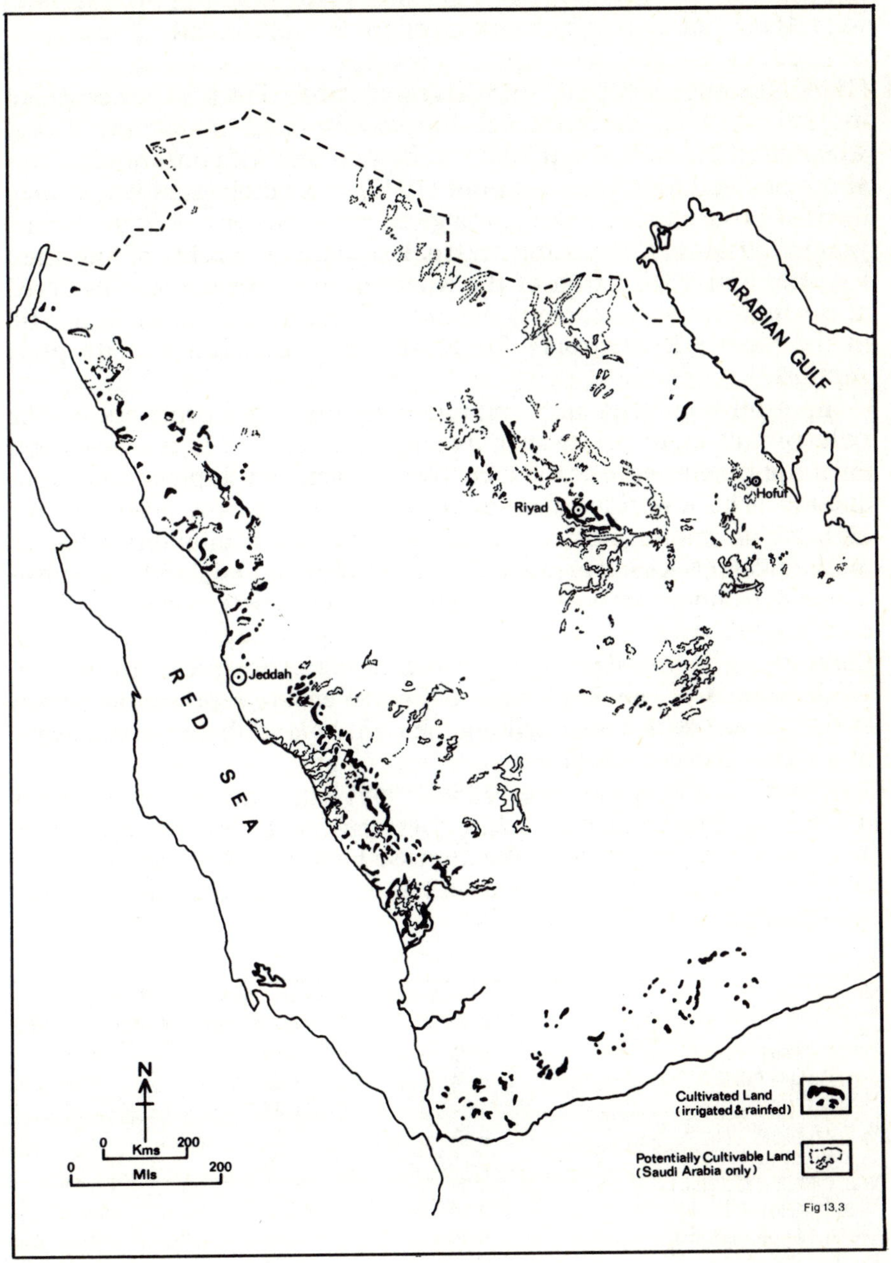

Fig 13.3

Saudi Arabian cultivated and cultivable land

Agricultural products account for about 30 per cent of the total imports for the Kingdom. In 1385–86H (1965–66), import subsidies were 16.67 per cent which amounts to 50 million SR. Those now covered, have only been reduced on wheat, rice and meat. In 1389H (1969), the import subsidy on wheat was reduced to 8.33 per cent and in 1391H (1971), the meat subsidy was stopped completely. Local wheat production is about 90,000 tons/year and the consumption was about 380,000 tons/year in 1390H (1970). An accelerated wheat production programme is planned to give a total increase of 75,000 tons/year in 1395H (1975) by using Mexipak seeds. The subsidy of imported fertilizer and a reduction of the wheat import subsidy is considered at the moment as an encouragement of local wheat production. Still in the picture is a subsidy for local rice production and its price support.

Input price controls also encourage and increase production. The reduction of input prices such as nutrition seeds (e.g. as wheat) and farm equipment serve as the incentive for farm development and production. The lowering of input prices can serve as a substitute for higher commodity price or resource of service availability (that is, mechanical service, farm practice or technology). The shift from subsidizing consumers' import commodities (by complete price stop or reduction) to local products could produce a significant breakthrough in the entire agricultural economy by increasing agricultural production.

All policies of this kind must of course ensure a profitable return to the farmers whilst also striking the right balance between the needs of a particular commodity.

Between 1380H (1960) and 1385H (1965) wheat and barley resulted in net losses to the farmer, while tomatoes, water melon and fruits showed positive net returns. We discussed before in Chapter Nine the effort and the programme set by the Government to increase wheat production.

Table No. (13–1) Average cost and return in 1380–83H (1960–63).

Crops	*Average Production Cost. SR/Kg*	*Average Farm Revenue. SR/Kg*	*Profit (+) or Loss (−). SR/Kg*
Wheat (Taif)	0.93	0.82	−0.11
Wheat (Qasim)	0.94	0.68	−0.26
Wheat (North)	1.04	0.86	−0.18
Barley (Taif)	0.85	0.68	−0.17
Tomato (Taif)	0.71	1.00	+0.29
Water Melon (Jeddah)	0.39	0.60	+0.21
Water Melon (North)	0.36	0.60	+0.24
Water Melon (Qasim)	0.45	0.60	+0.15
Fruits	0.61	0.96	+0.35

This Table illustrates the division into two parts of the effects of agricultural policy, that is, the return to individual farmers and the production of required commodities. Increased production must be achieved, as is expected in the National Plan, and a satisfactory balance between this and farm revenue must be reached.

The three elements, mentioned above, taken together interact to provide a greater incentive to increase production.

Financial allocations to the agricultural sector through the Development Plan period have reached 1,467.7 million SR whereas recurrent expenditures reached 973.8 million SR and project expenditures reached 493.9 million SR. These figures and the others following are illustrated in Table No. (7–11). The expenditure for agriculture is mainly channelled through MAW and the Agricultural Bank. Funds are 90 per cent for MAW and 10 per cent for the bank respectively. Allocations for the Bank reached 150.2 million SR. Its accelerated expansion calls for a major increase in capital and operating funds.

Allocations for several departments participating in land development and production are: 51.6 million SR for Research and Development; 331 million SR for Extension and Agricultural Services; 20.5 million SR for Water Resources Development; 5 million for Training; and 5.6 million SR for Public Land Management. Each Department has its area of concentration.

Research Development Department

Confines its applied research mostly to statistics, plant production, crops, veterinary and farm equipment. The three Research Centres are planned to provide more effective research administration. The laboratory available is analysing soil and water samples for Public Land and others. Other research is performed in several Departments of the Ministry.

Extension and Agricultural Services Department

Focuses on pest control, veterinary services, farm demonstrations and extension through its Agricultural Field Organizations. In the economic plan, the focus will be shifted to teaching the farmers through demonstrations of the production of vegetables, forage, animals and new varieties of wheat.

The Training Department is focusing now on a training programme for MAW personnel, extension agriculturists and demonstration workers. This is also besides the training programme for farmers and their sons.

Finally, the Water Resources Development Department is responsible for finding economic water for agriculture and the Water Conservation Department focusing on water control.

About 19 per cent of the total funds used in agriculture are obtained from subsidies at present. Most of the supporting subsidies of MAW increase by 10 to 15 per cent each year. Allocations for subsidies are 23 million SR for price support, 73.8 million SR for fertilizer, 75 million SR for farm equipment and 105 million SR for farm development (small irrigation development). All these figures are illustrated in Table No. (7–12).

Price support of newly imported Mexipak wheat seed by MAW might be introduced to maintain profitability. Practices including land preparation, mechanical planting, fertilizing, better water application, weed control and improved harvesting will be introduced by multiplication/demonstration teams of MAW.

Animal production is encouraging. Previous subsidies to live animal raising have been replaced by subsidies on concentrated fodders which could directly benefit both livestock and poultry production. This policy is clearly reflected in the approval of subsidizing the concentrated imported fodder by 50 per cent in 1394H (1974), a feature introduced since the issue of the National Plan. During the first six months, the fertilizer subsidy covers all kinds of imported fertilizers, after which MAW has to decide which kind of fertilizer should be subsidized according to the technical needs of production and development.

All in all, the policies outlined above have at least achieved the aim of increasing total agricultural production; present programmes are particularly concerned with encouraging the growth of livestock production.

Future possibilities

Where the bringing of new land into agricultural production is concerned, as is the case with PLD, there are other additional requirements for the future, the first of these being *specially focused* financial assistance.

Land development needs initial capital investment at the beginning for well drilling and land preparation and these problems of financing land utilization will remain important.

The encouragement by the State of the operation of credit facilities for land utilizers is perhaps the most important single procedure which the State can adopt for helping the utilizer. The first difficulty centres on the limited financial status and credit-worthiness of the new utilizers who predominate in the farms and production systems of several localities.

Tabuk and Qasim have better standing with capital to start with than does Al-Joaf.

Table No. (13–2) The distribution of income/year for utilizers in Tabuk.*

Income groups (in 000 SR pa)	*No. of Utilizers in Each Income Group*
Up to 5	67
More than 5–10	477
,, ,, 10–15	658
,, ,, 15–20	491
,, ,, 20–25	255
,, ,, 25–30	176
,, ,, 30–35	33
,, ,, 35–40	63
,, ,, 40	317
TOTAL	2,537

*Unpublished departmental data.

In many cases the utilizers' financial capabilities are limited. The most efficient and time-tested method for overcoming this difficulty is to grant credit facilities to these utilizers through payments in instalments, starting with well-drilling loans. Usually the successful execution of the programme will also call for the extension of credit to farmers for the purpose of acquiring equipment, buildings and other items of capital. The Agricultural Bank would also be the best medium to help in the supply of agricultural machinery by mobilizing subsidy systems. The Agricultural Bank already obtains profit from capital invested in agricultural enterprises, provided this investment does not contradict Islamic principles in general and that principle prohibiting usury in particular. Giving the Agricultural Bank the responsibility for the implementation of the farm machinery subsidy would be an effective step in drawing the Bank closer to the Ministry's plans and operations.

Agricultural co-operatives would be a further effective means through which direct communication for purposes of execution of social development programmes and the provision of concentrated services could be made. Co-operatives could concentrate on machine units necessary for land preparation, water distribution and harvesting or threshing operations which are not economic for ownership by individuals.

There is a need for developing agricultural marketing facilities in the PLD areas so as to ensure adequate markets and stable prices and improve incomes and standards of living for farmers. These would also provide incentives for the full and efficient utilization of the Nation's agricultural and water resources and help to meet consumers' needs for adequate and healthy supplies of food at reasonable prices. In brief, it may be said that the basic objective of any marketing programme is to have the right product in the right place in the right form at the right price.

This problem is complicated because of the factors involved in it and requires careful planning over a long period. For example, roads between producing and consuming areas are a factor limiting the development and expansion of market outlets for horticultural crops – especially in view of the vast distances involved, the high temperatures encountered and the high perishability of these crops. Where paved roads are available, truck transport is used and costs do not appear to be prohibitive since petrol costs are low and many trucks are available for hire. Building roads and road maintenance is expensive in a huge country like Saudi Arabia but an adequate freight-carrying road system remains essential. Until recently, road networks have mainly linked importing centres such as Jeddah with consumption centres and now a new emphasis is required.

The limited administrative manpower of the Government and the Ministry of Agriculture and Water at present cannot develop or handle a large network of storage, processing and marketing facilities since it can be used better where it has a greater comparative advantage. So these could be planned as a long-term policy.

Lastly, we should note that the technological requirements themselves have various further implications for the success of PLD. We may illustrate this by briefly mentioning the questions of the utilization of agricultural machinery and the designing of suitable production programmes for relatively small new farms and landholders.

The phenomenon of the great increase in the wages for agricultural labour, inconsistent with labour productivity, is symptomatic of the state of agriculture in Saudi Arabia and is caused by psychological and social factors and traditional customs even more than by rising oil revenues. Most of the public utilizers, even farmers in general, disdain to do manual work and rely on labour to work without efficient supervision.

This means that a large population works below capacity in the agricultural sector and this leads to disguised unemployment. In this situation, with existing capital and labour being attracted to the towns, mechanization is the only alternative on the new lands.

MAW had about 725 tractors (crawler and wheel) with various implements in 1390H (1970). Rentals charged to farmers (in 63 field organizations) cover about one-third of the operational cost. Out of this number of tractors, 50 per cent were not working due to the large variety of makes of tractors and the unavailability of spare parts. MAW decided to transfer this operation to the private sector and sold them to co-operative societies and farmers with 50 per cent and 25 per cent reduction of the actual cost respectively. The decision was also made because too many of the Ministry's personnel were occupied in purchasing, operating and maintaining this fleet of tractors and equipment. The Ministry is giving thought to the possibility of encouraging farm machinery co-operatives. A farm machinery subsidy was also started and the Agricultural Bank has begun to give loans.

Financial, social and technical matters are all involved. So far the PLD bringing of new land into production has meant that the immediate and specific production requirements for labour, machinery, credit, and so on, have been met on a piecemeal basis. As the youthful PLD programme matures and the immediate pressures diminish, so the possibilities of evaluating more integrated programmes appear.

The last points appear to be of importance if the newly utilized lands are to contribute effectively to development policies. They should be built into the framework of Land Distribution and Development, first taking into account predominant private enterprise and varying scales of production. The agricultural sector is, and should be, based on private entrepreneurship in agriculture. The decisions of what to produce, how much to produce, how to produce and how to sell products, are best made by each farmer. Farming by fiat and regulation is ineffective due to the existence of great numbers of farming units and the strength of agricultural traditions including following the example of others.[32]

Under the Ordinance, commercial farm companies, under special permission, may be allocated land to cultivate up to 400 ha in extent. This is so, even though it is known that the creation of very large farms might conflict with the broader goal of wide popular participation of large numbers of the Society in development. The experience gained during the first six years, however, is that no local, foreign or joint venture company has even tried to apply for a contribution.

Benefiting the masses by granting them land ownership of something of value increases both their social status and self-esteem. The stage and current environment of economic development does not, in fact, call for an agricultural structure of very large farms and PLD programmes in future will continue to concentrate on dealing with relatively small landholdings.

Secondly, flexible and differentiated production programmes are required. The restraints on, and opportunities for, production represent the effects of all of the physical resource supplies, water and soil of different types and qualities in each specific producing area and therefore there must be flexibility. Activity variables would cover all of the crop and livestock potentials and technologies in each region.

At the moment, for all practical purposes, we can divide Saudi Arabia into a series of agricultural regions in each of which there is at present some cultivation and in some of which there is a measure of unused potential (Fig. 13–4). It will be seen that each of these regions has its own special environment and locational characteristics which have to be taken into account. The production to be emphasized at each location must be related to natural resources and regional characteristics should be used for establishing priorities among investment alternatives. The programme should also be developed according to the extension service's experience, and its observations concerning the possibilities for introducing new crop and livestock varieties and production systems.

Already we can identify some measures which could be taken and which are based on regionally variable situations:[31]

1. Cultivate a greater range of crops and avoid concentration on one crop; this method guarantees the producer some return in case he experiences any physical difficulties or a drop in prices of particular commodities.
2. Raising forage crops because:
   (a) they give a profitable cash return, this over a longer period than food-grains;
   (b) they will assist the possibility of establishing livestock production in small farms.
3. The production of various vegetables especially the leafy varieties in areas near the main urban centres of consumption.
4. Winter crops as these require less water; moreover, the crops consume water during a relatively long period, and some of them, for example, potatoes and onions, can be easily stored for a long time without damage and with low cost.
5. Growing fruits suitable for particular areas identified by practical local experience and according to the available technical data:
   (a) Stone fruits in the Hejaz mountains; they flourish in this area and give an excellent crop. Moreover, this kind of crop is easily, physically and economically, transportable.
   (b) Pears and apple trees in the Asir mountains for the same reasons as in (a).
   (c) Other deciduous fruit trees, for example, peach, plum, pomegranate and apricot, in hilly and highland regions.
   (d) Citrus trees (orange, lemon, etc.) in regions of moderate

AGRICULTURAL AREAS IN SAUDI ARABIA

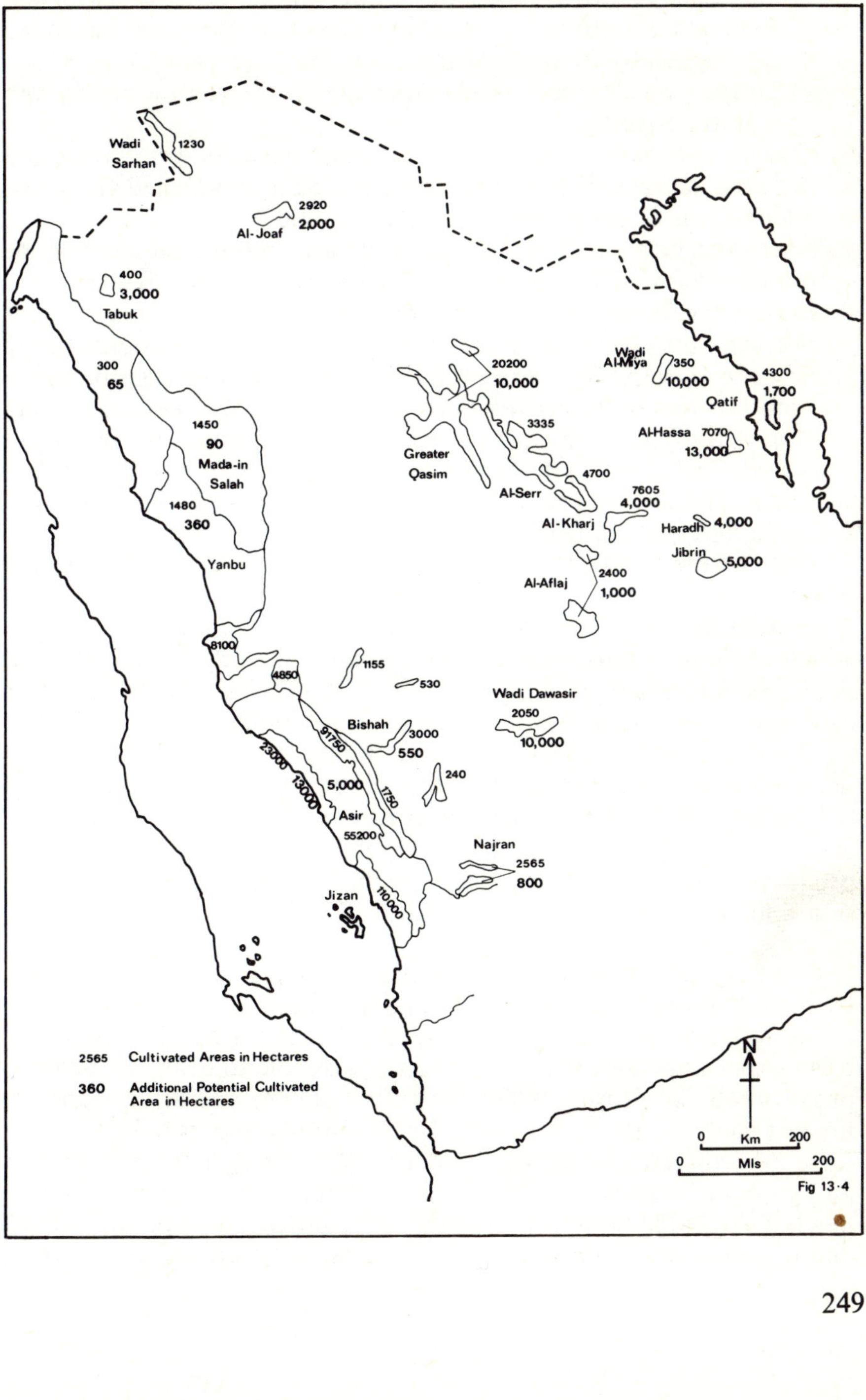

Fig 13·4

temperature, for example, Bishah, Turabah, Eastern and Middle regions.

(e) Bananas in hot regions especially along the coasts. Omani experience in mixed date and banana groves should be drawn on, especially in areas of traditional date growing.

(f) Grapes in calcareous lands especially in the central region and around Riyadh.

6. Choose varieties of fruit and vegetables both for very early and late production so that the cropping season is lengthened and gross fluctuations in price and supply are avoided.
7. Select the best possible and scientifically suitable varieties to be used even for palm trees, for example, Burhy and Sukkeriah.
8. Advise the farmer (producer) not to copy neighbouring farmers but, where possible, to avoid local reliance on a particular crop or even variety. For example, if farmers of the Qasim region prefer in general to grow melons, the individual is well-advised to choose another crop for this season; thus he reduces the risk of being affected by a glut causing low prices and he may avoid particular disease and pest infestations which are widespread in areas of limited crop-range.

Here we may apply the Arabic proverb, "If you contradict you will gain."

Needless to state, these points only indicate broad lines or principles which might be regarded as the basis for implementing the agricultural development policy for adoption in this Kingdom. The Ministry of Agriculture and Water may establish development programme criteria for each of the different regions, in which the above-mentioned points may be observed for the general betterment and education of the people. Within the framework of recommended programmes, the producers should have the liberty to select; as a result, agricultural production activities could be effectively controlled without oppression and the exploitation of new lands followed up directly or indirectly.

By such programmes, producers and consumers could benefit alike, both contributing towards the national income.

Saudi Arabia is experiencing dynamic change for development, and it is neither appropriate to our case nor possible to draw up detailed programmes or proposals for the future. From our discussion and modest analyses, the main lesson for the future appears to be the need for a type of interconnected, interrelated set of agricultural services and guidance offered to agriculture in general and to the holders of newly distributed land in particular. This process has already begun and will serve as a foundation for future land development. One may claim that, while the PLD programmes have inevitably had their problems and their limitations, a great deal has been achieved within a very short time. The avoidance of inflexibilities of the kind observed in many other countries gives one hope for the future evolution of PLD programmes from the level reached at the present time.

Appendix I: Sample Documents Concerning the Processing of an Application for Land

Form No. 1.

Contracting Registration Document
(*See facing page.*)

Form No. 2.

Application under Temporary Principles for Land Utilization

Region ....   Town ....   Village ....

1. Name of Public Land utilization applicant:
2. Age .... years.
3. Number of his dependants:
4. The tribe to which he belongs:
5. Financial status of the applicant
   (a) Good   (b) Fair   (c) Poor
6. Has the applicant any non-agricultural work?
   His approximate annual income ....
7. Does he farm other lands?
   (a) Owned lands   (b) Rented lands
   (c) Area in square metres ....
   (d) Approximate annual income ....
8. Does he own any lands rented to others?
   (a) Area of these lands in square metres ....
   (b) Approximate annual revenue ....
9. The Public Land he wishes to utilize:
   (a) Its location:
   (b) Its boundaries:
   (c) The claimed area in square metres:
10. Condition of the claimed land:
    (a) Soil type: Sand ....   Loam ....   Clay ....
    (b) Salinity: Slightly saline ....   Moderately saline ....
    Highly saline ....
    (c) Is the land arable or does it need reclamation?
    (d) Are irrigation means available on the land?

Form No.1.

Contracting Registration Document

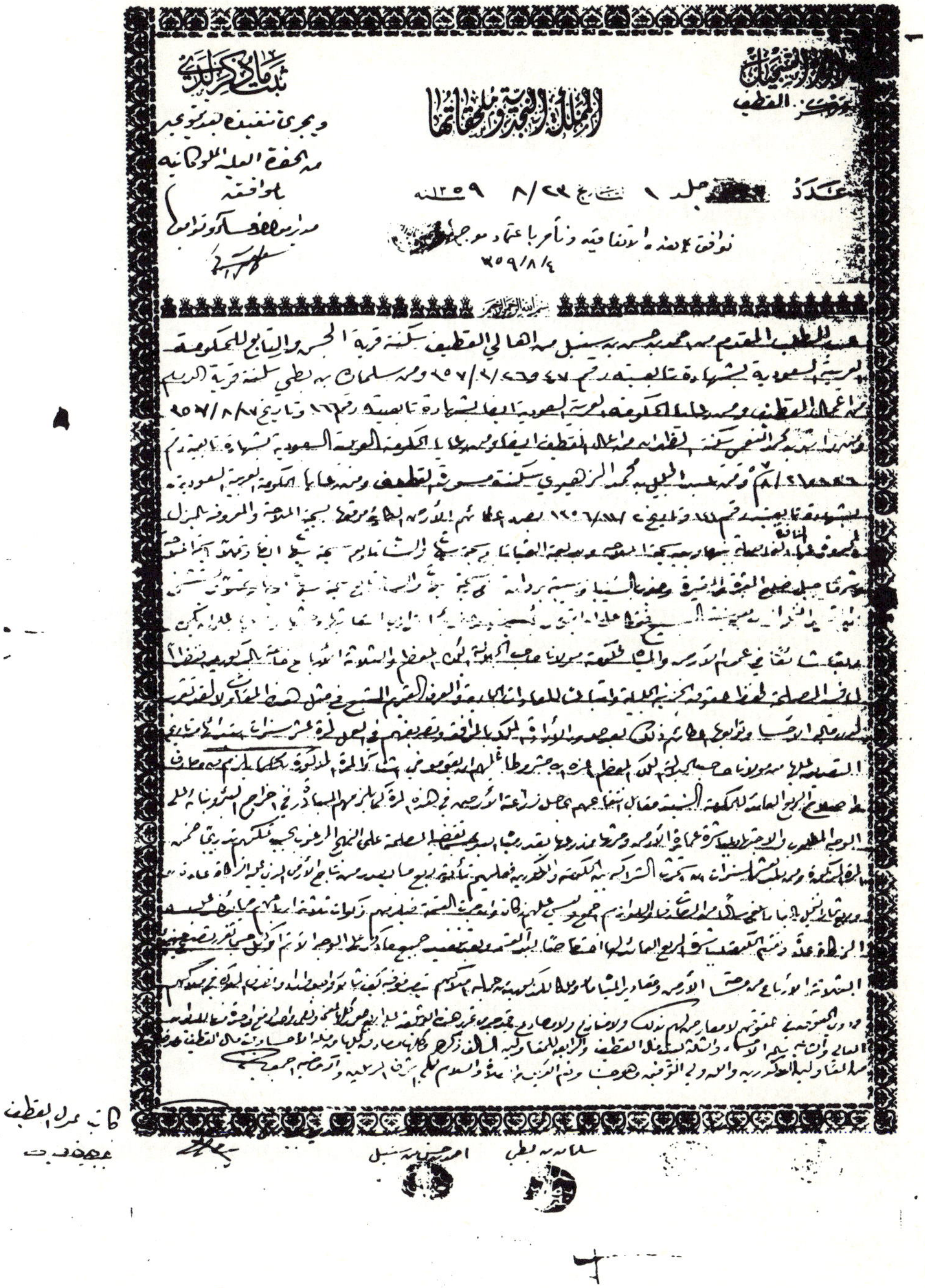

11. General water condition in the area in which the land lies:
    (a) Quality: Good .... Slightly saline ....
    Moderately saline .... Highly saline ....
    (b) Quantity: Rare .... Moderate .... Abundant ....
    (c) Water level:
    (d) Depth:

Note:
Water quality, quantity, water level and depth can be assessed from the condition of wells existing in the area where the land lies.

12. Is the land subject to any individual dispute or claim; or does it belong to the Public Domain?

We, the Public Land Inspection Committee, have inspected the above-mentioned land and we attest the truth of the information given above.

Member	Representative of the Ministry of Agriculture & Water	*Amir* of the Area

Form No. 3.

Information needed for Public Land Distribution

To: Director of Field Organization ....
please inspect and inform us whether Land (...............) being considered for distribution has been surveyed or studied or checked physically by one of your technicians, and if not please supply the following information.

1. Location of this Land with reference to the nearest known Town – the distance and direction – as well as its suitability for agricultural utilization.
2. Boundaries of the Land according to four compass directions and its approximate area.
3. Its distance from already settled lands and all relevant matters.
4. Whether there is any tribal or individual dispute affecting this land.
5. All information other than that mentioned above.

The survey or study of this Land does not imply donation, but the position should be reserved until the Ministry of Agriculture and Water gives a decision regarding distribution according to the Public Land Distribution Ordinance. If this Land is included in the Land Distribution which has been announced, it will be treated according to normal procedure.

Director General,
Public Land Management Department.

Form No. 4.

Laboratory analysis of soil samples

Serial No.	Sample Data	Chemical Analysis of Extracted Soil Paste							
	Sample name & location	Depth	EC	Ca & Mg Milli/ equ/L	$CaCO_3$ %	Exc. Na. %	pH	Texture	Notes

Form No. 5.

Public Land Distribution Announcement

The Ministry of Agriculture & Water, Public Land Management Department, announces that the Local Committee, formed according to Article Five of the Public Land Distribution Ordinance issued by the Royal Decree No. M/26 dated 6/7/1388H (1968), will study the Distribution of Agricultural Land plots in:...
....
.... Area.
Anyone who has a right of any kind to a plot of land or a portion of a plot should submit to ....
.... proof of his right within a period

of one month. Also, anyone who has a previous or recent application, and anyone who wishes to possess a plot of agricultural land in the mentioned area, for utilization purposes should submit to the Local Committee formed .... within a month from this date in order to file an Utilization Application. Survey maps for the Land meant for Distribution can be found in the possession of ....

Ministry of Agriculture & Water

Form No. 6.

Agricultural Land Utilization Application

Region.... Town.... Village....

Part One: This part is to be completed by the applicant in the presence of the relevant employee in the Field Organization of the Area:

1. Applicant's full name:
2. Identity Card:
3. The tribe to which he belongs (if there is any):
4. His permanent address:
5. His job:
6. His marital status, single, married or widowed:
7. Number of his dependants: Males Females Total
8. His family members in detail:

	Full name	*Male or Female*	*Relation to the family Head*	*Age*	*Recent work*
1.					
2.					
3.					
4.					
5.					
6.					

9. Does the applicant have any non-agricultural occupation? (Yes or No).
10. If he has other work, what is it?
11. What is his annual income from non-agricultural work, if he has any?
12. What is his annual income from agricultural work, if he has any?
13. Does the applicant farm a specific plot of agricultural land? (Yes or No).
    (a) If the answer is yes, what is the area of this land?
    (b) Where is it located?
14. If the applicant tills agricultural land, is the land he farms:
    (a) his own?
    (b) owned by others and rented by him?

(c) partly owned by him and the rest of the land owned by others? (In this case: the area he owns ....; the area owned by others ....)

15. Does the applicant own land which is rented to others? (Yes or No). If he owns such land:
    (a) What is its area?
    (b) Where is it located?
    (c) How much is his annual income from this land?
16. Does the applicant own any agricultural land? (Yes or No).
17. The land the applicant wishes to utilize:
    (a) Where is it located?
    (b) What are its boundaries?
    (c) What is its area in square metres?
18. Why does the applicant wish to utilize this specific plot of land?

I, the undersigned, testify that the information stated above is true, and in case all or part of it is proved untrue I will be responsible for the results.

Applicant's signature
Date....

Signature of the Field Organization employee who was present when this application was completed ....
Date of application delivery ....
Signature of the Director of the Field Organization ....

Part Two: This part is to be completed by the Local Committee according to information submitted by the Public Land Management Department, through the Field Organization, and according to the Committee's own data and investigations.

1. Total number of applications submitted to the Committee:
2. Number of applications lodged with the Committee when it discussed the individual applications:
3. Total distributable area according to data and maps given to the committee by the Public Land Management Department, through the Field Organization:
4. The applicant's principal job – according to the opinion and knowledge of the Committee, if the applicant is an official:
5. If an employee, his work, rank and place of work should be stated:
6. Is the applicant's own land adjacent to the Land he is claiming? (Yes or No).
   If the answer is yes:
   (a) What is the area of this land in square metres?
   (b) What are its boundaries?
7. Is the applicant a member of the regional community? (Yes or No).
   If the answer is "yes" does he live in the region? (Yes or No).
8. Does the applicant work only in agriculture?
9. If the applicant does not work totally in agriculture, what is his other work?

10. What is the applicant's annual income?
    (a) From agricultural work, if he has any:
    (b) From non-agricultural work, if he has any:
11. Is the applicant renting agricultural land from others? (Yes or No).
    If he rents agricultural land:
    (a) What is its area in square metres?
    (b) Where is it located?
    (c) What are its boundaries?
12. Does the applicant own agricultural land which he is renting to others? (Yes or No).
    If he owns agricultural land rented to others, what is its area in square metres?
13. Does the applicant own any agricultural land?
14. What is the number of the applicant's family members who are dependent on him and living with him?

Adult males (over 18 years old)	Minor males (under 18 years old)	Total (adults & minors)
Adult females (over 18 years old)	Minor females (under 18 years old)	Total (adults & minors)

Part Three:. The Committee's Decision.

Depending on conditions and priorities listed in the Public Land Distribution Ordinance issued by Royal Decree No. M/26 dated 6/7/1388H (1968) and its Operational Procedures, and depending on information given by the Public Land Management Department and on its own information, does the Committee see:

That the applicant deserves to be allotted Land? (Yes or No).

If the Committee recommends that the applicant be allotted land, the following section is to be completed:

1. Applicant's full name:
2. His identity card number:
3. His address:
4. Area of Land decided to be allotted to him (square metres):
5. Its location:
6. Its boundaries:
7. Utilization test period suggested by the Committee (two or three years):
8. Is this period the same suggested by Public Land Management Department (Yes or No).
9. (a) Land type in the Committee's opinion: (good, fair or poor).
   (b) Is the Land arable or does it need reclamation?
10. (a) Are irrigation systems available or could they be provided to irrigate the Land?
    (b) Type of water available or which could be provided to irrigate the Land: (good, slightly saline, moderately saline, highly saline).

(c) Water quantity: rare, moderate, abundant.
(d) Approximate water depth from Land surface:

11. Any other notes or comments the Committee wishes to add:

Committee members

Full name	Full name	Full name	Full name
signature	signature	signature	signature

Form No. 7.

Land Distribution Decision according to Public Land Distribution Ordinance

The Minister of Agriculture & Water,

Referring to Article Five of the Public Land Distribution Ordinance issued by Royal Decree No. M/26 dated 6/7/1388H (1968), and according to the recommendation of the Local Committee formed in .... Area, decides the following:

First: Name .... from .... village is to be allotted the Public Land located in ...., whose area is .... donums, and bounded by .... from north, ... from east, ... from west and .... from south. The Land location and boundaries are shown in the attached map.

Second: The named person has the right to utilize the Land stated in Section 1, for a period of ....; his rights on the Land are limited to the right of utilization only. He has no right to sell, gift or mortgage the Land except after obtaining written permission from the Minister of Agriculture & Water.

The Minister of Agriculture & Water has the right to recover the Land and allot it to another person if the utilizer fails to prove his capability for utilization of this Land according to the conditions stated in the Public Land Distribution Ordinance sanctioned by Royal Decree No. M/26 dated 6/7/1388H (1968), and according to the Ordinance's Operational Procedure.

Third: The utilization period begins from this date.

Minister of Agriculture & Water

Form No. 8.

Information needed for Land Claim Deeds

To: Director of Field Organization ....

Please study and inform us of the following:

1. Location of the claimed Land with reference to the nearest known Town,

the distance of the Land from this Town or village, as well as all other relevant data.

2. The boundaries of this Land with four compass directions, length of each boundary in metres and total area in donums; indicate, as well, the utilized portion, buildings, number of trees, the approximate age of trees, the non-utilized area, and whether the Land borders any Public Land and indicate the location of that boundary.
3. Whether any part of the Land under consideration is to be utilized in any Governmental project, the name of the project, the area taken, the location of the project; whether the person concerned is compensated for the part taken from his Land or whether he will apply for compensation in future.
4. Whether there is any dispute about this Land between tribes or persons dwelling in that area, as well as information concerning such a dispute if there is any.
5. Method of Land acquisition (i.e. inheritance, purchase, utilization or donation) and date of acquisition; copies of supporting documents are to be attached; attestation of the copies of documents issued by the judicial offices who arranged issue of the original documents after these have been compared with the records, and attestation of anything which may have happened to the originals; all this to avoid any harm or dispute and in accordance with the circular of Supreme Justice Authority to the courts and notary-public, vide No. 52/3T of 16/7/1390H (1970).
6. All other information you wish to add, noting that this request for information does not finalize the procedure, therefore we would wish to emphasize that the position is reserved on the application submitted, until the Ministry takes action in this regard and informs you accordingly. We wish the report to be signed by the person who prepared it, his name, date of preparation, your attestation on his signature and the official seal of the Department. We have to be supplied with two copies of the report. If there is any deficiency in the required information the documents will be returned to you and you will be held responsible for them according to the regulations.
7. All information mentioned in items (1, 2, 3) should be illustrated with sketches.

Director General,
Public Land Management Department.

Form No. 9.

Decision cancelling the Utilization right of Land Distributed according to the Public Land Distribution Ordinance

The Minister of Agriculture & Water,

Referring to Article Eight of the Public Land Distribution Ordinance issued by Royal Decree No. M/26 dated 6/7/1388H (1968), and depending on the date provided by the Seriousness of Utilization Committee formed by the Ministerial decision No .... dated ...., decides the following:

First: The utilization right given to .... by Ministerial decision No .... dated ...., is cancelled.

Second: The named person has to deliver the Land concerned to the person the Ministry of Agriculture and Water nominates.

Third: The sum of .... Riyals is to be paid by the person nominated by the Ministry to take the place of the first utilizer in the utilization right. This sum is compensation to be paid to the first utilizer for any increase in the Land value which resulted from his endeavours in the Land.

Fourth: The effect of this decision begins from the date of its issue, and any expenditure by the first utilizer after this date is not taken into consideration.

Minister of Agriculture & Water

Form No. 10.

Application for drilling/deepening/cleaning a drilled well

1. Name of applicant.
2. Date of application.
3. Field Organization receiving the application.
4. Location of the farm or land.
5. Boundary East West
   North South
6. Size .... donums
   Length .... m
   Width .... m
7. Area cultivated.
8. Type of crops cultivated.
9. Ownership of the farm or land.
10. Number of wells in this location.
11. Nearest distance between proposed well location and other existing drilled wells related to the owners or others.
12. Suggestions of the authorized personnel.

Name ....
Signature ....
Endorsement ....

Form No. 11.

Licence for drilling a well

To: Director of Field Organization.

With reference to the application of Citizen .... concerned with drilling an artesian well, located at .... for agricultural utilization; the technical division has no objection in accordance with the provisions of its standing regulations as long as Land ownership has been established and written consent is obtained from the applicant agreeing to the following:

1. Depth of the well should not exceed .... metres.
2. Casing should be fixed and the well wall should be cemented from the surface to the beginning of the aquifer.
   In case of any seepage, the owner will close this well at his own expense.
3. The distance between this well and any other should exceed .... metres. This is to make sure that no interference takes place.

A written and signed consent of the citizen concerned should be sent back to the Department.

Director General,
Water Conservation Department.

Appendix II: Tables

1. Chief tribes and names of their *Hejar*

Tribe: *Motir*

Al-Artawiyah, Al-Faruthi, Al-Namiriyah, Al-Ja'ala, Um Hazm, Mubaydh, Al-Haswa, Daban, Budha, Al-Ithla, Al-Artawi, Mulayih, Wadakh, Al-Tatuwi, Al-Shaflahiyah, Al-Ammar, Qarba, Al-Tamariyah, Al-Qariyah Al-Sifla, Al-Quariyah, Al-Ulya

Utaiba

Al-Dahnah, Al-Hufayrah, Al-Labib, Amsada, Sinam, Al-Ruwaydah, Usayla, Sajir, Arwa, Al-Rawdha, Kabshan, Al-Mukallat, Al-Suh, Arja, Nifi, Al-Hayd, Abu Jalal, Al-Qarara, Shabirma, Al-Qarayn

Harb

Al-Qarayn, Burud, Al-Ba'ayith, Al-Muhala'i, Al-Fawwara, Qatan, Al-Dulaymiyah, Biq-i-iyah, Al-Shabakiyah, Al-Thibiyah, Al-Faydah, Al-Bid'a, Al-Dakhna, Al-Khashibi, Al-Quwara, Al-Shubayhiyah, Al-Mahamalani, Al-Nahitiyah, Aqlah Al-Qasur, Al-Bamiri, Al-Dath, Al-Jirathamiyah, Ghasl, Al-Dulaymiyah, Al-Sam'uriyah, Thadiq, Al-Namariyah, Aqbah, Khashiba, Dhaida, Kuhaylah, Abu Mughir

Shammar

Al-Ajfar, Al-Safra, Um Al-Qalban, Jibba, Al-Hufayr, Al-Taym, Al-Khabba, Al-Sina, Al-Nifi, Al-Adhim, Al-Mak-hul, Al-Sahway, Al-Shafiq, Al-Qasir, Al-Faydha, Al-Aqlah

Anaza

Khibar, Al-Faydhah, Baydah Natil, Al-Sha'abiyah, Al-Samlí, Al-Sha'abiyah Al-Thania Al-Balaziyah

Qahtan

Al-Rayn Al-Asfal, Al-Rayn Al-'A'la, Al-Jufayr, Al-Hisah, Sabha, Al-Hayathim, Al-Hassa Al-Sifla, Al-Hassa Al-'Ulya, Al-Munaysif, Laban

Dawasir
Al-Hamr, Mushirfah, Al-Washita, Al-Hamarmah

Ajman
Al-Sarar, Al-Kahfa, Al-Wanan, Nunayth, Yakha, Al-Zaghin, Al-Air'arah, Al-Ayyanah, Anwa, Al-Faradi, Al-Sahaf, Um Rabi'ah, Al-Barah, Matnanah

Al-Awazim
Atiq, Thaz

Al Murrah
Jibrin, Al-Sikak, Niyal, Al-Badu

Bani Khalid
Al-Wafi, Jalmud

Bani Hageer
Ayndar, Yakrib, Fudah, Salasal

2. Soil Survey of Wadi Sarhan area.[37]

Location	Land Class	Hectares	Soil Profile	Limitations	Recommendations prior to Development
Rashrashiyah	3 s 3 d	1,536 806	Silt loam 0–40 cm Sandy loam 40–150 cm	Moderate salt content with considerable gypsum. May develop uneven surface when irrigated.	1. Detailed soil and drainage investigations necessary in all areas prior to land development. 2. Removal of salt from root zone will require (a) construction of adequate drainage (b) proper irrigation with good quality water.
Ghatty	3 s	1,775	Sandy loam 0–40 cm Silt loam 40–150 cm	Moderate salt content and flood hazard.	
	3 sd	160	Silt loam 0–150 cm	High salt content and flood hazard.	
Jemajim	3 s	1,143	Silt loam 0–150 cm	Moderate to high salt content.	
	3 sd	2,698	Silt loam 0–150 cm	High salt content and impeded drainage.	
Qalib Khidr	3 sd	404	Silt loam 0–150 cm	High salt content and impeded drainage.	
	3 sd	1,123	Silt loam 0–20 cm Sandy loam 20–80 cm Loam 80–150 cm	Moderate to high salt content, impeded drainage. Some areas under-lain by bedrock above 150 cm.	
Isawiyah	3 sd	1,385	Silt loam 0–110 cm Sandy loam 20–80 cm	Moderate salt content and impeded drainage because of shallow bedrock.	
	3 sd	1,512	Silt loam 0–140 cm Bedrock at 140 cm	Moderate salt content and impeded drainage.	
Al-Feyidah	3 sd	550	Silt loam 0–80 cm Clay 80–120 cm Bedrock at 120 cm	No drainage outlet – Impeded drainage because of underlying bedrock.	
Tabarjal	3 s	1,196	Sandy loam 0–120 cm	Moderate to high salt content.	
	3 sd	1,101	Sandy loam 0–20 cm Loam 20–50 cm Sandy loam 50–90 cm Bedrock at 90 cm	High salt content and impeded drainage.	

cm = centimetre

3. Soil Survey of Buraidah and Tabuk areas.[37]

Area	Location	Land Class	Hectares	Soil Profile	Limitations	Recommendations Prior to Development
BURAIDAH	Ad Dugh-maniyah	2 s	707	Sandy loam 0–10 cm Silt loam 10–120 cm Sandy loam 120–150 cm	None.	1. Detailed soil and drainage studies needed. 2. Removal of salt from the root zone will require (a) installation of adequate drains, (b) proper irrigation with good quality water, and (c) rough tillage where possible (use suitable salt tolerant crops). 3. Consideration should be given to increased grape production along the edge of the sand dune near Buraidah.
		2 d	1,258	Sandy loam 0–40 cm Sandy clay loam 40–150 cm	May require drainage when fully developed.	
		3 s	5,788	Sandy loam 0–50 cm Loamy sand 50–150 cm	Moderate to high salt content.	
	Vicinity of Buraidah	3 d	633	Sandy loam 0–150 cm	High salt content.	
		3 sd	6,873	Sandy clay loam 0–70 cm Impervious bed-rock at 70 cm	Slight to moderate salt content, impeded drainage, flood hazard.	
		3 sfd	77	Loam 0–50 cm Silt loam bedrock at 70 cm	High salt content, impeded drainage, flood hazard.	
TABUK	Surrounding Tabuk	3 s	287	Loamy sand 0–20 cm Sandy loam 20–50 cm Clay loam 50–150 cm	Impeded drainage.	Detailed soil and drainage investigations needed because of the high salt content and poor drainage on much of the arable land. A detailed soil map of the area may show areas (additional) of arable land of sufficient size for development.
		3 sd	6,307	Clay 0–50 cm Silty clay 50–150 cm	High salt content, impeded drainage.	

cm = centimetre

Bibliography

The published literature relevant to this study and concerned with Saudi Arabia is limited. Much of the data concerning Public Land Distribution and the social, economic, administrative and resource fields is only to be found in unpublished documents. These documents include:

(a) Royal Decrees and Orders
(b) Government Ordinances
(c) Ministry and Department papers.

Whenever Decrees, Orders and Ordinances have been publicly promulgated they have been referred to in the manuscript. However, footnotes were omitted in this book and the references in question are listed in section (B) of this Bibliography, each followed by the page number where such reference was first mentioned.

A. List of major works referred to in the text

1. ABD, S., *Community Development in Saudi Arabia, report to the Government*, Ministry of Labour and Social Affairs, Riyad, 1384H (1964).
2. ABD, S., *Human Settlements in the Newly Reclaimed Areas at the UAR, Their Design and Development*. Middle East Office of FAO. Document No. HSWL 9A, Cairo, 1971.
3. ABDO, A. S., "A Geographical Study of Transport in Saudi Arabia with Special Reference to Road Transport PhD" thesis, University of Durham, 1969.
4. AL-ASHIEKH, A. A., "Agriculture and Economic Development with Special emphasis on a Strategy for Saudi Arabian Economic Development", PhD thesis, University of Edinburgh, 1970.
5. AL-FRRAA, ABY-YAALA, M., *Sultanic Rules*, Al-Halaby Library, Egypt, 1938, pp. 1–20, 193–225 (*in Arabic*).
6. AL-JERRASH, M. A., "Soils and Agricultural Development in the Region of Al-Qassim, Saudi Arabia", MA thesis, University of Durham, 1968.
7. AL-MAWDUDY, A., *Land Tenure in Islam*, Damascus, 1966.
8. AL-QASIM, A. B. S., *Kitab al-amwal, A Classical Work on Money, Ownership, and Public Finance in Islamic Law*. Edited by M. K. Harās, Cairo, 1968, pp. 386–423.
9. ARAMCO, *Aramco handbook*, Revised Edition, Dhahran, 1388H (1968).

10. ASADALLAH, M. M. A., "Land and Maritime Boundaries of North and North Eastern Saudi Arabia", PhD thesis, University of Newcastle-upon-Tyne, 1971.
11. ASHBY, A. W., *Public Lands*, FAO, Agricultural studies No. 31, Rome, 1956.
12. ASSADR, M. B., *Our Economy*, Dar Al-Fekr, Beirut, Third Edition, 1389H 1969, pp. 400–461 (*in Arabic*).
13. ASSAH, A., *Miracle of the Desert Kingdom*, Johnson, London, 1969, pp. 122–132, 190–210.
14. AWAD, M., "The assimilation of nomads in Egypt", *Geographical Review*, **XLIV,** 1954, pp. 240–250.
15. AWAD, M., "Settlement of nomadic and semi-nomadic tribal groups in the Middle East", *The Int. Lab. Rev.*, **79,** 1959, pp. 25–56.
16. AWAD, M., "Nomadism in the Arab lands of the Middle East", UNESCO, *The Problems of the Arid Zone, Proceedings of the Paris Symposium, 1960, Arid Zone Research*, **18,** 1962, pp. 325–339.
17. BASTONS, A., WALPOLE, N. C. and other co-authors, *Area Handbook for Saudi Arabia.* The American University, Foreign Area Studies, Washington, Government Printing Office, 1971.
18. CAPONERA, D. A., *Water Laws in Moslem Countries*, FAO Development Papers No. 43, Third Edition, Rome, 1954.
19. CENTRAL PLANNING ORGANIZATION, *Kingdom of Saudi Arabia, Development Plan*, Riyad, 1390H (1970).
20. CENTRAL PLANNING ORGANIZATION, *Kingdom of Saudi Arabia, Economic Report*, 1390–1391H (1970–1971).
21. COLE, D. P., "The Social and Economic Structure of the Al-Murrah: A Saudi Arabian Bedouin Tribe", PhD thesis, University of California, Berkeley, 1971.
22. DAWSON, E., *An Enquiry into Land Tenure and Related Questions*, Government of Iraq, The Garden City Press Limited, Letchworth, England, 1932.
23. EL-GHONEMY, M. R., *The Development of Tribal Lands and Settlements in Libya, Information on Land Reform, Land Settlement and Co-operatives*, No. 1, Rome, 1965.
24. EL-GHONEMY, M. R., *The role of Land Policy in Agricultural Production and Income Distribution in the Near East*, FAO, Rome, Paper No. 6, 1965.
25. EL-GHONEMY, M. R. (compiler), *Land Policy in the Near East*, FAO, Rome, 1967.
26. FADEL, M., *Islamic Law and Modern Life*, Beirut, 1964.
27. FAO/LIBYA/FUNDS-IN-TRUST 20, *Development of Tribal Lands and Settlements Project*, Report to the Government of Libya, Vols. I, II, III and IV, Rome, 1969.
28. FILALI, M., *Settlement and Urbanization of Nomadic Tribes in the Kingdom of Saudi Arabia*, Ministry of Labour and Social Affairs, Riyad, 1384H (1964).
29. HAJJAJI, S. A., "The land use patterns and rural settlement in the Benghazi plain", PhD thesis, University of Durham, 1969.

30. HAJRAH, H. H., *Quality of Irrigation Water*, Ministry of Agiculture and Water, Riyad 1390H (1970).
31. HAJRAH, H. H., *Possibilities of Agricultural Potential in Saudi Arabia*, Ministry of Agriculture, Riyad, 1392H (1972) (*in Arabic*).
32. HEADY, E. O., *A synthesis of Policies to Attain Goals of the Five Year Plan for the Ministry of Agriculture and Water, Kingdom of Saudi Arabia*, Stanford Research Institute, California, 1970.
33. INSTITUTE of PUBLIC ADMINISTRATION, *Regulations, Shari'a Jurist Division from 1345–1357H*, Riyad, 1357 H (1938).
34. INTERNATIONAL BANK FOR RECONSTRUCTION AND DEVELOPMENT, *Approach to the Economic Development of Saudi Arabia*, Report No. AS–82a, 1960.
35. ILO, *Agricultural Organizations and Economic and Social Development in Rural Areas*, New Series, No. 77, Geneva, 1971.
36. KHAFFAJI, S. AL-DIN, *Agricultural Reform Legislation and Property Control*, Youth Library, Cairo, 1971 (*in Arabic*).
37. KINGERY, C. E., *Possibilities for Development and Management of Public Range Lands: A Review of Resources*, Survey Reports, 1971.
38. KRASHEVSHI, S. H., *Soil–Water–Plant–Relationship in Area I*, Ministry of Agriculture and Water, Riyad, 1388H (1968).
39. LEWIS, W. A., *Thoughts on Land Settlement, Agriculture in Economic Development*, Ed. C. Eicher and L. Witt, McGraw-Hill Book Co., New York, 1964.
40. MAKTARI, A. M. A., *Water Rights and Irrigation Practices in Lahj, A Study of the Application of Customary and Shari'a Law in Southern West Arabia*, Cambridge University Press, 1971.
41. MCLACHLAN, K. S., "A Geographical Study of the Coastal Zone Between Khoms and Misurata, Tripolitania. A Geography of Economic Growth", PhD thesis, University of Durham, 1961.
42. MEDAWAR, G. S., *Agriculture in Saudi Arabia, A Report to the Ministry of Agriculture*, Economic Research Institute, American University of Beirut, Beirut, 1965.
43. MINISTRY OF AGRICULTURE AND WATER, *Statistical Bulletins*, Research Department, Riyad, 1382–1388H (1962–1968).
44. MINISTRY OF AGRICULTURE AND WATER, *Public Land Distribution Ordinance and Operational Procedure*, Public Land Management Department, Riyad, 1388H (1968).
45. MOURAD, F., "The Attitude of Village Population in Saudi Arabia Towards Community Development: A Study in the Social Psychology or Development", PhD thesis, University of Southern California, 1969.
46. PARSONS, BASIL, *Kingdom of Saudi Arabia, Ministry of Agriculture and Water, Agricultural and Water Resources, the Great Nafud Sedimentary Basin*, **I, II & III,** Riyad, 1388H (1968).
47. PARSONS, K. H., PENN, R. J., RAUP, P. M. (Editors), *Land Tenure, Proceedings of the International Conference on Land Tenure and Related Problems in Agriculture held at Madison, Wisconsin, 1951*, The University of Wisconsin Press, Third Printing, 1963.

48. PASSEUR, J. E., *Summary of Land Classification Report on Area I.* The Great Nafud Sedimentary Basin contract consultant Parsons-Basil, Consultant 1391H (1971).
49. PEPPELENBOSCH, P. G. N., *Nomadism on the Arabian Peninsula: A General Appraisal.* Tijdschrift voor En Soc. Geografie, **59,** 1968, pp. 335–346.
50. SADEQ, M. T., *Development of Government and Administration in Saudi Arabia*, Institute of Public Administration, Riyad, 1385H (1965) (*in Arabic*).
51. SHARBINY, S. T., "Credit and education in the development of agriculture: The potential role of the Saudi Arabian agricultural bank", MA thesis, American University of Beirut, 1970.
52. SOLAIM, S. A., "Constitutional and Judicial Organization in Saudi Arabia", PhD thesis, The Johns Hopkins University, Washington, DC, 1970.
53. TANNOUS, A. I., "Land reform: key to the development and stability of the Arab world", *Middle East Journal*, **V,** 1951, pp. 1–20.
55. UN, *Progress in Land Reform.* Fifth Report, New York, 1970.
56. WATT, W. M., *Islam and the Integration of Society*, Routledge and Kegan Paul, London, 1960.
57. WARRENER, D., *Land and Poverty in the Middle East*, Broadwater Press, Hertfordshire, 1948.
58. WARRENER, D., *Land Reform and Development in the Middle East, 1962*, Second Edition, Oxford University Press, London, 1962.
59. WARRENER, D., *Land Reform in Principle and Practice*, Clarendon Press, Oxford, 1969.
60. WILSON-MURROW, *Feeder Road Study Areas I, II & III*, Ministry of Communication, Kingdom of Saudi Arabia, Riyad, 1390H (1970).
61. YAMANI, A. Z., *Islamic Law and Contemporary Issues*, The Saudi Publishing House, Jeddah, Saudi Arabia, 1388H (1968).

B. List of other works to which reference is made in the text

ABUL ELA, M. T., "A Geographical Study of Man and His Environment in Al-Ahssa Province (Saudi Arabia)", PhD thesis, Trinity College, Dublin, 1959, (p. 102).

ALI, M. I. A., "Social Responsibility of the Individual and State in Saudi Arabian Law", PhD thesis, University of London, 1971, (p. 246).

AL-RASHEED, M. C., "Criminal Procedure in Saudi Arabian Judicial Institutions", PhD thesis, University of Durham, April, 1973, (p. 16).

AL-TURKI, M. I., "Accelerating Agricultural Production in Saudi Arabia", PhD, Colorado State University, 1971, (p. 184).

EDENS, D. G. AND SNAVELEY, W. P., "Planning for economic development in Saudi Arabia", *The Middle East Journal*, **24** (1), 1970, (p. 40).

GHIASSI, M., "Land reform and output, the Iranian Case", MA thesis, University of Durham, 1972, (p. 188).

HABIB, J. S., "The Ikhwan Movement of Najd: Its Rise, and Decline", PhD thesis, University of Michigan, 1970, (p. 40).

HOBBES, T., *Leviathan or the Matter, Form and Power of Common Wealth Ecclesiastical*, 1935 Edition, pp. 176–177, (p. 19).
HUNTER, G., *Modernizing Peasant Societies: A Comparative Study in Asia and Africa*, The Institute of Race Relations, London, Oxford University Press, 1969, (p. 229).
JACOBY, E. H., *Man and Land*, André Deutsch, London, 1971, (p. 228).
KING, R., *Land Reform, the Italian Experience*, The Butterworth Group, London, 1973, (p. 169).
RA ANA, I. M., *Economic System under Omar the Great*, Ashraf Press, Lahore, Pakistan, 1970, (p. 159).
RAYES, R., *Annual Report from 1970, for the inter-Agency Consultative Board*, United Nations Development Programme in Saudi Arabia, 1971, (p. 108).
SAUDI ARABIA AGRICULTURAL BANK, *Eighth Annual Report*, Al-Asfahani Press, Jeddah, 1391–1392H (1971–1972), (p. 154).
SAUDI ARABIAN MONETARY AGENCY, *Annual Reports 1390–1391H* (1970–1971), *1391–1392H* (1971–1972), *and 1392–1393H* (1972–1973), Jeddah; (p. 108).
THE FORD FOUNDATION, *An Evaluation of the Economic Feasibility and Technical Requirements for an Accelerated Wheat Production Programme in Saudi Arabia*, Riyad, 1390H (1970), (p. 242).
UN, *Nomadic Population in Selected Countries in the Middle East and Related Issues of Sedentarization and Settlement*, New York, 1970, (p. 177).
YAMANI, A. Z., *Administrative Organization in Saudi Arabia*, Riyad, University Magazine, No. 3, 1380H (1960) (*in Arabic*), (p. 237).

C. List of other works consulted

AL-AWAJI, I. M., "Bureaucracy and Society in Saudi Arabia", PhD thesis, University of Virginia, 1971.
AMER, M., "The Oases of Central Arabia with Special Reference to Trade and Pilgrim Routes", PhD thesis, University of Liverpool, 1921.
ASFOUR, E. Y., *Preliminary Estimate of Gross National Product of Saudi Arabia in 1380H (1960)*, Economic Research Institute, American University of Beirut, 1964.
ASFOUR, E. Y., *Saudi Arabia: Long-term Projections of Supply and Demand for Agricultural Products*, Economic Research Institute, American University of Beirut, Beirut, 1965.
ASFOUR, E. Y., "Prospects and problems of economic development of Saudi Arabia, Kuwait and the Gulf principalities", in C. A. Cooper and S. S. Alexander (Eds), *Economic Development and Population Growth in the Middle East*, American Elsevier, 1972.
BINNS, B., *Land Settlement for Agriculture*, FAO Development Paper No. 9, Rome, 1951.
BOWEN-JONES, H., DEWDNEY, J. C., FISHER, W. B., *Malta*, Department of Geography, Durham Colleges, Durham, 1962.
CENTRAL DEPARTMENT OF STATISTICS, *The Gross Domestic Product of Saudi Arabia*, Ministry of Finance and National Economy, Riyad, 1390H (1970).

CLAUSON, G., *Communal Land Tenure*, FAO Agricultural Studies, No. 17, FAO, Rome, 1953.

DENMAN, D. R., *Origins of Ownership*, George Allen & Unwin, London, 1958.

FISHER, W. B., *The Middle East*, Methuen & Co Ltd, London, Sixth Edition, 1971.

FAO, *Agrarian Reconstruction*, Basic study No. 18, Rome, 1968.

FAO, *Development Centre on Land Policy and Settlement for the Near East*, Report No. A2160, Rome, 1966.

FAO, *Funds in trust for Saudi Arabia, Development of Water Resources and Agriculture*. Report to the Government of Saudi Arabia, Rome, 1966.

FAO, *Information on Land Reform, Land Settlement and Co-operatives*, No. 1, Rome, 1969.

FAO, *Mediterranean Development Project, The Integrated Development of Mediterranean Agriculture and Forestry in Relation to Economic Growth, A Study and Proposals for Action*, Rome, 1959.

FAO, *Saudi Arabian Funds in Trust*, FAO, SAA/TF 26, The organization and programme of work of the agricultural marketing section, Report to the Government of Saudi Arabia, Rome, 1970.

HASHEM, M. A., *Analysis of Community Development Programme in Saudi Arabia*, Report to the Government, Ministry of Labour and Social Affairs, Riyad, 1383–1385H (1963–1965) (Restricted Report).

HELAISSI, A. S., "The bedouins and tribal life in Saudi Arabia", *International Social Science Journal*, UNESCO, **XI,** No. 4, Paris, 1959, pp. 532–538.

INDUSTRIAL STUDIES & DEVELOPMENT CENTRE, *Feasibility and Opportunity Studies*, Riyad, 1390H (1970).

ITALCONSULT, *Final Reports, Water and Agricultural Development Surveys, For Areas I & II, IV, VI*, Ministry of Agriculture & Water, Riyad, 1389H (1969).

LITTLE, ARTHUR D., *Inc. Agri-Industry opportunities in Saudi Arabia*, Report to the Ministry of Commerce and Industry of Saudi Arabia, Riyad, 1389H (1969).

MINISTRY OF AGRICULTURE & WATER, *Study of Manpower of the Ministry of Agriculture and Water*, Training Department, Riyad, 1390H (1970).

MUGHRAM, A. A., "Assarah, Saudi Arabia: Change and Development in a Rural Context", PhD thesis, Durham University, 1973.

SHARI'A COURTS, *Regulations for Determining Responsibilities and Organization of Administrative Functions in the Shari'a Court System*, Royal Decree No. 109, Government Press, Mecca, 1372H (1972).

SOGREAH, *Soil and Land Classification for Area VI*, Ministry of Agriculture & Water, Riyad, 1391H (1971).

SPRAGUE, H. B., *Improvement of Livestock Production on Semi-desert Forage Lands of Saudi Arabia*, Report to Ministry of Agriculture & Water, Riyad, 1390H (1970).

TANNOUS, A. I., "The Arab tribal community in a nationalist State", *Middle East Journal*, **I,** 1949, pp. 5–17.

TUMA, E. H., *Twenty-six Centuries of Agrarian reform, A Comparative Analysis*, University of California, 1972.

UN, "North African Sub-region", *Economic survey of Africa*, **11,** New York, 1968, pp. 27–35.

WAHBA, H., *Arabian Peninsula in Twentieth Century*, Second Edition, Authorship, Translation and Publishing Committee, Cairo, 1967 (*in Arabic*).

WAZAN, S., *Basic Points Concerning Development of the Re-settlement Process in Some Areas of Land Reclamation in the Syrian Arab Republic*, Middle East Office of FAO, Document HSNL 12A, Cairo, 1971.

Index